# Second Chinese Language Processing Workshop 2000



**Held in conjunction with the 38th Annual Meeting of the Association for Computational Linguistics (ACL 2000)**

## Hong Kong
## 8 October 2000

## Editors:

**Martha Palmer**
**Aravind Joshi**
**Mitch Marcus**
**Fei Xia**

**ISBN: 978-1-62748-371-1**

**Printed from e-media with permission by:**

Curran Associates, Inc.
57 Morehouse Lane
Red Hook, NY 12571

**Some format issues inherent in the e-media version may also appear in this print version.**



Printed by Curran Associates, Inc. (2013)

For permission requests, please contact the Association for Computational Linguistics at the address below.

Association for Computational Linguistics
209 N. Eighth Street
Stroudsburg, Pennsylvania 18360

Phone: 1-570-476-8006
Fax: 1-570-476-0860

acl@aclweb.org

**Additional copies of this publication are available from:**

Curran Associates, Inc.
57 Morehouse Lane
Red Hook, NY 12571 USA
Phone: 845-758-0400
Fax: 845-758-2634
Email: curran@proceedings.com
Web: www.proceedings.com

ACL 2000

Proceedings of the

# Second Chinese Language Processing Workshop

Held in conjunction with
The 38th Annual Meeting of the
Association for Computational Linguistics

Edited by
Martha Palmer
Mitch Marcus
Aravind Joshi
Fei Xia

8 October 2000
Hong Kong University of Science and Technology (HKUST)
Hong Kong

**SPONSORS:**

SIGDAT
SIGLEX
SIGPARSE

**INDUSTRY SPONSOR:**

Intel China Research Center

**INVITED SPEAKER:**

Chin-Chuan Cheng (City University of Hong Kong)

**ORGANIZERS:**

Martha Palmer
Mitch Marcus
Aravind Joshi
Fei Xia

**PROGRAM COMMITTEE:**

| | | | |
|---|---|---|---|
| Srinivas Bangalore | (AT&T Research Labs) | Keh-Yih Su | (Behavior Design Corporation) |
| Keh-Jiann Chen | (Academia Sinica) | Maosong Sun | (Tsinghua Univ.) |
| Zhengdong Dong | (Hownet) | Chew Lim Tan | (National Univ. of Singapore) |
| Shengli Feng | (Univ. of Kansas) | Benjamin K Tsou | (City Univ. of Hong Kong) |
| Kok Wee Gan | (HKUST) | Amy Weinberg | (Univ. of Maryland) |
| Laurie Gerber | (Univ. of Southern CA/ISI) | Ralph Weischedel | (BBN) |
| Changning Huang | (Microsoft Research China) | Andi Wu | (Microsoft) |
| Chu-Ren Huang | (Academia Sinica) | Dekai Wu | (HKUST) |
| Wanying Jin | (New Mexicon State Univ.) | Nianwen Xue | (Univ. of Delaware) |
| Kim-Teng Lua | (National Univ. of Singapore) | Jin Yang | (Systran) |
| John Kovarik | (Department of Defense) | Shiwen Yu | (Peking Univ.) |
| K.L. Kwok | (Queens College) | Chunfa Yuan | (Tsinghua Univ.) |
| Mary Ellen Okurowski | (Department of Defense) | Joe Zhou | (Intel China Research Center) |
| Fuji Ren | (Hiroshima City Univ.) | Qiang Zhou | (Tsinghua Univ.) |
| Richard Sproat | (AT&T Research Lab) | | |

**FURTHER INFORMATION:**

Martha Palmer, Mitch Marcus, Aravind Joshi, and Fei Xia
Department of Computer and Information Science
University of Pennsylvania
Philadelphia, PA 19104, USA
Email: {mpalmer,mitch,joshi,fxia}@linc.cis.upenn.edu

**ACKNOWLEDGMENT:**

Special thanks to Yen-Lin Yin at the Univ. of Pennsylvania for helping us to organize this workshop.

# WORKSHOP PROGRAM

**Sunday, 8 October 2000**

| | |
|---|---|
| 8:45-9:00 | Welcome |
| 9:00-9:50 | *Invited Talk: Zero Anaphors in Chinese Discourse Processing*<br>Chin-Chuan Cheng |
| 9:50-10:10 | *Sense-Tagging Chinese Corpus*<br>Hsin-Hsi Chen and Chi-Ching Lin |
| 10:10-10:30 | *Enhancement of a Chinese Discourse Marker Tagger with C4.5*<br>Benjamin K. T'sou, Tom B.Y. Lai, Samuel W.K. Chan, Weijun Gao and Xuegang Zhan |
| 10:30-11:00 | *Break* |
| 11:00-11:20 | *Two Statistical Parsing Models Applied to the Chinese Treebank*<br>Daniel M. Bikel and David Chiang |
| 11:20-11:40 | *Using Co-occurence Statistics as an Information Source for Partial Parsing of Chinese*<br>Elliott Franco Drabek and Qiang Zhou |
| 11:40-12:00 | *Statistics Based Hybrid Approach to Chinese Base Phrase Identification*<br>Tie-jun Zhao, Mu-yun Yang, Fang Liu, Jian-min Yao and Hao Yu |
| 12:00-12:20 | *A Block-Based Robust Dependency Parser for Unrestricted Chinese Text*<br>Ming Zhou |
| 12:20-1:30 | *Lunch* |
| 1:30-2:30 | *Poster session* |
| 2:30-2:50 | *Knowledge Extraction for Identification of Chinese Organization Names*<br>Keh-Jiann Chen and Chao-jan Chen |
| 2:50-3:10 | *Statistically-Enhanced New Word Identification in a Rule-Based Chinese System*<br>Andi Wu and Zixin Jiang |
| 3:10-3:30 | *A Trainable Method for Extracting Chinese Entity Names and Their Relations*<br>Yimin Zhang and Joe F Zhou |
| 3:30-4:00 | *Break* |
| 4:00-4:20 | *Sinica Treebank: Design Criteria, Annotation Guidelines, and On-line Interface*<br>Chu-Ren Huang, Feng-Yi Chen, Keh-Jiann Chen, Zhao-ming Gao and Kuang-Yu Chen |
| 4:20-4:40 | *Comparing Lexicalized Treebank Grammars Extracted from Chinese, Korean, and English*<br>Fei Xia, Chunghye Han, Martha Palmer and Aravind Joshi |
| 4:40-5:00 | *The Research of Word Sense Disambiguation Method Based on Co-occurrence Frequency of Hownet*<br>Erhong Yang, Guoqing Zhang and Yongkui Zhang |
| 5:00-6:00 | *Panel: Prioritizing Chinese Language Processing Resources*<br>Keh-Jiann Chen, Chu-Ren Huang, Bing Swen, Benjamin K. T'sou, Joe Zhou and Ming Zhou |

# Table of Contents

PRESENTATIONS



POSTERS

## INVITED TALK

# Two Statistical Parsing Models Applied to the Chinese Treebank

**Daniel M. Bikel** **David Chiang**
Department of Computer & Information Science
University of Pennsylvania
200 South 33rd Street
Philadelphia, PA 19104-6389
{dbikel,dchiang}@cis.upenn.edu

## Abstract

This paper presents the first-ever results of applying statistical parsing models to the newly-available Chinese Treebank. We have employed two models, one extracted and adapted from BBN's SIFT System (Miller et al., 1998) and a TAG-based parsing model, adapted from (Chiang, 2000). On sentences with ≤40 words, the former model performs at 69% precision, 75% recall, and the latter at 77% precision and 78% recall.

## 1 Introduction

Ever since the success of HMMs' application to part-of-speech tagging in (Church, 1988), machine learning approaches to natural language processing have steadily become more widespread. This increase has of course been due to their proven efficacy in many tasks, but also to their *engineering* efficacy. Many machine learning approaches let the data speak for itself (*data ipsa loquuntur*), as it were, allowing the modeler to focus on what features of the data are important, rather than on the complicated interaction of such features, as had often been the case with hand-crafted NLP systems. The success of statistical methods in particular has been quite evident in the area of syntactic parsing, most recently with the outstanding results of (Charniak, 2000) and (Collins, 2000) on the now-standard English test set of the Penn Treebank (Marcus et al., 1993). A significant trend in parsing models has been the incorporation of linguistically-motivated features; however, it is important to note that "linguistically-motivated" does not necessarily mean "language-dependent"—often, it means just the opposite. For example, almost all statistical parsers make use of lexicalized nonterminals in some way, which allows lexical items' indiosyncratic parsing preferences to be modeled, but the paring between head words and their parent nonterminals is determined almost entirely by the training data, thereby making this *feature*—which models preferences of particular words of a particular language—almost entirely language-independent. In this paper, we will explore the use of two parsing models, which were originally designed for English parsing, on parsing Chinese, using the newly-available Chinese Treebank. We will show that the language-dependent components of these parsers are quite compact, and that with little effort they can be adapted to produce promising results for Chinese parsing. We also discuss directions for future work.

## 2 Models and Modifications

We will briefly describe the two parsing models employed (for a full description of the BBN model, see (Miller et al., 1998) and also (Bikel, 2000); for a full description of the TAG model, see (Chiang, 2000)).

### 2.1 Model 2 of (Collins, 1997)

Both parsing models discussed in this paper inherit a great deal from this model, so we briefly describe its "progenitive" features here, describing only how each of the two models of this paper differ in the subsequent two sections.

The lexicalized PCFG that sits behind Model 2 of (Collins, 1997) has rules of the form

$$P \rightarrow L_n L_{n-1} \cdots L_1 H R_1 \cdots R_{n-1} R_n \quad (1)$$

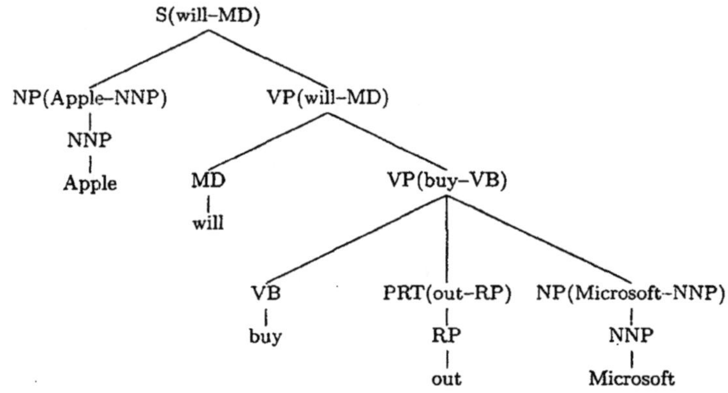


Figure 1: A sample sentence with parse tree.

where $P$, $L_i$, $R_i$ and $H$ are all lexicalized nonterminals, and $P$ inherits its lexical head from its distinguished head child, $H$. In this generative model, first $P$ is generated, then its head-child $H$, then each of the left- and right-modifying nonterminals are generated from the head outward. The modifying nonterminals $L_i$ and $R_i$ are generated conditioning on $P$ and $H$, as well as a distance metric (based on what material intervenes between the currently-generated modifying nonterminal and $H$) and an incremental subcat frame feature (a multiset containing the complements of $H$ that have yet to be generated on the side of $H$ in which the currently-generated nonterminal falls). Note that if the modifying nonterminals were generated completely independently, the model would be very impoverished, but in actuality, by including the distance and subcat frame features, the model captures a crucial bit of linguistic reality, *viz.*, that words often have well-defined sets of complements and adjuncts, dispersed with some well-defined distribution in the right hand sides of a (context-free) rewriting system.

## 2.2 BBN Model

### 2.2.1 Overview

The BBN model is also of the lexicalized PCFG variety. In the BBN model, as with Model 2 of (Collins, 1997), modifying nonterminals are generated conditioning both on the parent $P$ and its head child $H$. Unlike Model 2 of (Collins, 1997), they are also generated conditioning on the previously generated modifying nonterminal, $L_{i-1}$ or $R_{i-1}$, and there is no subcat frame or distance feature. While the BBN model does not perform at the level of Model 2 of (Collins, 1997) on Wall Street Journal text, it is also less language-dependent, eschewing the distance metric (which relied on specific features of the English Treebank) in favor of the "bigrams on nonterminals" model.

### 2.2.2 Model Parameters

This section briefly describes the top-level parameters used in the BBN parsing model. We use $p$ to denote the unlexicalized nonterminal corresponding to $P$ in (1), and similarly for $l_i$, $r_i$ and $h$. We now present the top-level generation probabilities, along with examples from Figure 1. For brevity, we omit the smoothing details of BBN's model (see (Miller et al., 1998) for a complete description); we note that all smoothing weights are computed via the technique described in (Bikel et al., 1997).

The probability of generating $p$ as the root label is predicted conditioning on only +TOP+, which is the hidden root of all parse trees:

$$P\left(p \mid +\text{TOP}+\right), \; e.g., \; P(\text{S} \mid +\text{TOP}+). \quad (2)$$

The probability of generating a head node $h$ with a parent $p$ is

$$P(h \mid p), \; e.g., \; P(\text{VP} \mid \text{S}). \quad (3)$$

The probability of generating a left-modifier $l_i$ is

$$P_L(l_i \mid l_{i-1}, p, h, w_h), , \; e.g., \quad (4)$$
$$P_L(\text{NP} \mid +\text{BEGIN}+, \text{S}, \text{VP}, \text{will})$$

when generating the NP for NP(Apple–NNP), and the probability of generating a right modifier $r_i$ is

$$P_R(r_i \mid r_{i-1}, p, h, w_h),\ e.g., \quad (5)$$
$$P_R(\mathrm{NP} \mid \mathrm{PRT}, \mathrm{VP}, \mathrm{VB}, \mathrm{buy})$$

when generating the NP for NP(Microsoft–NNP).[1]

The probabilities for generating lexical elements (part-of-speech tags and words) are as follows. The part of speech tag of the head of the entire sentence, $t_h$, is computed conditioning only on the top-most symbol $p$:[2]

$$P(t_h \mid p). \quad (6)$$

Part of speech tags of modifier constituents, $t_{l_i}$ and $t_{r_i}$, are predicted conditioning on the modifier constituent $l_i$ or $r_i$, the tag of the head constituent, $t_h$, and the word of the head constituent, $w_h$

$$P(t_{l_i} \mid l_i, t_h, w_h) \text{ and } P(t_{r_i} \mid r_i, t_h, w_h). \quad (7)$$

The head word of the entire sentence, $w_h$, is predicted conditioning only on the top-most symbol $p$ and $t_h$:

$$P(w_h \mid t_h, p). \quad (8)$$

Head words of modifier constituents, $w_{l_i}$ and $w_{r_i}$, are predicted conditioning on all the context used for predicting parts of speech in (7), as well as the parts of speech themsleves

$$P(w_{l_i} \mid t_{l_i}, l_i, t_h, w_h)$$
$$\text{and} \quad P(w_{r_i} \mid t_{r_i}, r_i, t_h, w_h). \quad (9)$$

The original English model also included a word feature to help reduce part-of-speech ambiguity for unknown words, but this component of the model was removed for Chinese, as it was language-dependent.

The probability of an entire parse tree is the product of the probabilities of generating all of the elements of that parse tree, where an element is either a constituent label, a part of speech tag or a word. We obtain maximum-likelihood estimates of the parameters of this model using frequencies gathered from the training data.

[1]The hidden nonterminal +BEGIN+ is used to provide a convenient mechanism for determining the initial probability of the underlying Markov process generating the modifying nonterminals; the hidden nonterminal +END+ is used to provide consistency to the underlying Markov process, *i.e.*, so that the probabilities of all possible nonterminal sequences sum to 1.

[2]This is the one place where we altered the original model, as the lexical components of the head of the entire sentence were all being estimated incorrectly, causing an inconsistency in the model. We corrected the estimation of $t_h$ and $w_h$ in our implementation.

### 2.3 TAG Model

The model of (Chiang, 2000) is based on stochastic TAG (Resnik, 1992; Schabes, 1992). In this model a parse tree is built up not out of lexicalized phrase-structure rules but by tree fragments (called *elementary trees*) which are lexicalized in the sense that each fragment contains exactly one lexical item (its *anchor*).

In the variant of TAG we use, there are three kinds of elementary tree: initial, (predicative) auxiliary, and modifier, and three composition operations: substitution, adjunction, and sister-adjunction. Figure 2 illustrates all three of these operations. $\alpha_1$ is an initial tree which substitutes at the leftmost node labeled NP↓; $\beta$ is an auxiliary tree which adjoins at the node labeled VP. See (Joshi and Schabes, 1997) for a more detailed explanation.

Sister-adjunction is not a standard TAG operation, but borrowed from D-Tree Grammar (Rambow et al., 1995). In Figure 2 the modifier tree $\gamma$ is sister adjoined between the nodes labeled VB and NP↓. Multiple modifier trees can adjoin at the same place, in the spirit of (Schabes and Shieber, 1994).

In stochastic TAG, the probability of generating an elementary tree depends on the elementary tree itself and the elementary tree it attaches to. The parameters are as follows:

$$\begin{aligned} \sum_\alpha P_i(\alpha) &= 1 \\ \sum_\alpha P_s(\alpha \mid \eta) &= 1 \\ \sum_\beta P_a(\beta \mid \eta) + P_a(NONE \mid \eta) &= 1 \end{aligned}$$

where $\alpha$ ranges over initial trees, $\beta$ over auxiliary trees, $\gamma$ over modifier trees, and $\eta$ over nodes. $P_i(\alpha)$ is the probability of beginning a derivation with $\alpha$; $P_s(\alpha \mid \eta)$ is the probability of substituting $\alpha$ at $\eta$; $P_a(\beta \mid \eta)$ is the probability of adjoining $\beta$ at $\eta$; finally, $P_a(NONE \mid \eta)$ is the probability of nothing adjoining at $\eta$.

Our variant adds another set of parameters:

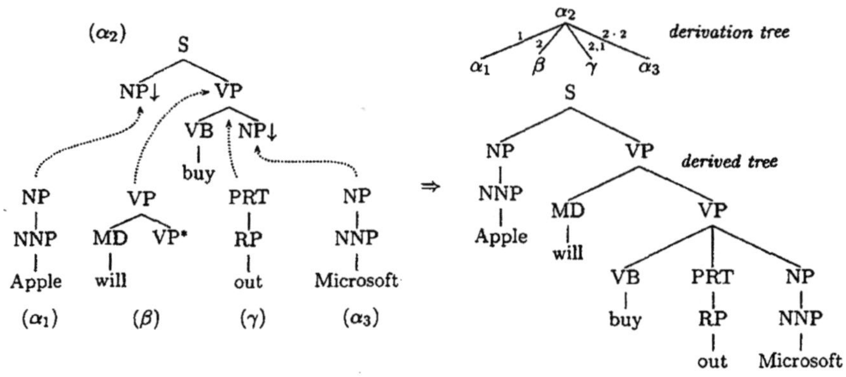


Figure 2: Grammar and derivation for "Apple will buy out Microsoft."

$$\sum_{\gamma} P_{sa}(\gamma \mid \eta, i, f) + P_{sa}(STOP \mid \eta, i, f) = 1$$

This is the probability of sister-adjoining $\gamma$ between the $i$th and $i+1$th children of $\eta$ (allowing for two imaginary children beyond the leftmost and rightmost children). Since multiple modifier trees can adjoin at the same location, $P_{sa}(\gamma)$ is also conditioned on a flag $f$ which indicates whether $\gamma$ is the first modifier tree (i.e., the one closest to the head) to adjoin at that location.

For our model we break down these probabilities further: first the elementary tree is generated without its anchor, and then its anchor is generated. See (Chiang, 2000) for more details.

During training each example is broken into elementary trees using head rules and argument/adjunct rules similar to those of (Collins, 1997). The rules are interpreted as follows: a head is kept in the same elementary tree in its parent, an argument is broken off into a separate initial tree, leaving a substitution node, and an adjunct is broken off into a separate modifier tree. A different rule is used for extracting auxiliary trees; see (Chiang, 2000) for details. Xia (1999) describes a similar process, and in fact our rules for the Xinhua corpus are based on hers.

### 2.4 Modifications

The primary language-dependent component that had to be changed in both models was the head table, used to determine heads when training. We modified the head rules described in (Xia, 1999) for the Xinhua corpus and substituted these new rules into both models.

The (Chiang, 2000) model had the following additional modifications.

- The new corpus had to be prepared for use with the trainer and parser. Aside from technicalities, this involved retraining the part-of-speech tagger described in (Ratnaparkhi, 1997), which was used for tagging unknown words. We also lowered the unknown word threshold from 4 to 2 because the Xinhua corpus was smaller than the WSJ corpus.
- In addition to the change to the head-finding rules, we also changed the rules for classifying modifiers as arguments or adjuncts. In both cases the new rules were adapted from (Xia, 1999).
- For the tests done in this paper, a beam width of $10^{-4}$ was used.

The BBN model had the following additional modifications:

- As with the (Chiang, 2000) model, we similarly lowered the unknown word threshold of the BBN model from its default 5 to 2.
- The language-dependent word-feature was eliminated, causing parts of speech for unknown words to be predicted solely on the head relations in the model.
- The default beam size in the probabilistic CKY parsing algorithm was widened. The default beam pruned away chart entries whose scores were not within a factor of $e^{-5}$ of the top-ranked subtree; this

| Model, test set | ≤40 words | | | | |
|---|---|---|---|---|---|
| | LR | LP | $\overline{\text{CB}}$ | 0CB | ≤2CB |
| BBN-all†, WSJ-all | 84.7 | 86.5 | 1.12 | 60.6 | 83.2 |
| BBN-small†, WSJ-small* | 79.0 | 80.7 | 1.66 | 47.0 | 74.6 |
| **BBN, Xinhua‡** | **69.0** | **74.8** | **2.05** | **45.0** | **68.5** |
| Chiang-all, WSJ-all | 86.9 | 86.6 | 1.09 | 63.2 | 84.3 |
| Chiang-small, WSJ-small | 78.9 | 79.6 | 1.75 | 44.8 | 72.4 |
| **Chiang, Xinhua** | **76.8** | **77.8** | **1.99** | **50.8** | **74.1** |
| | ≤100 words | | | | |
| | LR | LP | $\overline{\text{CB}}$ | 0CB | ≤2CB |
| BBN-all†, WSJ-all | 83.9 | 85.7 | 1.31 | 57.8 | 80.8 |
| BBN-small†, WSJ-small* | 78.4 | 80.0 | 1.92 | 44.3 | 71.3 |
| **BBN, Xinhua‡** | **67.5** | **73.5** | **2.87** | **39.9** | **61.8** |
| Chiang-all, WSJ-all | 86.2 | 85.8 | 1.29 | 60.4 | 81.8 |
| Chiang-small, WSJ-small | 77.1 | 78.8 | 2.00 | 43.25 | 70.5 |
| **Chiang, Xinhua** | **73.3** | **74.6** | **3.03** | **44.8** | **66.8** |

Table 1: Results for both parsing models on all test sets. Key: LR = labeled recall, LP = labeled precision, $\overline{\text{CB}}$ = avg. crossing brackets, 0CB = zero crossing brackets, ≤2CB = ≤2 crossing brackets. All results are percentages, except for those in the $\overline{\text{CB}}$ column. †Used larger beam settings and lower unknown word threshold than the defaults. *3 of the 400 sentences were not parsed due to timeouts and/or pruning problems. ‡3 of the 348 sentences did not get parsed due to pruning problems, and 2 other sentences had length mismatches (scoring program errors).

tight limit was changed to $e^{-9}$. Also, the default decoder pruned away all but the top 25-ranked chart entries in each cell; this limit was expanded to 50.

## 3 Experiments and Results

The Chinese Treebank consists of 4185 sentences of Xinhua newswire text. We blindly separated this into training, devtest and test sets, with a roughly 80/10/10 split, putting files 001–270 (3484 sentences, 84,873 words) into the training set, 301–325 (353 sentences, 6776 words) into the development test set and reserving 271–300 (348 sentences, 7980 words) for testing. See Table 1 for results.

In order to put the new Chinese Treebank results into context with the unmodified (English) parsing models, we present results on two test sets from the Wall Street Journal: WSJ-all, which is the complete Section 23 (the *de facto* standard test set for English parsing), and WSJ-small, which is the first 400 sentences of Section 23 and which is roughly comparable in size to the Chinese test set. Furthermore, when testing on WSJ-small, we trained on a subset of our English training data roughly equivalent in size to our Chinese training set (Sections 02 and 03 of the Penn Treebank); we have indicated models trained on all English training with "-all", and models trained with the reduced English training set with "-small". Therefore, by comparing the WSJ-small results with the Chinese results, one can reasonably gauge the performance gap between English parsing on the Penn Treebank and Chinese parsing on the Chinese Treebank.

The reader will note that the modified BBN model does significantly poorer than (Chiang, 2000) on Chinese. While more investigation is required, we suspect part of the difference may be due to the fact that currently, the BBN model uses language-specific rules to guess part of speech tags for unknown words.

## 4 Conclusions and Future Work

There is no question that a great deal of care and expertise went into creating the Chinese Treebank, and that it is a source of important grammatical information that is unique to the Chinese language. However, there are definite similarities between the grammars of English and Chinese, especially when viewed through the lens of the statistical models we employed here. In both languages, the nouns, adjectives, adverbs, and verbs have preferences for certain arguments and adjuncts, and these preferences—in spite of the potentially vastly-different configurations of these items—are effectively modeled. As discussed in the introduction, lexical items' idiosyncratic parsing preferences are modeled by lexicalizing the grammar formalism, using a lexicalized PCFG in one case and a lexicalized stochastic TAG in the other. Linguistically-reasonable independence assumptions are made, such as the independence of grammar productions in the case of the PCFG model, or the independence of the composition operations in the case of the LTAG model, and we would argue that these assumptions are no less reasonable for the Chinese grammar than they are for that of English. While results for the two languages are far from equal, we believe that further tuning of the head rules, and analysis of development test set errors will yield significant performance gains on Chinese to close the gap. Finally, we fully expect that absolute performance will increase greatly as additional high-quality Chinese parse data becomes available.

## 5 Acknowledgements

This research was funded in part by NSF grant SBR-89-20230-15. We would greatly like to acknowledge the researchers at BBN who allowed us to use their model: Ralph Weischedel, Scott Miller, Lance Ramshaw, Heidi Fox and Sean Boisen. We would also like to thank Mike Collins and our advisors Aravind Joshi and Mitch Marcus.

## References

Daniel M. Bikel, Richard Schwartz, Ralph Weischedel, and Scott Miller. 1997. Nymble: A high-performance learning name-finder. In *Fifth Conference on Applied Natural Language Processing*, pages 194–201, , Washington, D.C.

Daniel M. Bikel. 2000. A statistical model for parsing and word-sense disambiguation. In *Joint SIGDAT Conference on Empirical Methods in Natural Language Processing and Very Large Corpora*, Hong Kong, October.

Eugene Charniak. 2000. A maximum entropy-inspired parser. In *Proceedings of the 1st Meeting of the North American Chapter of the Association for Computational Linguistics*, pages 132–139, Seattle, Washington, April 29 to May 4.

David Chiang. 2000. Statistical parsing with an automatically-extracted tree adjoining grammar. In *Proceedings of the 38th Annual Meeting of the Association for Computational Linguistics*.

Kenneth Church. 1988. A stochastic parts program and noun phrase parser for unrestricted text. In *Second Conference on Applied Natural Language Processing*, pages 136–143, Austin, Texas.

Michael Collins. 1997. Three generative, lexicalised models for statistical parsing. In *Proceedings of ACL-EACL '97*, pages 16–23.

Michael Collins. 2000. Discriminative reranking for natural language parsing. In *International Conference on Machine Learning*. (to appear).

Aravind K. Joshi and Yves Schabes. 1997. Tree-adjoining grammars. In A. Salomma and G. Rosenberg, editors, *Handbook of Formal Languages and Automata*, volume 3, pages 69–124. Springer-Verlag, Heidelberg.

Mitchell P. Marcus, Beatrice Santorini, and Mary Ann Marcinkiewicz. 1993. Building a large annotated corpus of English: The Penn Treebank. *Computational Linguistics*, 19:313–330.

Scott Miller, Heidi Fox, Lance Ramshaw, and Ralph Weischedel. 1998. SIFT – Statistically-derived Information From Text. In *Seventh Message Understanding Conference (MUC-7)*, Washington, D.C.

Owen Rambow, K. Vijay-Shanker, and David Weir. 1995. D-tree grammars. In *Proceedings of the 33rd Annual Meeting of the Assocation for Computational Linguistics*, pages 151–158.

Adwait Ratnaparkhi. 1997. A simple introduction to maximum entropy models for natural language processing. Technical Report IRCS Report 97–08, Institute for Research in Cognitive Science, May.

Philip Resnik. 1992. Probabilistic tree-adjoining grammar as a framework for statistical natural language processing. In *Proceedings of COLING-92*, pages 418–424.

Yves Schabes and Stuart M. Shieber. 1994. An alternative conception of tree-adjoining derivation. *Computational Linguistics*, 20(1):91–124.

Yves Schabes. 1992. Stochastic lexicalized tree-adjoining grammars. In *Proceedings of COLING-92*, pages 426–432.

Fei Xia. 1999. Extracting tree adjoining grammars from bracketed corpora. In *Proceedings of the 5th Natural Language Processing Pacific Rim Symposium (NLPRS-99)*.

# Sense-Tagging Chinese Corpus

**Hsin-Hsi Chen**
Department of Computer Science and Information Engineering
National Taiwan University
Taipei, TAIWAN
hh_chen@csie.ntu.edu.tw

**Chi-Ching Lin**
Department of Computer Science and Information Engineering
National Taiwan University
Taipei, TAIWAN
cclin@nlg2.csie.ntu.edu.tw

**Abstract**

Contextual information and the mapping from WordNet synsets to Cilin sense tags deal with word sense disambiguation. The average performance is 63.36% when small categories are used, and 1, 2 and 3 candidates are proposed for low, middle and high ambiguous words. The performance of tagging unknown words is 34.35%, which is much better than that of baseline mode. The sense tagger achieves the performance of 76.04%, when unambiguous, ambiguous, and unknown words are tagged.

## 1 Introduction

Tagging task, which adds lexical, syntactic or semantic information to raw text, makes materials more valuable. The researches on part of speech (POS) tagging have been a long history, and achieve very good results. Many POS-tagged corpora are available. The accuracy for POS-tagging is in the range of 95% to 97%[1]. In contrast, although the researches on word sense disambiguation (WSD) are also very early (Kelly and Stone, 1975), large-scale sense-tagged corpus is relatively few. In English, only some sense-tagged corpora such as HECTOR (Atkins, 1993), DSO (Ng and Lee, 1996), SEMCOR (Fellbaum, 1997), and SENSEVAL (Kilgarriff, 1998) are available. For evaluating word sense disambiguation systems, the first SENSEVAL (Kilgarriff and Rosenzweig, 2000) reports that the performance for a fine-grained word sense disambiguation task is at around 75%.

Tagging accuracy depends on several issues (Manning and Schutze, 1999), e.g., the amount of training data, the granularity of the tagging set, the occurrences of unknown words, and so on. Three approaches have been proposed for WSD, including dictionary/thesaurus-based approach, supervised learning, and unsupervised learning. The major differences are what kinds of resources are used, i.e., dictionary versus text corpus, and sense-tagged corpus versus untagged corpus. A good survey refers to the paper (Ide and Veronis, 1998). Compared with English, Chinese does not have large-scale sense-tagged corpus. The widely available corpus is Academic Sinica Balanced Corpus abbreviated as ASBC hereafter (Huang and Chen, 1995), which is a POS-tagged corpus. Thus, a computer-aided tool to sense-tag Chinese corpus is indispensable.

This paper presents a sense tagger for Mandarin Chinese. It is organized as follows. Section 2 discusses the degree of polysemy in Mandarin Chinese from several viewpoints. Section 3 presents WSD algorithms for tagging ambiguous words and unknown words. Section 4 shows our experimental results. Finally, Section 5 concludes the remarks.

## 2 Degree of Polysemy in Mandarin Chinese

The degree of polysemy is defined as the average number of senses of words. We adopt tagging set from tong2yi4ci2ci2lin2 (同義詞詞林) abbreviated as Cilin (Mei, *et al.*, 1982). It is composed of 12 large categories, 94 middle categories, and 1,428 small categories.

Small categories (more fine granularity) are used to compute the distribution of word senses. Besides Cilin, ASBC is employed to count frequency of a word. Total 28,321 word types appear both in Cilin and in ASBC corpus. Here a word type corresponds to a dictionary

[1] The performance includes tagging unambiguous words. Marshall (1987) reported that the performance of CLAWS tagger is 94%. Approximately 65% of words were tagged unambiguously, and the disambiguation program achieved better than 80% success on the ambiguous words.

**Table 1. The Distribution of Word Senses**

| Low Ambiguity | | Middle Ambiguity | | High Ambiguity | | | |
|---|---|---|---|---|---|---|---|
| Degree | #Word Types | Degree | #Word Types | Degree | #Word Types | Degree | #Word Types |
| 2 | 4261 (71.95%) | 5 | 186 (3.14%) | 9 | 14 (0.24%) | 14 | 1 (0.02%) |
| 3 | 948 (16.01%) | 6 | 77 (1.30%) | 10 | 8 (0.14%) | 15 | 1 (0.02%) |
| 4 | 344 (5.81%) | 7 | 42 (0.71%) | 11 | 3 (0.05%) | 17 | 1 (0.02%) |
| | | 8 | 25 (0.42%) | 12 | 4 (0.07%) | 18 | 1 (0.02%) |
| | | | | 13 | 5 (0.08%) | 20 | 1 (0.02%) |
| Sum | 5553 (93.77%) | Sum | 330 (5.57%) | Sum | | | 39 (0.66%) |
| Total Word Types | | 5922 | | | | | |

**Table 2. The Distribution of Word Senses with Consideration of POS**

| Degree \ POS | | N | V | A | F | K |
|---|---|---|---|---|---|---|
| Low | 2 | 1441 (81.05%) | 1056 (71.79%) | 580 (79.67%) | 14 (77.78%) | 101 (73.72%) |
| | 3 | 238 (13.39%) | 238 (16.18%) | 115 (15.80%) | 4 (22.22%) | 25 (18.25%) |
| | 4 | 55 (3.09%) | 99 (6.73%) | 20 (2.75%) | | 7 (5.11%) |
| Middle | 5 | 26 (1.46%) | 41 (2.79%) | 9 (1.24%) | | 3 (2.19%) |
| | 6 | 12 (0.67%) | 13 (0.88%) | 2 (0.27%) | | 1 (0.73%) |
| | 7 | 3 (0.17%) | 13 (0.88%) | 2 (0.27%) | | |
| | 8 | 2 (0.11%) | 6 (0.40%) | | | |
| High | 9 | 1 (0.06%) | 1 (0.07%) | | | |
| | 11 | | 1 (0.07%) | | | |
| | 12 | | 1 (0.07%) | | | |
| | 13 | | 1 (0.07%) | | | |
| | 19 | | 1 (0.07%) | | | |
| Total Word Types | | 1778 | 1471 | 728 | 18 | 137 |

entry. Of these, 5,922 words are polysemous, i.e., they have more than one sense. Table 1 lists the statistics. We divide the ambiguity degree into three levels according to the number of senses of a word. It includes low (2-4), middle (5-8), and high ambiguity (>8). The statistics shows that 93.77% of word types belong to the class of low ambiguity.

We further consider POS when computing the distribution of word senses. Table 2 shows the statistics. N, V, A, F, and K denote nouns, verbs, adjectives, numerals, and auxiliaries (adverbs), respectively. We can find most of words belong to the class of low ambiguity no matter which POSes they are. Besides, the ambiguity is decreased when POS is considered. The number of polysemous words is down to 4,132. For A and K, the number of senses is no more than 7, and the percentages in the class of low degrees are 98.22% and 97.08%, respectively. For N and V, there are some high ambiguous words. In particular, the verb (打, da3) has 19 senses[2]. The percentages in the class of low degrees are 97.53% and 94.70%, respectively.

Then, the frequency of word types is considered. ASBC corpus is used to compute the occurrences of word types. Table 3 lists the statistics. A word token is an occurrence of a type in the corpus. On the average, the words of low, middle and high ambiguity appear 205.96, 1926.65, and 4480.28 times, respectively. Table 1 shows 93.77% of polysemous words belong to the class of low ambiguity, but Table 3 illustrates they only

[2] The word (打, da3) has 20 senses. Besides verb usage, it also functions as an auxiliary.

**Table 3. The Distribution of Word Senses with Consideration of Frequencies**

| Low Ambiguity | | | Middle Ambiguity | | | High Ambiguity | | |
|---|---|---|---|---|---|---|---|---|
| Types | Tokens | #Tokens/ #Types | Types | Tokens | #Tokens/ #Types | Types | Tokens | #Tokens/ #Types |
| 5553 | 1143686 | 205.96 | 330 | 635796 | 1926.65 | 39 | 174731 | 4480.28 |
| 93.77% | 58.52% | | 5.57% | 32.53% | | 0.66% | 8.94% | |

**Table 4. The Distribution of Word Senses and Frequencies with Consideration of POS**

| Ambiguity \ Frequency | | Low | Middle | High | Sum | Percentage |
|---|---|---|---|---|---|---|
| Low | Types (C) | 3112 | 734 | 147 | 3993 | 96.64% |
| | Tokens (A) | 70131 | 230955 | 735819 | 1036905 | 85.52% |
| | A/C | 22.54 | 314.65 | 5005.57 | 259.68 | |
| Middle | Types (C) | 42 | 62 | 29 | 133 | 3.22% |
| | Tokens (A) | 1905 | 14667 | 153307 | 169879 | 14.01% |
| | A/C | 45.36 | 236.56 | 5286.45 | 1277.29 | |
| High | Types (C) | 0 | 2 | 4 | 6 | 0.15% |
| | Tokens (A) | 0 | 843 | 4847 | 5690 | 0.47% |
| | A/C | 0 | 421.5 | 1211.75 | 948.33 | |
| Sum | Types (C) | 3154 | 798 | 180 | 4132 | |
| | Tokens (A) | 72036 | 246465 | 893973 | 1212474 | |
| | A/C | 22.84 | 308.85 | 4966.52 | | |
| % | Types (C) | 76.33% | 19.31% | 4.36% | | |
| | Tokens (A) | 5.94% | 20.33% | 73.73% | | |

occupy 58.52% of tokens in ASBC corpus.

Table 4 summarizes the distribution of word senses and frequencies. Low frequency denotes the number of occurrences less than 100, middle frequency denotes the number of occurrences between 100 and 1000, and high frequency denotes the number of occurrences more than 1000. Rows C and A in Table 4 denote number of word types and word tokens, respectively. The last column denotes percentage for each ambiguity degree. For example, the percentage of word types with low ambiguity is 96.64% (i.e., 3993/4132). This table shows the following two phenomena:

(1) POS information reduces the degree of ambiguities. Total 8.94% of word tokens are high ambiguous in Table 3. It decreases to 0.47% in Table 4.

(2) High ambiguous words tend to be high frequent. From the row of low ambiguity, there are 3,112 low-frequent words. They occur 70,131 times in ASBC corpus. Comparatively, there are only 881 middle- or high-frequent words, but they occur 966,774 times. That is, 23.67% of word types are middle- or high-frequent words, and they occupy 94.06% of word tokens. From the row of high ambiguity, there are only a few words, but they occur frequently in the ASBC corpus. It shows that semantic tagging is a challengeable problem in Mandarin Chinese.

## 3 Semantic Tagging

### 3.1 Tagging Unambiguous Words

In the semantic tagging, the small categories are selected. We postulate that the sense definition for each word in Cilin is complete. That is, a word that has only one sense in Cilin is called an *unambiguous* word or a *monosemous* word. If POS information is also considered, a word may be unambiguous under a specific POS. Because we do not have a semantically tagged corpus for training, we try to acquire the context for each semantic tag starting from the unambiguous words.

ASBC corpus is the target we study. At the first stage, only those words that are unambiguous in Cilin, and also appear in ASBC corpus are tagged. Figure 1 shows this case.

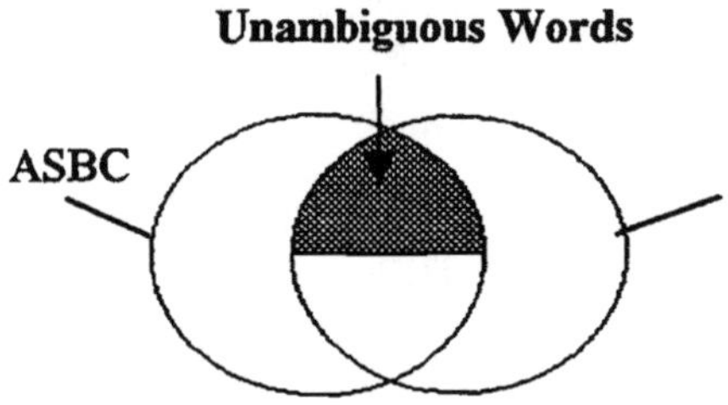


**Figure 1. Tagging Unambiguous Words**

An unambiguous word (and hence its sense tag) is characterized by the words surrounding it. The window size is set to 6, and stop words are removed. A list of stop words is trained from ASBC corpus. The words of POSes Neu (數詞), DE (的，之，得，地), SHI (是), FW (外文標記), C (連接詞), T (語助詞), and I (感嘆詞) are regarded as stop words. A sense tag *Ctag* is in terms of a vector ($w_1$, $w_2$, ..., $w_n$), where n is the vocabulary size and $w_i$ is a weight of word *cw*. The weight can be determined by the following two ways.

(1) MI metric (Church, *et al.*, 1989)

$$MI\,(Ctag\,,cw) = \log_2 \frac{P(Ctag\,,cw)}{P(Ctag\,)P(cw)} = \log_2 \frac{f(Ctag\,,cw)}{f(Ctag\,)f(cw)} \times N$$

where *P*(*Ctag*) is the probability of *Ctag*,
*P*(*cw*) is the probability of *cw*,
*P*(*Ctag*, *cw*) is the cooccurrence probability of *Ctag* and *cw*,
*f*(*Ctag*) is the frequency of *Ctag*,
*f*(*cw*) is the frequency of *cw*,
*f*(*Ctag*, *cw*) is the cooccurrence frequency of *Ctag* and *cw*, and
*N* is total number of words in the corpus.

(2) EM metric (Ballesteros and Croft, 1998)

$$em(Ctag, cw) = \max\left( \frac{f(Ctag, cw) - En(Ctag, cw)}{f(Ctag) + f(cw)}, 0 \right)$$

$$En\,(Ctag\,, cw) = \frac{f(Ctag\,)\,f(cw)}{N}$$

### 3.2 Tagging Ambiguous Words

At the second stage, we deal with those words that have more than one sense in the Cilin. Figure 2 shows the words we consider.

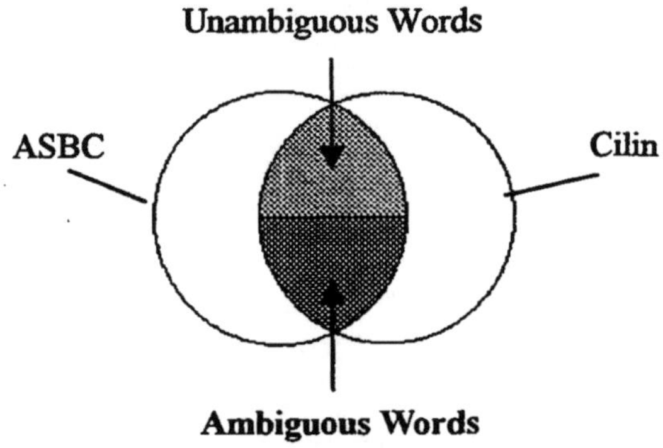


**Figure 2. Tagging Ambiguous Words**

The approach we adopted on semantic tagging rests on an underlying assumption: each sense has a characteristic context that is different from the context of all the other senses. In addition, all words expressing the same sense share the same characteristic context. We will apply the information trained at the first stage to selecting the best sense tag from the candidates of each ambiguous word. Recall that a vector corresponds to a sense tag. We employ the similar way specified in Section 3.1 to identify the context vector of an ambiguous word. A cosine formula shown as follows measures the similarity between a sense vector and a context vector, where *w* and *v* are a sense vector and a context vector, respectively. The sense tag of the highest similarity score is chosen.

$$\cos\,(w\,,\,v\,) = \frac{w\,\cdot v}{|w\,|\,|v\,|}$$

We retrain the sense vector for each sense tag after the unambiguous words are resolved.

### 3.3 Tagging Unknown Words

Those words that appear in ASBC corpus, but are not gathered in Cilin are called *unknown words*. All the 1,428 sense tags are the possible candidates. Intuitively, the algorithm in Section 3.2 can be applied directly to select a sense tag from the 1,428 candidates. However, the candidate set is very large. Here we adopt outside evidences from the mapping among WordNet synsets (Fellbaum, 1998) and Cilin

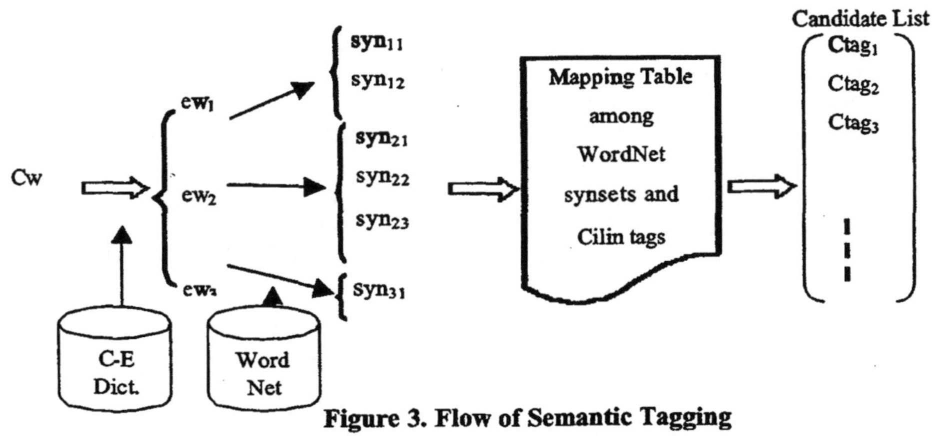


**Figure 3. Flow of Semantic Tagging**

sense tags to narrow down the candidate set. Figure 3 summarizes the flow of our algorithm. It is illustrated as follows.

(1) Find all the English translations of an unknown Chinese word by looking up a Chinese-English dictionary.

(2) Find all the synsets of the English translations by looking up WordNet. We do not resolve translation ambiguity and target polysemy at these two steps, thus the retrieved synsets may cover more senses than that of the original Chinese word.

(3) Transform the synsets back to Cilin sense tags by looking up a mapping table. How the mapping table is set up will be discussed in Section 3.3.1.

(4) Select a sense tag from the candidates proposed at step (3) by using the WSD in Section 3.2.

Figure 4 shows the unknown words we deal with at this stage. Those words that are not gathered in our Chinese-English dictionary are not considered, so that only parts of unknown words are resolved. In other words, there remain words without sense tags.

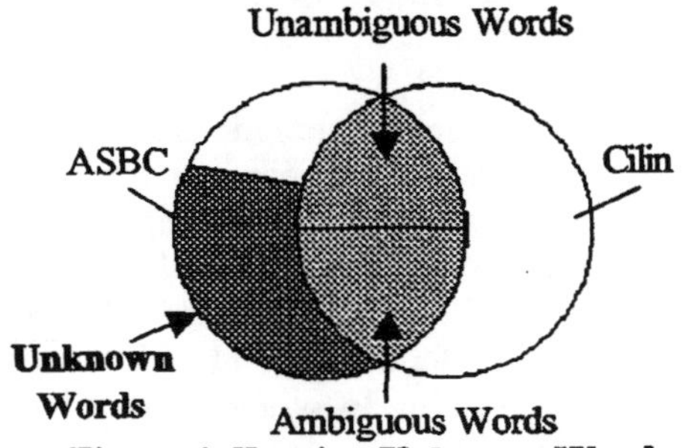


**Figure 4. Tagging Unknown Words**

### *3.3.1 Mapping SynSets to Cilin Sense Tags*

At first, we put unambiguous words (specified in Section 3.1) into WordNet by looking up a Chinese-English dictionary. Although these words do not have translation ambiguity, the corresponding English translation may have target polysemy problem. In other words, the English translation may cover irrelevant senses besides the correct one. The following algorithm will find the most similar synset with Chinese sense tag.

(1) If the English translation corresponds to only one synset, this synset is the solution.

(2) If the English translation corresponds to more than one synset, POS is considered:

(a) If the Chinese sense tag belongs to one of categories A-D in Cilin (i.e., a noun sense), and there is only one noun synset, then the synset is adopted. Otherwise, we translate the context vector of the Chinese sense into English, compare it with vectors of the synsets, and select the most similar synset.

(b) If the Chinese sense tag belongs to one of categories F-J in Cilin (i.e., a verb sense), we try to find a verb synset in the similar way as (a). If it fails, we try noun and adjective synsets instead.

(c) If the Chinese sense tag belongs to category E in Cilin (i.e., an adjective sense), we try adjective, adverb, noun and verb synsets in sequence.

(d) If the Chinese sense tag belongs to category K in Cilin (i.e., an adverb sense), only adverb synsets are considered.

Next, we consider the ambiguous words. Chinese-English dictionary lookup finds all the English translations. WordNet search collects the synset candidates for the translations. Some synsets are selected and regarded as the mapping of the Cilin sense tag. Here the problems of translation ambiguity and target polysemy must be faced. In other words, not all English translations cover the Cilin sense. Because the goal is to find a mapping table between WordNet synsets and Cilin sense tags, we neglect the problem of translation ambiguity and follow the method in the previous paragraph to choose the most similar synsets.

During mapping, English translations of a word may not be found in the Chinese-English dictionary, and WordNet may not gather the English translations even dictionary look-up is successful. Thus, only 1,328 of 1,428 Cilin tags are mapped to WordNet synsets. From the other view, there remains some WordNet synsets that do not correspond to any Cilin sense tags. Let such a synset be $S_i$. We follow the relational pointers like hypernym, hyponym, similar, derived, antonym, or participle to collect the neighboring synsets denoted by $S_j$. The following method selects suitable Cilin tag(s) for $S_i$.

(1) If $S_j$ is the only one synset that has been mapped to Cilin tags, we choose a Cilin tag and map $S_i$ to it.

(2) If there exists more than one $S_j$ (say, $S_{j1}$, $S_{j2}$, ..., $S_{jn}$) that has been mapped to Cilin tags, we choose the Cilin tags that more synsets map to.

The above method is called a *more restrictive* scheme. An alternative method (called *less restrictive* method) is: all the Cilin tags that the neighboring synsets map to are selected. If Cilin tags cannot be found from neighboring synsets, we extend the range one more, and repeat the selection procedure again until all the synsets are considered.

## 4 Experiments

### 4.1 Test Materials

We sample documents of different categories from ASBC corpus, including philosophy (10%), science (10%), society (35%), art (5%), life (20%) and literary (20%). There are 35,921 words in the test corpus. Research associates tag this corpus manually. At first, they mark up the ambiguous words by looking up the Cilin dictionary. Next, they tag the unknown words. A list of candidates is proposed by looking up the mapping table. Because the mapping table may have errors, the annotators assign a tag "none" when they cannot choose a solution from the proposed candidates. Total 435 of 1,979 words are tagged with "none" with the more restrictive method. In contrast, only 346 words are labeled with "none" with the less restrictive method. The tag mapper achieves 82.52% of performance approximately.

### 4.2 Tagging Ambiguous Words

Table 5 shows the performance of tagging ambiguous words. MI defined in Section 3.1 is used. Total 11,101 words are tagged. The performance of tagging low, middle, and high ambiguous words are 62.60%, 31.36%, and 27.00%, respectively. Table 6 shows that the performance is improved, in particular, the classes of middle- and high- ambiguity, when EM (defined in Section 3.1) is used. The overall performance is increased from 49.55% to 52.85%.

In the previous experiments, only one sense is reported for each word. If we report more than one sense for middle and high ambiguous words, the performance is improved. Table 7 shows that the first 2 and 3 candidates are selected. From the diagonal of this table, the performance for tagging low ambiguity (2-4), middle ambiguity (5-8) and high ambiguity (>8) is similar (i.e., 63.98%, 60.92% and 67.95%) when 1 candidate, 2 candidates, and 3 candidates are proposed, respectively. In this case, 7,034 of 11,101 words are tagged correctly. That is, the performance is 63.36%.

In the next experiment, we adopt middle categories (i.e., 94 categories) rather than the above small categories (i.e., 1428 categories). Table 8 shows that the overall performance is improved by 11.05%. It also lists the results with the combinations of first-n and middle categories. Under the middle categories and 1-3 proposed candidates, the performance for tagging low, middle and high ambiguous words are 71.02%, 73.88%, and 75.94%, respectively. Total 8,033 of 11,101 words are tagged correctly. In other words, the performance is 72.36%.

**Table 5. Performance of Tagging Ambiguous Words using MI**

| Ambiguity / Word Tokens | Low | Middle | High | Summary |
|---|---|---|---|---|
| Total Tokens | 6601 | 3511 | 989 | 11101 |
| Correct Tokens | 4132 | 1101 | 267 | 5500 |
| Correct Rate | 62.60% | 31.36% | 27.00% | 49.55% |

**Table 6. Performance of Tagging Ambiguous Words using EM**

| Ambiguity / Word Tokens | Low | Middle | High | Summary |
|---|---|---|---|---|
| Total Tokens | 6601 | 3511 | 989 | 11101 |
| Correct Tokens | 4223 | 1334 | 310 | 5867 |
| Correct Rate | 63.98% | 37.99% | 31.34% | 52.85% |

**Table 7. Performance of Tagging using the First-n and EM**

| Ambiguity / First-n | Low | Middle | High | Middle and High |
|---|---|---|---|---|
| 1 | **63.98%** | 37.99% | 31.34% | 36.53% |
| 2 | | **60.92%** | 53.99% | 59.40% |
| 3 | | 71.35% | **67.95%** | 70.60% |

**Table 8. Performance of Tagging using First-n and Middle Categories**

| Ambiguity / First-n/Categories | | Low | Middle | High | Middle and High |
|---|---|---|---|---|---|
| 1 | Small | **63.98%** | 37.99% | 31.34% | 36.53% |
| | Middle | **71.02%** | 56.19% | 43.78% | 53.47% |
| 2 | Small | | **60.92%** | 53.99% | 59.40% |
| | Middle | | **73.88%** | 65.72% | 72.09% |
| 3 | Small | | 71.35% | **67.95%** | 70.60% |
| | Middle | | 79.27% | **75.94%** | 78.53% |

### 4.3 Tagging Unknown Words

There are 1,979 unknown words in our test corpus. Total 1,663 words have been tagged manually. In the experiments, we consider the effects from training corpus and mapping table. Table 9 shows the performance. M1 and P1 employ more restrictive mapping table, while M2 and P2 adopt less restrictive mapping table. M1 and M2 use the training result in Section 3.1 (i.e., unambiguous words), while P1 and P2 utilize the training result in Section 3.2 (i.e., unambiguous and ambiguous words). In the baseline model, all 1428 Cilin tags are the candidates of unknown words. The performance is worse. On the average, the precision is 1.22%. M1 is the best because more restrictive mapping table reduces the possibility of mapping errors. This table also lists the performance of each category. It meets our expectation, i.e., tagging verb is harder than tagging other categories. Next we use POS to improve the performance. POS narrows down the number of candidates, so that the overall performance is enhanced from 27.13%% to 34.35%%.

In summary, we consider the overall performance of tagging our sample data. Recall that there are 35,921 words in the test corpus. Except the stop words that are not tagged by the sense tagger, there remain 13,586 unambiguous words, 11,101 ambiguous words, and 1,633 unknown words for tagging. From Tables 6 and 9, we know 5,867 unambiguous words and 561 unknown words are tagged correctly. The sense tagger achieves the performance of 76.04%.

### 5. Conclusion

This paper analyzes the polysemy degree in Mandarin Chinese. We consider the distribution of word senses from POS and frequency. Under the Cilin small categories, 23.67% of word types in ASBC corpus are

Table 9. Performance of Tagging Unknown Words

| Categories | #Tokens | | Baseline | M1 | M2 | P1 | P2 | M1(POS) |
|---|---|---|---|---|---|---|---|---|
| All | 1633 | Correct | 20 | 443 | 395 | 438 | 396 | 561 |
| | | Precision | 1.22% | 27.13% | 24.19% | 26.82% | 24.25% | 34.35% |
| N | 858 | Correct | 11 | 255 | 228 | 255 | 231 | 320 |
| | | Precision | 1.28% | 29.72% | 26.57% | 29.72% | 26.92% | 37.30% |
| V | 619 | Correct | 5 | 144 | 124 | 137 | 120 | 167 |
| | | Precision | 0.81% | 23.26% | 20.03% | 22.13% | 19.39% | 26.98% |
| A | 58 | Correct | 0 | 5 | 5 | 5 | 5 | 28 |
| | | Precision | 0 | 8.62% | 8.62% | 8.62% | 8.62% | 48.28% |
| F | 4 | Correct | 1 | 1 | 1 | 1 | 1 | 4 |
| | | Precision | 25.00% | 25.00% | 25.00% | 25.00% | 25.00% | 100.00% |
| K | 94 | Correct | 3 | 38 | 37 | 40 | 39 | 42 |
| | | Precision | 3.19% | 40.43% | 39.36 | 42.55 | 41.49 | 44.68% |

middle or high frequent words, but they occupy 94.06% of word tokens. We adopt contextual information and mapping from WordNet synsets to Cilin sense tags to deal with this challengeable problem. The performances for tagging low, middle and high ambiguous words are 63.98%, 60.92%, and 67.95% when small proposed. Comparatively, the performances categories are used and 1-3 candidates are 71.02%, 73.88%, and 75.94% by using middle categories. The performance of tagging unknown words is 34.35%. It is worse than that of tagging ambiguous words, but is much better than that of the baseline mode. The overall performance is the sense tagger is 76.04%. Although sense tagging does not achieve the performance of POS tagging, the sense tagger proposed in this paper is still a useful computer-aided tool to reduce the human cost on tagging a large-scale corpus.

## References


Atkins, S. (1993) "Tools for Computer-Aided Lexicography: the Hector Project," *Acta Linguistica Hungarica*, 41, pp. 5-72.

Ballesteros, L. and Croft, W.B. (1998) "Resolving Ambiguity for Cross-Language Information Retrieval," *Proceedings of the 21st Annual International ACM SIGIR Conference*, pp. 64-71.

Church, K.W., *et al.* (1989) "Parsing, Word Associations and Typical Predicate-Argument Relations." *Proceedings of International Workshop on Parsing Technologies*, pp. 389-398.

Huang, C.R. and Chen, K.J. (1995) "Academic Sinica Balanced Corpus," Technical Report 95-02/98-04, Academic Sinica, Taipei, Taiwan.

Fellbaum, C. editor (1998) *WordNet: An Electronic Lexical Database*, MIT Press, Cambridge, Mass.

Ide, N. and Veronis, J. (1998) "Word Sense Disambiguation: The State of Art," *Computational Linguistics*, 24(1), pp. 1-40.

Kelly, E. and Stone, P. (1975) *Computer Recognition of English Word Senses*, North-Holland, Amsterdam.

Kilgarriff, A. (1998) "SENSEVAL: An Exercise in Evaluating Word Sense Disambiguation Programs," *Proceedings of First International Conference on Language Resources and Evaluation*, Granada, pp. 581-588.

Kilgarriff, A. and Rosenzweig, J. (2000) "English SENSEVAL: Report and Results," *Proceedings of Second International Conference on Language Resources and Evaluation.*

Manning, C.D. and Schutze, H. (1999) *Foundations of Statistical Natural Language Processing*, MIT Press, Cambridge, Mass.

Marshall, I. (1987) "Tag Selection using Probabilistic Methods," in Roger Garside, Geoffrey Leech and Geoffrey Sampson (editors), *The Computational Analysis of English*, Longman, pp. 42-56.

Mei, J.; *et al.* (1982) *tong2yi4ci2ci2lin2.* Shanghai Dictionary Press.

Ng, H.T. and Lee, H.B. (1996) "Integrating Multiple Knowledge Sources to Disambiguate Word Sense: An Exemplar-Based Approach," *Proceedings of 34th Annual Meeting of Association for Computational Linguistics*, pp. 40-47.

# Knowledge Extraction for Identification of Chinese Organization Names

*Keh-Jiann Chen & Chao-jan Chen*

kchen@iis.sinica.edu.tw richard@iis.sinica.edu.tw

Institute of Information Science, Academia Sinica, Taipei

**ABSTRACT**

In this paper, a knowledge extraction process was proposed to extract the knowledge for identifying Chinese organization names. The knowledge extraction process utilizes the structure property, statistical property as well as partial linguistic knowledge of the organization names to extract new organizations from domain texts. The knowledge extraction processes were experimented on large amount of texts retrieved from WWW. With high standard of threshold values, new organization names can be identified with very high precision. Therefore the knowledge extraction processes can be carried out automatically to self improve the performance in the future.

## 1. INTRODUCTION

The occurrences of unknown words cause difficulties in natural language processing. The word set of a natural language is open-ended. There is no way of collecting every words of a language, since new words will be created for expressing new concepts, new inventions, newborn babies, new organizations. Therefore how to identify new words in a text will be the most challenging task for natural language processing. It is especially true for Chinese. Each Chinese morpheme (usually a single character) carries meanings and most are polysemous. New words are easily constructed by combining morphemes and their meanings are the semantic composition of morpheme components. However there are also semantically non-compositional compounds, such as proper names. In Chinese text, there is no blank to mark word boundaries and no inflectional markers nor capitalization markers to denote the syntactic or semantic types of new words. Hence the unknown word identification for Chinese became one of the most difficult and demanding research topic.

There are many different types of unknown words and each has different morph-syntactic and morph-semantic structures. In principle their syntactic and semantic categories can be determined by their content and contextual information, but there are many difficult problems have to be solved. First of all it is not possible to find a uniform representational schema and categorization algorithm to handle different types of unknown words due to their different morph-syntactic structures. Second, the clues for identifying different type of unknown words are also different. For instance, identification of names of Chinese people is very much relied on the surnames, which is a limited set of characters. The statistical methods are commonly used for identifying proper names (Chen & Lee 1996, Chang et al. 1994, Sun et al. 1994). The identification of general compounds is more relied on the morphemes and the semantic relations between morphemes (Chen & Chen 2000). The third difficulty is the problems of ambiguities, such as structure ambiguities, syntactic ambiguities and semantic ambiguities. For instances, usually a morpheme character/word has multiple meaning and syntactic categories and may play the roles of common words or proper names. Therefore the ambiguity resolution became one of the major tasks.

In this paper we focus our attention on the identification of the organization names. It is considered to be a hard task to identify organization names in comparing with the identification of other types of unknown words, because there are not much morph-syntactic and morph-semantic clues to indicate an organization name. There is no significant preference on the selection of morphemes/ characters and the semantic of the morphemes, which gives no clue leading toward the identification. For instance, '微軟, micro-soft' (Microsoft) has the character by character (morpheme by morpheme) translation of 'slightly soft' and there is no marker, such as capitalization, to indicate that it is a proper name. The only reliable clue is its context information. However an organization's full names usually occur at its first mention, unless it is a well-known organization. A full name contains its proper name and organization type, such as '宏碁 電腦 公 司 , Acer Computer-Company'. The organization types became the major clue of identifying a new organization name. However abbreviated shorter names usually will be used, such as a) omit part of the organization type, for instances '宏碁 電腦, Acer Computer', '宏碁 公司, Acer Company', b) omit the organization type totally, for instance '宏碁, Acer', or c) the abbreviation, for instance '宏電, global-electric (Acer-computer)'. Therefore the task became not only the identification of organization names in different forms but also finding their meaning equivalence classes. To achieve the above goal, the knowledge of 1) proper names of organizations, 2) different lines of the businesses, and 3) different organization types, should be equipped. Unfortunately there is no well-prepared knowledge sources containing the above information. Therefore a knowledge extraction model is proposed to extract the above mentioned knowledge from the dictionary and domain texts.

## 2. STRUCTURES OF ORGANIZATION NAMES

There is no rigid structure for an organization name as mentioned in the previous section. Roughly speaking an organization name is composed by two major components. The first part is the proper name and the second part is the organization type. The second part contains the major key words lead toward the identification of an organization, since the organization types, such as '公司, company', '基金會 foundation', '小組 group', '集團 enterprise' etc, tells what kind of organizations they are. If it is a company, to be more informative the line of business usually goes with the key word '公司 company', for instances '食品公司 food company', '電腦 公司 computer company', '投資顧問公司 investment consultant company', but in most cases the keyword '公司 company' will be ignored, such as 統一食品( President food). Sometimes the line of business and the organization type go together to become a single word, such as '中學 middle school'，'銀行 bank'，'醫院 hospital'. By observing the structure of the organization name, it seems that once a complete list of the organization types is well prepared, then it is not hard to identify the organizations by their full names. The only complication is that abbreviated names occur more frequently than full names. The identifier '公司 company' is usually ignored in real text. The lines of business became the major identifier for a company and many business lines are common words, such as '食品 food', '電腦 computer', '水泥 cement'. Therefore it is necessary to make the distinction between a common compounds and a company name, for examples, '健康食品 health food' vs. '統一食品 President food', '個人電腦 personal computer' vs. '宏碁電腦 Acer computer'. Although they are two-way ambiguous, usually they have only one preference reading.

In conclusion, the types and the proper names of organizations will be the major clues lead toward the identification of the organizations. In addition, it is also better to have a list of well known organization names, such that the well known company names, like '微軟 Microsoft', can be identified immediately. Most of the knowledge preparation works should be done by offline approaches. The prepared knowledge would be utilized to online identification of newly coined organizations. The equivalent classes of the well-known organizations are also classified by a similarity-based approach.

## 3. KNOWLEDGE EXTRACTION

There are two knowledge sources. One is the CKIP Chinese lexicon and another is the Chinese text from WWW. The lexicon provides a partial list of important organizations and the information extracted from them will be the initial knowledge of the identification system. The texts from WWW provide ample of new organization names implicitly. The problem is how to extract some, if not all, of them from the texts. Once we have a list of organization names. The proper names for organizations and the organization types will be extracted by analyzing the morphological structures of the organization names. However an effective morphological analyzer depends upon the availability of the knowledge of the organization types, but the lists of the organization types are not available yet.

As we mentioned before the complete organization names have two parts. The first part is the proper name and the second part is the organization type. The number of different proper names is unlimited and on the other hand the number of different organization types is limited. This property will be utilized to separate the variable parts, i.e. the proper name, and the constant parts, i.e. the organization type, from the organization names.

The numbers of organization names in the lexicon is very limited, since only the important organizations in the common domain will be collected. Therefore the initial knowledge extracted from lexicon is also very limited. To make the sources of knowledge more adequate, vast amount of new organization names should be extracted from each different domain corpus. Unfortunately none of the existing corpora had tagged the organization names. Therefore we are going to design a semi-automatic method to extract the high frequency organization names from text corpora.

The locality of occurrences of keywords in a text will be utilized for keyword extraction. Once an organization name occurring in a text it is very probably reoccurred in the same text. The recurrence property had been utilized to extract keywords or key-phrases from text (Chien 1999, Fung 1998, Smadja 1993). However not all keywords are organization names. The knowledge extracted from the lexicon, i.e. the list of the organization types will be the initial knowledge for identifying organization names. In addition to the initial knowledge, the structure property of the organization names will be also utilized in classifying extracted keywords into organization names and non-organization names. The extraction processes will be repeated for extracting new organizations and therefore extracting new organization types. The more knowledge would have been extracted the more accurate of the organization identification will achieve.

### 3.1 Morphological Analysis for Organization Names

There are 1391 number of words in the CKIP lexicon classified as organizations. Table 1 shows some of the examples.

一女中 人代會 人民公社 人事行政局 人事室
人事處 人事部 十信 八號分機 三軍總醫院
三商隊 三商銀 三專 三輕 三總 下院 下議院
上議院 土木系土地局 土地銀行 土銀 大仁藥專
大同工學院 大同商專 大同盟 大使館 大英國協
大英博物館 大專 大通銀行 大華工專 大漢工商
大學 女青年會

Table 1. The samples of organizations from the CKIP dictionary

As we observed, the morphological structure of an organization name usually is a compounding of a proper name and a organization type. The organization type might be a compounding of a line of business and a type, for instances 電腦公司 (computer company), 銀行(bank), 中學 (middle school), or simply a line of business, for instances 食品(food), 電腦(computer), 水泥 (cement). The proper names are variables, since each organization type may have many different institutions with different names. The types are constants. There is a limited number of constants attached with many different proper names to form different organization names. Therefore to extract the organization types is equivalent to extract the high frequency ending morphemes. Table 2 shows the top 20 high frequency ending morphemes extracted from the 1391 organization names and in deed they are organization types.

| | | | | |
|---|---|---|---|---|
| 52 會 | 38 局 | 36 部 | 30 社 | 29 大學 |
| 21 黨 | 21 處 | 20 院 | 17 科 | 16 署 |
| 16 校 | 16 委會 | 15 所 | 15 系 | 15 工專 |
| 13 隊 | 12 協 | 12 司 | 12 公司 | 11 大 |

Table 2. The top 20 organization types ranked with their occurrence frequencies extracted from the 1391 organization names

### 3.2 Automatic Extraction of Organization Names

A Web spider can extract text from each different domain through WWW. Then keyword extraction technique is applied on domain texts to retrieve possible keywords. The keyword set includes organization names, personal names, general compounds, and also error extraction. Most of which are not organization names. It is supposed that the available list of the organization types will be the source of knowledge to identify candidates of organizations. However such a method only identifies the organizations of the known organization types and provides new proper names only. It will not identify new types of organizations. Therefore we use a new method to extract the organization names by using the structure property of organization names.

**Extraction Algorithm for Organization Types:**

Step 1. Using a Web spider to collect Chinese texts of a fixed domain, such as domain of finance and business, from WWW.

Step 2. Extract high frequency keywords in the text (Smadja 93, Chang & Su 97, Chien 99).

Step 3. For the keywords of length 3,4, and 5, each keyword is divided into two parts X and Y. X is a candidate of proper name and

Y is a candidate of organization type. The X is the initial two-characters of the keyword and Y is the remained characters. (Since most proper names of organizations have two characters, we can extract the organization types of the lengths 1, 2 and 3 from three different groups of keywords with lengths 3, 4 and 5 respectively.)
Extract the organization type Y, if for some keywords X+Y, the following conditions hold.

a) X satisfies one of the following cases.
   1. X is not in the lexicon, i.e. X is an unknown word.
   2. X has the categories of Nb or Nc, i.e. it is a known proper name (Nb) or a location name (Nc).
b) For each Y, assumed to be the organization type, there must have more than n number of different X, such that X+Y in the extracted keyword list. In practice, the threshold value n was set to 2.

In general, Chinese company names like most proper names are non-common word (unknown words). However sometimes they are place names (Nc), but rarely they are common nouns, adjectives, or verbs. Therefore in order to avoid too many false alarms, such as "超級電腦 super computer", to be considered as a company name, the condition a) of step 3 is set. The reason to setup the condition b) is that each organization type Y should have many different organizations which have the same organization type Y, such as '宏碁電腦 Acer computer', '國眾電腦 Leo computer', '藍天電腦 Blue-sky computer', ...etc.. The real implementation shows the different threshold value n gives the different precision and recall for identification.

For the first iteration of knowledge extraction, we suggest to have higher recall rate. Set the threshold value low and manually select the final list of the organization types. For the future automatic knowledge extraction, in order to increase the precision of the information extraction higher threshold values are suggested.

## 4. EXPERIMENTAL RESULTS

The knowledge extraction processes for Chinese organization names are carried out by different stages. At the first stage, the words marked with semantic category of organization were accessed from the CKIP dictionary. There are 1391 word organization types. As mentioned in section 3.1, a pseudo morphological analysis process was carried out, which try to find the high frequency ending morphemes. Since the structure of an organization name is a composition of X+Y, where X is a proper name and Y is a organization type. There are 546 different ending morphemes. The high frequency ending morphemes are exactly to be the morphemes for common organization types. Many of them are monosyllabic words and they are polysemous, as shown in Table 1. For the future identification, the disambiguation process has to be carried out for those polysemous ending morphemes (Chen & Chen 2000). The extracted morphemes and list of organizations will be the first collection of the organization types.

At the second stage, we try to extract new organizations names from different domain text. Each different domain has many new organization types. For instance in the domain of finance and business, there are many company names, which have completely different word strings for the organization types as in the extracted list by the first stage.

The algorithm shown in the section 3.2 was carried out. At the step 1, 31787 texts of news of the finance and business domain were extracted from http://www.cnyes.com. At step 2, 40675 keywords were extracted from the news corpus. At step 3, organization names were identified and the organization types were extracted. If the threshold value n = 2, 92 types were extracted and among them 83 are correct organization types. The precision is 90%. If the threshold was set to 3, only 56 types were extracted and all of them happen to be correct. The precision increased to 100%, but of course the recall rate dropped. We don't know the exact recall rate, since there are too many keywords in the training set. However the recall rate is not important, since the whole knowledge extraction process is a recurrent process. The knowledge extraction procedures should be repeatedly applied on the different set of text and at each iteration more information will be extracted. Hence the precision is much more important than the recall. The knowledge sources for future identification of organizations are the accumulated lists of the organization names, the proper names of organizations and the organization types.

Table 3 contains the extracted organization types while the threshold value n=3. The organization types are classified by their lengths and sorted by their frequencies of uses. Table 4 contains the extracted organization types which associated with exactly two different names and the last line shows the error extractions. Among newly extracted organization types only 23 of them are already in the old list.

| | | | | | | | | | | | |
|---|---|---|---|---|---|---|---|---|---|---|---|
| 證 | 24 | 銀 | 14 | 電 | 9 | 市 | 6 | 網 | | | |
| 證券 | 81 | 科技 | 74 | 集團 | 46 | 銀行 | 41 | 電子 | 40 | 公司 | 36 |
| 電腦 | 19 | 建設 | 18 | 電訊 | 17 | 企業 | 16 | 汽車 | 15 | 國際 | 15 |
| 資訊 | 15 | 電信 | 15 | 航空 | 14 | 投信 | 13 | 實業 | 11 | 日報 | 10 |
| 工業 | 9 | 基金 | 9 | 光電 | 8 | 通信 | 7 | 控股 | 6 | 開發 | 6 |
| 電機 | 6 | 精密 | 6 | 人壽 | 5 | 紡織 | 5 | 商銀 | 5 | 網絡 | 5 |
| 興業 | 5 | 化學 | 4 | 石化 | 4 | 企銀 | 4 | 百貨 | 4 | 重工 | 4 |
| 時報 | 4 | 電力 | 4 | 電工 | 4 | 工程 | 3 | 化工 | 3 | 瓦斯 | 3 |
| 石油 | 3 | 金屬 | 3 | 電話 | 3 | 電器 | 3 | 網路 | 3 | 數碼 | 3 |
| 線上 | 3 | | | | | | | | | | |
| 半導體 | 7 | 交易所 | 6 | | | | | | | | |

Table 3. The extracted organization types associated with the number of different names >=3

| | | | | | | | | |
|---|---|---|---|---|---|---|---|---|
| 中心 | 五金 | 水泥 | 委員會 | 房屋 | 信託 | 保全 | 保險 | |
| 旅遊網 | 海運 | 紙業 | 動力 | 商事 | 啤酒 | 組織 | 貨運 | 貨櫃 |
| 郵報 | 塑膠 | 新聞 | 精工 | 寬頻 | 廣場 | 數碼港 | 聯網 | |
| 證券報 | 證監會 | | | | | | | |
| *大西洋 | *先生 | *先進 | *明珠 | *指數 | *添惠 | *概念股 | | |
| *總統 | *創業板 | | | | | | | |

Table 4. The extracted organization types associated with two different names and the last lines show the error extractions.

### 4.1 Strategies for On-line Identification of Organization Names

The knowledge about organizations extracted from the dictionaries and domain texts will be used to identify organization names at on-line sentence processing. During the word segmentation process, an organization name is either identified immediately (if it is a known organization name), or it will be segmented into two segments of X+Y or several segments of (x1+x2+…+xn)+Y, where X is a proper names, Y is the organization type. When the proper name X is a new word, it will be segmented into shorter segments (x1+x2+…+xn). To simplify the experiment process, we assume the proper names X are either the words of categories Nb (i.e. proper names) or Nc (i.e. the place names) or a two-character unknown word. For the identification experiment, a corpus extract from a T.V. news（http://www.ttv.com.tw）

The patterns of X+Y in the testing corpus were searched. 117 different organizations were identified. Among them 56 are known organizations, i.e. they are in the organization name list. 61 of them are identified by the composition of X+Y and 52 of them are correct. It counts the precision of 52/61=85% for identifying new names. The total performance is the precision of 108/117=92%.

The knowledge-based approach for identifying organization names seems very promising. It outperforms the reports of the precision of 61.79% and the recall of 54.50% in (Chen & Lee 1996) and the experiment was carried out under the condition that the knowledge extraction process is in its initial stage. We expect that performance of the algorithm will become better and better while the knowledge extraction process continuously performs.

### 4.2 Automatic Extraction of Name Equivalent Classes

The abbreviated names are very frequently occurred in the real text especially in the domain of the stock market. By observing the abbreviation names, the heuristic rules for abbreviating a company name can be concluded as follows.

Abbreviation rule: If the proper name of a company is unique, then take the proper name as its abbreviation name, such as '微軟, Microsoft'. Otherwise the abbreviation will be a compound of key-characters from part of its proper name and part of its line of business, such as 中油 is the abbreviation of '中國石油, China petroleum'.

An experiment was carried out to find the full names of the abbreviations of company names shown in the price table of the Taiwan stock market. The purposes of this experiment are a) to find the equivalent classes of company names and b) to have some idea about the recall rate of the current knowledge extraction process.

The matching process between the abbreviations and the extracted organization name lists is as follows.

1. For each abbreviation name matches the organization names in the organization name list. Find all the organization names containing the abbreviation name.
2. Rank the matched organization names according to the following criterion.
   The first rank: The proper name of the organization name is exactly matched with the abbreviation name.
   The second rank: The abbreviation is compounding of key-characters from part of the proper name and part of the line of business of the matched organization names.
   If there are many candidates with the same rank, then rank them according to their frequencies occurring in the training corpus.

There are 471 abbreviated company names in the price list of the stock market. 302 of them have matched candidates. Each abbreviation name may match many different organization names. The recall rate for the top ranked candidate is 282/471=60%. The precision of the first rank candidate is 282/302=93%. Table 5 shows some of the results.

| Abbr. | Candidates arranged in the order of their ranks |
|---|---|
| 泰山 | **泰山企業** 8 泰山集團 3 泰山電子 2 |
| 福壽 | **福壽實業** 7 幸福人壽 9 宏福人壽 2 |
| 惠勝 | **惠勝實業** 11 |
| 南亞 | **南亞科技** 101 南亞興業 2 |
| 國喬 | **國喬石化** 48 國喬石油 2 |
| 中石化 | **中國石化** 10 中間石化 2 中油石化 1 |
| 宏電 | **宏電集團** 5 宏碁電腦 22 宏泰電工 22 |
| | 旺宏電子 21 |
| 台達電 | **台達電子** 6 |
| 華通 | **華通電腦** 15 華南通信 2 華智通信 2 |
| 台揚 | **台揚科技** 11 |
| ?大眾 | 大眾電信 67 **大眾電腦** 29 大眾銀行 17 |
| | 大眾集團 6 大眾網路 2 大眾科技 2 |
| | 大眾投信 2 |

Table 5. Some examples of the abbreviations and the matched candidates (the correct answer is highlighted by the boldface characters)

## 5. CONCLUSIONS

The knowledge extraction process will be continuously carried on in the future. The accumulated knowledge will be utilized for the on-line unknown word identification as well as for the off-line knowledge extraction. The proposed knowledge extraction processing model can be generalized to extract other types of linguistics or morphological knowledge, for instances, to extract the transliterate foreign names, to extract the titles of people.

Some of the errors are caused by that the titles of the people are wrongly identified as organization types, since the patterns of people's name followed by their title are commonly occurred in real text. These patterns are similar to the structures of organization names. Such kind of errors can be avoid, if the titles of people are known and in fact the titles of people can be extracted by the same extraction model except that most of people's names have three characters instead of two.

In the future, the knowledge extraction processes will be automatically carried out. We expect that it will be one of the major building blocks for automatic learning systems for Chinese morphology and sentence processing.

## REFERENCES

[1] Bai, M.H., C.J. Chen & K.J. Chen, 1998, "POS tagging for Chinese Unknown Words by Contextual Rules" *Proceedings of ROCLING*, pp.47-62.

[2] Chang, J. S.,S.D. Chen, S. J. Ker, Y. Chen, & J. Liu,1994 "A Multiple-Corpus Approach to Recognition of Proper Names in Chinese Texts", *Computer Processing of Chinese and Oriental Languages*, Vol. 8, No. 1, pp. 75-85.

[3] Chang, Jing Shin and Keh-Yih Su, 1997," An Unsupervised Iterative Method for Chinese New Lexicon Extraction," Computational Linguistics and Chinese Language Processing, Vol. 2 #2, pp97-147.

[4] Chen, Keh-Jiann, Ming-Hong Bai, 1997, "Unknown Word Detection for Chinese by a Corpus-based Learning Method." *Proceedings of the 10th Research on Computational Linguistics International Conference*, pp159-174.

[5] Chen, K.J. & Chao-jan Chen, 2000," Automati Semantic Classification for Chinese Unknown Compound Nouns," Coling 2000.

[6] Chen, K.J. & S.H. Liu, 1992,"Word Identification for Mandarin Chinese Sentences," *Proceedings of 14th Coling*, pp. 101-107.

[7] Chen, Hsin-His & Jen-Chang Lee, 1996," Identification and Classification of Proper Nouns in Chinese Texts," Proceedings of Coling-96, Vol. 1., pp. 222-229.

[8] Chien, Lee-feng, 1999," PAT-tree-based Adaptive Keyphrase Extraction for Intelligent Chinese Information Retrieval," Information Processing and Management, Vol. 35, pp. 501-521.

[9] Fung P., 1998," Extracting Key Terms from Chinese and Japanese Texts," Computer Processing of Oriental Languages, Vol. 12, #1, pp 99-122.

[10] Lee, J.C. , Y.S. Lee and H.H. Chen, 1994, "Identification of Personal Names in Chinese Texts." *Proceedings of 7th ROC Computational Linguistics Conference.*

[11] Lin, M. Y., T. H. Chiang, & K. Y. Su, 1993," A Preliminary Study on Unknown Word Problem in Chinese Word Segmentation" *Proceedings of Rocling VI*, pp 119-137.

[12] McDonald D., 1996, " Internal and

External Evidence in the Identification and Semantic Categorization of Proper Names", in *Corpus Processing for Lexical Acquisition*, J. Pustejovsky and B. Boguraev Eds, MIT Press 1996.

[13] Smadja, Frank, 1993,"Retrieving Collocations from Text: Xtract," Computational Linguistics, vil. 19, #1, pp. 143-177.

[14] Sun, M. S., C.N. Huang, H.Y. Gao, & Jie Fang, 1994, "Identifying Chinese Names in Unrestricted Texts", *Communication of COLIPS*, Vol.4 No. 2. 113-122.

# Using Co-occurrence Statistics as an Information Source for Partial Parsing of Chinese

**Elliott Franco DRÁBEK**
The State Key Laboratory
for Intelligent Technology and Systems
Department of Computer Science
Tsinghua University, Beijing 100084
elliott_drabek@ACM.org

**Qiang ZHOU**
The State Key Laboratory
for Intelligent Technology and Systems
Department of Computer Science
Tsinghua University, Beijing 100084
zhouq@s1000e.cs.tsinghua.edu.cn

**Abstract**

Our partial parser for Chinese uses a learned classifier to guide a bottom-up parsing process. We describe improvements in performance obtained by expanding the information available to the classifier, from POS sequences only, to include measures of word association derived from co-occurrence statistics. We compare performance using different measures of association, and find that Yule's coefficient of colligation Y gives somewhat better results over other measures.

## Introduction

In learning-based approaches to syntactic parsing, the earliest models developed generally ignored the individual identities of words, making decisions based only on their part-of-speech classes. On the other hand, many later models see each word as a monolithic entity, with parameters estimated separately for each word type. In between have been models which attempt to generalize by considering similarity between words, where knowledge about similarity is deduced from hand-written sources (e.g. thesauri), or induced from text. For example, The SPATTER parser (Magerman, 1995) makes use of the output of a clustering algorithm based on co-occurrence information. Because this co-occurrence information can be derived from inexpensive data with a minimum of pre-processing, it can be very inclusive and informative about even relatively rare words, thus increasing the generalization capability of the parser trained on a much smaller fully annotated corpus.

The current work is in this spirit, making complementary use of a relatively small treebank for syntactic information and a relatively large collection of flat text for co-occurrence information. However, we do not use any kind of clustering, instead using the co-occurrence data directly. Our parser is a bottom-up parser whose actions are guided by a machine-learning-based decision-making module (we use the SNoW learner developed at the University of Illinois, Urbana-Champaign (Roth, 1998) for its strength with potentially very large feature sets and for its ease of use). The learner is able to directly use statistics derived from the co-occurrence data to guide its decisions.

We collect a variety of statistical measures of association based on bigram co-occurrence data (specifically, mutual information, t-score, $X^2$, likelihood ratio and Yule's coefficient of colligation Y), and make the statistics available to the decision-making module. We use labelled constituent precision and recall to compare performance of different versions of our parser on unseen test data. We observe a marked improvement in some of the versions using the co-occurrence data, with strongest performance observed in the versions using Yule's coefficient of colligation Y and mutual information, and more modest improvements in those using the other measures.

## 1 Background

### 1.1 Our Task — Partial Parsing

The current work has developed in the context of developing a partial or "chunk" parser for Chinese, whose task is to identify certain kinds of local syntactic structure. The syntactic analysis we use largely follows the outline of Steven Abney's work (Abney, 1994). We adopt the concept of a "c-head" and an "s-head" for each phrase, where the c-head corresponds roughly to the generally used concept of head (e.g., the main verb in a verb phrase, or the preposition in a prepositional phrase), and the s-head is the "main content word" of a phrase (e.g., the main verb in a verb phrase, but the object of the preposition in a prepositional phrase). The core of our chunk definition is also in line with Abney's: A chunk is essentially the contiguous range of words s-headed by a given major content word. Within this basic framework, we make some accommodations to the Chinese language and to practicality. For example, by our understanding of Abney's definition, a numeral-classifier phrase followed immediately by the noun it modifies should constitute two separate chunks. However such units seem likely to be useful in further processing, and easy to accurately identify, so we chose to include them in our definition of chunk.

For simplicity and consistency, we adopt a very restricted phrase-structured syntactic formalism, somewhat similar to a phrase-structured formulation of a dependency grammar. In our formalism, all constituents are binary branching, and the purpose of the non-terminal labels is restricted to indicating the direction of dependency between the two children. Figure 1 shows an example sentence with some indicative structures.

Dependencies within individual chunks are shown with heavy arrows. A right-pointing dependency, such as the three dependencies within the noun phrase "瓜类蔬菜栽培方法", corresponds to a constituent labelled "right-headed". A left-pointing dependency, such as that between the verb "发生" and its aspect particle "了", corresponds to a constituent labelled "left-headed". These are cases where the s-head and the c-head of the phrase are identical. When they are not identical, we have a "two-headed" dependency, like those in the phrase "根本上的". Here, the relation between "根本" and "上" (and between "根本上" and "的") is that the left constituent provides the s-head of the phrase, while the right constituent provides the c-head.

These four non-terminal categories can describe high- or low- level syntactic structures. However, for chunking we wish to leave the higher-level structures of a sentence unspecified, leaving only a list of local structures. We treat this in a consistent way by adding a fifth non-terminal category "unspecified", and replacing all higher structures with a backbone of strictly left-branching "unspecified" nodes, anchored to a special "wall" token to the left of the sentence. This backbone structure is shown by the light lines in the figure.

### 1.2 Our Data Sources — One Large and One Small

During development, we made use of two corpora. The first is a relatively small-scale treebank of approximately 3500 sentences, 39,000 words, and 55,000 characters (Zhou, 1996). We transformed this corpus by annotating each phrase with c-heads and s-heads, using a large collection of hand-written rules, and then extracted chunks from this transformed version.

The second corpus, which we use only as a source of co-occurrence statistics, is much larger, with approximately 67,000 sentences, 1.5 million words, and 2.2 million characters, with sentences separated and words separated and marked with parts-of-speech, but with no further syntactic annotation (Zhou and Sun, 1999). In the current work we make no use of the part-of-speech annotation, taking co-occurrence counts of word-types alone.

### 1.3 Our Framework — Classifier-Guided Shift-Reduce Parsing

The parsing framework we use has been chosen for maximum simplicity, aided by the simplicity of the syntactic framework. In parsing, we model a left-to-right shift-reduce automaton which builds a parse-tree constituent-by-constituent in a deterministic left-to-right process. The parsing process is thus reduced to making a series of decisions of exactly what to build.

For training, we extract the series of actions the shift-reduce parser would have had to make to produce the trees from the surface structure of the sentences. This gives a long series of state-action pairs: "when the parser was in state X, it took action Y". The state description X is set of binary predicates describing the local surface structure of the sentence and the contents

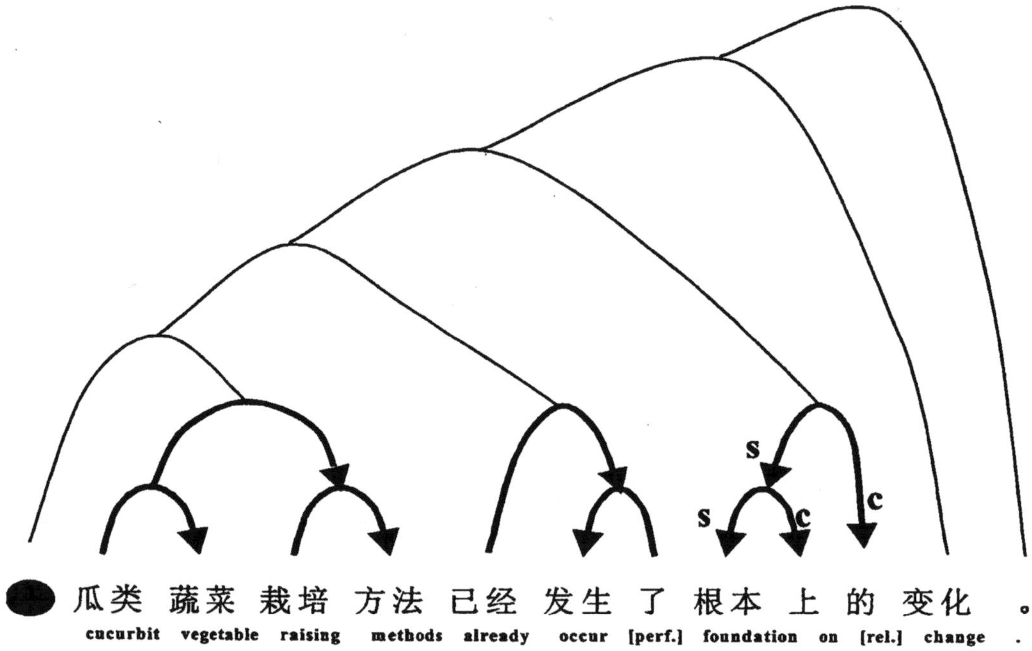


**Methods of raising cucurbit vegetables have changed fundamentally.**

**Figure 1. An example sentence annotated according to our system.**

of the stack. We describe these predicates in detail below. This series of state-action pairs is presented to the SNoW learner, which tries to learn to predict the parser actions from the parser states, attempting to find a linear discriminant over these binary predicates which best accounts for the corresponding actions in the training data.

These parse actions can be either "shift a word from the right on to the stack", or "reduce the top elements of the stack" into a single constituent. Because our syntactic framework is strictly binary branching, each reduce action operates on exactly the top two items on the stack, so the automaton need only choose a category for the new constituent. This decision turns out to be nearly trivial, and we were able to achieve 100% accuracy on our test set using only part-of-speech information, so in the remainder of this paper we discuss only issues relating to the more difficult decision of whether to shift or reduce.

Within the shift-reduce decisions, over half are pre-determined by the basic requirements of the framework. For example, if there are no words left to shift, we can only reduce. If there is only one item on the stack, we can only shift. These decisions are handled by simple deterministic rules within the parser and are not shown to the classifier either in training or in parsing.

In the first version of the parser, prior to the introduction of co-occurrence statistics, the information available to the classifier is limited to parts-of-speech of words in the surface structure of the sentence, nonterminal categories of constituents already built on the stack, and parts-of-speech of the s- and c-heads of constituents already built on the stack. These are collected into schemas representing sets of possible binary predicates. Table 1 shows a representative subset of this original set of 18 predicate schemas (space does not allow us to present all of them). The total of all the instantiations of all these templates presents a potentially huge feature set, so we rely on an important property of the SNoW architecture, that it can handle an indefinitely large set of

| Predicate Schema | Range of Parameters |
| --- | --- |
| POS(Surface-word[k]) = t | $-1 \le k \le 2$ |
| POS(Surface-word[k]) = $t_1$ ∧ POS(Surface-word[k + 1]) = $t_2$ | $-2 \le k \le 1$ |
| Category(Stack[k]) = c | $0 \le k \le 1$ |
| Category(Stack[k]) = $c_1$ ∧ Category(Stack[k + 1]) = $c_2$ | $0 \le k \le 1$ |
| POS(S-head(Stack[k])) = t | $0 \le k \le 2$ |
| POS(S-head(Stack[k])) = $t_1$ ∧ POS(S-head(Stack[k + 1])) = $t_2$ | $0 \le k \le 1$ |
| POS(S-head(Stack[$k_1$])) = $t_1$ ∧ POS(Surface-word[$k_2$]) = $t_2$ | $0 \le k_1 \le 1$<br>$-1 \le k_2 \le 0$ |
| Category(Stack[$k_1$]) = c ∧ POS(C-head(Stack[$k_1$])) = $t_1$ ∧ POS(Surface-word[$k_2$]) = $t_2$ | $0 \le k_1 \le 1$<br>$-1 \le k_2 \le 0$ |

**Table 1. A Subset of the Feature Schemas in the Original Version of the Parser. The variables t, $t_1$, and $t_2$ range over the set of part-of-speech categories, while the variables c, $c_1$, and $c_2$ range over the set of non-terminal categories. Surface words are indexed relative to the parsing position, such that Surface-word[0] is the next word to be shifted.**

features, actually using only those features which are active. The set of these actually active features is reasonable for our set of schemas.

## 2 Enriching the Feature Set with Co-occurrence Statistics

### 2.1 Measures of Association

Table 2 shows the definitions of the five measures we have chosen to compare in the current work, taken from (Manning and Shütze, 1999), (Kageura, 1999).

These measures are based on empirical counts of word occurrences and co-occurrences. Because these events are very prone to zero-counts, both for unseen bigrams and for unseen words, we applied Simple Good-Turing smoothing (Gale and Sampson, 1995) to both bigram and word counts.

### 2.2 Making Measures of Association Available to the Parser

To make the measures of association available to the parser, we started by discretizing each measure, that, is substituting for each continuous measurement a set of binary predicates coarsely describing its approximate value. We used a very simple form of discretization, counting occurrences of each value, and then dividing the values into bins of approximately equal counts. Informal exploration showed consistently better performance when bin membership was made cumulative; that is, using non-mutually-exclusive predicates of the form:

$\text{statistic}(w_1, w_2) \leqslant X_1$
$\text{statistic}(w_1, w_2) \leqslant X_2$
. . .

rather than mutually-exclusive predicates of the form:

$X_0 < \text{statistic}(w_1, w_2) \leqslant X_1$
$X_0 < \text{statistic}(w_1, w_2) \leqslant X_2$
. . .

Using these cumulative predicates, parsing accuracy consistently improved with increases in the number of bins, though the rate of improvement slowed at the same time. The cost of increasing the number of bins came primarily in the algorithm's training time. We chose thirty-two to be a good number of bins.

The predicates resulting from discretization are predicates over values of a statistic. To apply these predicates in parsing, we created features relating to particular slots within parse-state descriptions. Specifically, we made three new feature schemas available to the Winnow learner, as shown in Table 3. Each of these feature schemas is an extension to one available to the original parser. In each case, the original schema was of the form:

$\text{POS}(w_1) = t_1 \wedge \text{POS}(w_2) = t_2$

And the extended schema was of the form:

$\text{POS}(w_1) = t_1 \wedge \text{POS}(w_2) = t_2 \wedge \text{statistic}(w_1, w_2) \leqslant X$

In this way, the learner is able to condition separately depending on the parts-of-speech of the two words in question. This is based on the intuitions that different cases for part-of-speech combinations would behave very differently, and that the training data was sufficient that

| Measure | Definition |
| --- | --- |
| MI | $\log\left(\frac{c(w_1,w_2)}{c(w_1,\bullet)c(\bullet,w_2)}\right)$ |
| T-score | $\sqrt{c(w_1,w_2)}\left(\frac{c(w_1,\bullet)c(\bullet,w_2)}{c(w_1,w_2)}-1\right)$ |
| $X^2$ | $\frac{c(\bullet,\bullet)\left(c(w_1,w_2)c(\neg w_1,\neg w_2)-c(w_1,\neg w_2)c(\neg w_1,w_2)\right)^2}{c(w_1,\bullet)c(\neg w_1,\bullet)c(\bullet,w_2)c(\bullet,\neg w_2)}$ |
| Likeli-hood Ratio | $2\begin{bmatrix} LogL\left(\frac{c(w_1,w_2)}{c(\bullet,w_2)};c(w_1,w_2);c(\bullet,w_2)\right)+LogL\left(\frac{c(w_1,\neg w_2)}{c(\bullet,\neg w_2)};c(w_1,\neg w_2);c(\bullet,\neg w_2)\right) \\ -LogL\left(\frac{c(w_1,\bullet)}{c(\bullet,\bullet)};c(w_1,w_2);c(\bullet,w_2)\right)-LogL\left(\frac{c(w_1,\bullet)}{c(\bullet,\bullet)};c(w_1,\neg w_2);c(\bullet,\neg w_2)\right)\end{bmatrix}$ |
| Note: | $LogL(p;n;k)=k\log(p)+(n-k)\log(1-p)$ |
| Yule's Y | $\frac{\sqrt{\alpha}-1}{\sqrt{\alpha}+1}$ |
| Note: | $\alpha=\frac{c(\bullet,\bullet)c(w_1,w_2)}{c(w_1,\overline{w_2})c(\overline{w_1},w_2)}$ |

**Table 2. Definitions of the Five Measures of Association. $c(x_1,w_2)$ represents the count of the event that x and y occur adjacent and in this order in the training corpus. $\neg w$ represents summation over all words other than w, and • represents summation over all words.**

performance would not be hurt by the resulting sub-division; however we have no specific empirical support for this.

### 2.3 Experimental Results

We trained a series of SNoW networks using features sets extended with each of the five measures, and tested five versions of our parser, one using each of the resulting networks. This was done on a held-out test set comprising approximately ten percent of our treebank. The resulting measurements for labeled constituent precision and recall are shown in Table 4, arranged according to the geometric mean of the two measurements.

It is clear from the table that co-occurrence information can be made useful, and that the measure used to represent this information has a large influence on its usefulness. There is also a large disparity between the improvement in precision, 1.7%, and the improvement in recall, 4.1%. We conjecture that this is because the parser originally tended to err in the direction of splitting words into separate chunks, the commoner case, while with the co-occurrence information, it is able to pick out some cases where a strong association suggests that words be joined in the same chunk.

## 3 Related Work

Statistical measures of association applied to bigram co-occurrence counts have been used most extensively in terminology and collocation extraction. (Manning and Shütze, 1999) contains a good introduction to this topic. (Kageura, 1999) is an especially good empirical comparison of the performance of several measures of association on a set of tasks in both terminology extraction and in morpheme splitting of Chinese character sequences. This latter task, which can be seen as a very restricted form of parsing, has been treated in a body of interesting work, including (Sun, Shen and Tsou, 1998), (Lee, 1999) . This work has generally used very simple heuristic control policies, such as repeatedly splitting at the point of lowest mutual information. The use of similar

| Predicate Schema | Range of Parameters |
|---|---|
| POS(Surface-word[k]) = $t_1$ ∧ POS(Surface-word[k + 1]) = $t_2$ ∧ Statistic(Surface-word[k], Surface-word[k + 1]) ⩽ X | $-2 \le k \le 1$ |
| POS(S-head(Stack[k])) = $t_1$ ∧ POS(S-head(Stack[k + 1])) = $t_2$ ∧ Statistic(S-head(Stack[k]), S-head(Stack[k + 1])) ⩽ X | $0 \le k \le 1$ |
| POS(S-head(Stack[$k_1$])) = $t_1$ ∧ POS(Surface-word[$k_2$]) = $t_2$ ∧ Statistic(S-head(Stack[$k_1$]), Surface-word[$k_2$]) ⩽ X | $0 \le k_1 \le 1$<br>$-1 \le k_2 \le 0$ |

**Table 3. Augmented Feature Schemas.**

approaches for general parsing received some early exploration (Brill, Magerman, Marcus and Santorini, 1990), (Magerman and Marcus, 1990), but this approach seems to have lost popularity. This may be because using co-occurrence statistics as a sole source of guidance may become insufficient as the object of parsing moves from the very local structure of word splitting to the longer-distance dependencies of general parsing. The current work attempts to remedy this by using a general learning device to balance co-occurrence statistics with other information to be integrated into a larger control policy.

### Conclusions and Future Work

Our experiments show that simple statistical information gathered from the unprocessed surface structure of large-scale text has value in guiding parsing decisions. However, we feel that there is still a great deal of further advantage to be gained from this approach. Our next step will be to include co-occurrence information from a much larger corpus, containing on the order of $10^8$ characters.

We would also like to experiment with other definitions of co-occurrence. (Yuret, 1998) describes some very interesting work, in a different framework from ours, in which a parser using only co-occurrence mutual information was able to achieve a high precision but low recall when co-occurrence was defined as adjacent co-occurrence, and low precision but high recall when co-occurrence was defined as occurrence within the same sentence. We would like to experiment with ways of balancing these two measures.

We also suspect that significant gains are possible through a more sophisticated inclusion of the statistics in the decision making process. The current discretization scheme is very simple, but there is ample empirical evidence that discretization which takes into account target categories can significantly improve classification accuracy (Dougherty, Kohavi, and Sahami, 1995).

The several articles we have cited which use exclusively co-occurrence information to predict constituent boundaries are very interesting for the simplicity of their control structures, but in one important way they are more complex than the current work: they make decisions by explicitly comparing the measures of association between different pairs of words. We predict that augmenting the feature set to allow our parser to be sensitive to this kind of information would be a very valuable extension.

A related issue is the choice of learning methodology. The Winnow learner has served us well with its ability to handle very large feature sets, but it is weak in its ability to take advantage of the interaction between features. We would like to experiment with learning methods which do not suffer from this weakness, and with methods for automatic feature extraction which could supplement Winnow.

We experimented with a nondeterministic control policy for the parser, using cost-front search to find the most probable series of parsing decisions, but we found this not to be very useful. Over a series of comparative experiments, the non-deterministic control policy consistently raised precision by a small margin, lowered recall by a small margin, increased run times by an order of magnitude or more, and for about 10% of the test-set sentences exhausted system resources before finding any parse at all. We posit that these problems may in part be due to the fact that while the Winnow learner is otherwise quite well adapted for our purposes, its output is not intended to be interpreted probabilistically. In the future we intend to run parallel experiments with more probabilistically oriented learners; we

| Measure of Association | Precision | Recall | Geometric Mean |
|---|---|---|---|
| Yule's Y | 0.882 | 0.875 | 0.879 |
| Mutual Information | 0.885 | 0.857 | 0.871 |
| Likelihood Ratio | 0.879 | 0.845 | 0.862 |
| $X^2$ | 0.870 | 0.848 | 0.859 |
| T-score | 0.870 | 0.836 | 0.853 |
| None (Original Feature Set) | 0.868 | 0.834 | 0.851 |

**Table 4. Accuracy Measurements of Parsing with Different Measures of Association**

are especially interested in experimenting with a Maximum Entropy model.

In the larger context, we plan to experiment with more sophisticated, model-based unsupervised learning methods, including clustering and beyond, and ways of providing their gathered knowledge to the parser, to make the fullest possible use of the vast wealth of un-annotated text available.


### Acknowledgements

The research was supported by National Natural Science Foundation of China (NSFC) (Grant No. 69903007) and National 973 Foundation (Grant No. G1998030507-2).


### References


Steven Abney (1994) *Parsing by Chunks.* http://www.sfs.phil.uni-tuebingen.de/~abney/

Eric Brill, David Magerman, Mitch Marcus and B. Santorini (1990) *Deducing Linguistic Structure from the Statistics of Large Corpora.* Proceedings of the DARPA Speech and Natural Language Workshop, pp. 275-281.

Kenneth W. Church and P. Hanks (1990) *Word Association Norms, Mutual Information, and Lexicography.* Computational Linguistics, Computational Linguistics, 16/1, pp. 22-29.

Ted Dunning (1993) *Accurate Methods for the Statistics of Surprise and Coincidence.* Computational Linguistics, Computational Linguistics, 19/1, pp. 61-74.

Kyo Kageura (1999) *Bigram Statistics Revisited: A Comparative Examination of Some Statistical Measures in Morphological Analysis of Japanese Kanji Sequences.* Journal of Quantitative Linguistics, 6/22, pp. 149-166.

James Dougherty, Ron Kohavi and Mehran Sahami (1995) *Supervised and Unsupervised Discretization of Continuous Features.* In "Machine Learning: Proceedings of the Twelfth International Conference", Morgan Kaufmann Publishers.

William A. Gale and Geoffrey Sampson (1995) *Good-Turing Frequency Estimation without Tears.* Journal of Quantitative Linguistics, 2, pp. 217-237.

Christopher D. Manning and Hinrich Shütze (1999) *Foundations of Statistical Natural Language Processing.* The MIT Press, Cambridge, Massachusetts.

David M. Magerman (1995) *Natural Language Parsing as Statistical Pattern Recognition.* Ph.D. Dissertation, Stanford University.

David Magerman and Mitch Marcus (1990) *Parsing a Natural Language Using Mutual Information Statistics.* In "Proceedings, Eighth National Conference on Artificial Intelligence (AAAI 90)".

Adwait Ratnaparkhi (1997) *A Linear Observed-Time Statistical Parser Based on Maximum Entropy Models.* In "Proceedings of the Second Conference on Empirical Methods in Natural Language Processing".

Dan Roth (1998) *Learning to Resolve Natural Language Ambiguities, a Unified Approach.* In "AAAI'98".

K-Y. Su, M-W. Wu, and J-S. Chang (1994) *A Corpus-Based Approach to Automatic Compound Extraction.* In "Proceedings of the 32nd Annual Meeting of the ACL", pp. 27-30.

Maosong Sun, Dayang Shen, and Benjamin K. Tsou (1998) *Chinese Word Segmentation without Using Lexicon and Hand-Crafted Training Data.* In "Proceedings of the 36th Annual Meeting of the ACL", pp. 1265-1271.

Aboy Wong, Dekai Wu (1999) *Are Phrase Structured Grammars Useful in Statistical Parsing?.* In "Proceedings of the Fifth Natural Language Processing Pacific Rim Symposium", pp. 120-125.

Deniz Yuret (1998) *Discovery of Lexical Relations Using Lexical Attraction.* Ph.D. Thesis, Massachusetts Institute of Technology.

Qiang Zhou (1996) *Phrase Bracketing and Annotating on Chinese Language Corpus.* (in Chinese), Ph.D. Thesis, Beijing University.

# Sinica Treebank:
# Design Criteria, Annotation Guidelines, and On-line Interface

*Chu-Ren Huang*[1], *Feng-Yi Chen*[2], *Keh-Jiann Chen*[2], *Zhao-ming Gao*[3], & *Kuang-Yu Chen*[2]

churen@sinica.edu.tw, apple@iis.sinica.edu.tw, kchen@iis.sinica.edu.tw, zmgao@ccms.ntu.edu.tw, sasami@iis.sinica.edu.tw

[1]Institute of Linguistics, Academia Sinica, Taipei, Taiwan
[2]Institute of Information Science, Academia Sinica, Taipei, Taiwan
[3]Dept. of Foreign Languages & Literatures, National Taiwan University, Taipei, Taiwan

## Abstract

This paper describes the design criteria and annotation guidelines of Sinica Treebank. The three design criteria are: Maximal Resource Sharing, Minimal Structural Complexity, and Optimal Semantic Information. One of the important design decisions following these criteria is the encoding of thematic role information. An on-line interface facilitating empirical studies of Chinese phrase structure is also described.

## 1. Introduction

The Penn Treebank (Marcus et al. 1993) initiated a new paradigm in corpus-based research. The English Penn Treebank has enabled and motivated corpus and computational linguistic research based on information extractable from structurally annotated corpora. Recently, the research has focused on the following two issues: first, when and how can a structurally annotated corpus of language X be built? Second, what information should or can be annotated? A good sample of issues in these two directions can be found in the papers collected in Abeille (1999).

The construction of the Sinica Treebank deals with both issues. First, it is one of the first structurally annotated corpora in Mandarin Chinese. Second, as a design feature, the Sinica Treebank annotation includes thematic role information in addition to syntactic categories. In this paper, we will discuss the design criteria and annotation guidelines of the Sinica Treebank. We will also give a preliminary research result based on the Sinica Treebank.

## 2. Design Criteria

There are three important design criteria for the Sinica Treebank: maximal resource sharing, minimal structural complexity, and optimal semantic information.

First, to achieve maximal resource sharing, the construction of the Sinica Treebank is bootstrapped from existing

Chinese computational linguistic resources. The textual material is extracted from the tagged Sinica Corpus (http://www.sinica.edu.tw/ftms-bin/kiwi.sh, Chen et al. 1996). In other words, the tasks and issues involving tokenization / word segmentation and category assignment are previously resolved. It is worth noting that the segmentation and tagging of Sinica Corpus have undergone vigorous post-editing. Hence the precision of category-assignment is much higher than with an automatically tagged corpora. In addition, since the same research team carried out the tagging of Sinica Corpus and annotation of Sinica Treebank, consistency of the interpretation of texts and tags are ensured. For structure-assignment, an automatic parser (Chen 1996) is applied before human post-editing.

Second, the criterion of minimal structural complexity is motivated to ensure that the assigned structural information can be shared regardless of users' theoretical presupposition. It is observed that theory-internal motivations often require abstract intermediate phrasal levels (such as in various versions of the X-bar theory). Other theories may also call for an abstract covert phrasal category (such as INFL in the GB theory for Chinese). In either case, although the phrasal categories are well-motivated within the theory, their significance cannot be maintained in the context of other theoretical frameworks. Since a primary goal of annotated corpora is to serve as the empirical base of linguistic investigations, it is desirable to annotate structure divisions that are the most commonly shared among theories. We came to the conclusion that the minimal basic level structures are the ones that are shared by all theories. Thus our annotation is designed to achieve minimal structural complexity. All abstract phrasal levels are eliminated and only canonical phrasal categories are marked.

Third, a critical issue involving Treebank construction as well as theories of NLP is how much semantic information, if any, should be incorporated. The original Penn Treebank took a fairly straightforward syntactic approach. A purely semantic approach, though tempting in terms of theoretical and practical considerations, has never been attempted yet. A third approach is to annotate partial semantic information, especially those pertaining to argument-relations. This is an approach shared by us and the Prague Dependency Treebank (e.g. Bohmova and Hajikova 1999). In this approach, the thematic relation between a predicate and an argument is marked in addition to grammatical category. Note that the predicate-argument relation is usually grammatically instantiated and generally considered to be the semantic relation that interacts most closely with syntactic behavior. This allows optimal semantic information to be encoded without going too beyond the partially automatic process of argument identification.

## 3. Annotation Guidelines I: Category and Hierarchy

The basic structure of a tree in a treebank is a hierarchy of nodes with categorical denotation. As in any standard phrase structure grammar, the lexical (i.e. terminal) symbols are defined by the lexicon (CKIP 1992). And following the recent lexicon-driven and information-based trends in linguistic theory, linguistic information will be projected from encoded lexical information. Please refer to CKIP (1993) for the definition of lexical categories that we followed. We will give below the inventory of the restricted set of phrasal categories used and their interpretation. This set defines the domain of expressed syntactic information (instead of projected or inherited information). Readers can also consult Chen et al.'s (2000) general description of how the Sinica Treebank is constructed for a more complete list of tags as well as explanation in Chinese.

### 3.1. Defining Phrasal Categories

There are only 6 non-terminal phrasal categories annotated in the Sinica Treebank.

(1) Phrasal Categories

1. S: An S is a complete tree headed by a predicate (i.e. S is the start symbol).
2. VP: A VP is a phrase headed by a predicate. However, it lacks a subject and cannot function alone.
3. NP: An NP is headed by an N.
4. GP: A GP is a phrase headed by locational noun or locational adjunct. Since the thematic role is often determined by the governing predicate and not encoded locally; nominal phrases are given a tentative role of DUMMY so that it can inherit the correct role from the main predicate.
5. PP: A PP is headed by a preposition. The thematic role of its argument is inherited from the mother, hence its argument is marked with a DUMMY.
6. XP: A XP is a conjunctive phrase that is headed by a conjunction. Its syntactic head is the conjunction. However, since the actual category depends on the interactive inheritance from possibly non-identical conjoined elements, X in XP stands for an under-specified category.

### 3.2. Defining Inheritance Relations

Following unification-based grammatical theories, categorical assignments in Sinica Treebank are both lexicon-driven and head-driven. In principle, all grammatical information is lexically encoded. Structurally heads indicate the direction of information inheritance and define possible predicate-argument relations. However, since the notion 'head' can have several different linguistic definitions, we attempt to allow at least the discrepancy between syntactic and semantic heads. In Sinica Treebank, three different kinds of grammatical heads are annotated.

(2) Heads

1. **Head**: indicates a grammatical head in an endocentric phrasal category. Unless a different semantic head is explicitly marked, a Head marks a category that serves simultaneously as the syntactic and semantic heads of the construction.
2. **head**: indicates a semantic head which does not simultaneously function as a syntactic head. For instance in constructions involving grammaticalized 'particles,' such as in the 'VP-de' construction, the grammatical head ('de' in this case) does not carry any semantic information. In these cases, the head marks the semantic head ('VP' in this case) to indicate the flow of content information.
3. **DUMMY**: indicates the semantic head(s) whose categorical or thematic identity cannot be locally determined. The two most likely scenarios involving DUMMY are (a) in a coordination construction, where the head category depends on the sum of all conjuncts. And (b) in a non-NP argument phrase, such as PP, where the semantic head carries a thematic role assigned not by the immediate governing syntactic head ("P" in this case), but by a higher predicate. In these cases, DUMMY allows a parser to determine the correct categorical / thematic relation later, while maintaining identical local structures.

### 3.3. Beyond Simple Inheritance

When simple inheritance fails, the following principles derived from our design criteria serve to predict the structural assignments of a phrasal category: default inheritance, sisters only, and left most.

#### 3.3.1. Default Inheritance

This principle deals primarily and most effectively with coordinations and conjunctions. The theoretical motivation of this account follows Sag et al.'s (1985) proposal. In essence, the category of a conjunctive construction must be inherited from its semantic heads. However, since conjunctions are not restricted to same categories, languages must have principled ways to determine the categorical identity when different semantic heads carry different information.

First, in the trivial case when all head daughters are of the same category, the mother will inherit that category.

Second, when the different head daughters are an elaboration of the same basic category (e.g. both Nd and Ne are elaboration of N), then the basic category is the default inheritance category for the mother. This can be illustrated by (3).

(3) [[[*da4*]VH11[*er2*]Caa [*yuan2*]VH13]] VP

big and round

Third, when other inheritance mechanisms fail to provide a clear categorical choice, the default inheritance is activated. There are two default hierarchies. The first one deals with when the head daughters are all lexical categories (4a), and the second one deals with when they are all phrasal categories (4b). If there is a disparity between lexical and phrasal categories, then a lexical category will be expanded to a phrasal category first.

(4) Default Inheritance Hierarchy for Categories

a) Lexical Categories: V > N > P > Ng

b) Phrasal Categories: S> VP> NP> PP> GP

When phrasal conjuncts are involved, S is the privileged category since it is the start symbol of the grammar. VP comes next since its structural composition is identical to that of S. If the structure involved is not a predicate (i.e. head of a sentence), then it must be a role. For argument roles, NP's are more privileged than PP's, and PP's are more privileged than GP's. (5) is an instance of the application of this default hierarchy.

(5) [[*da4liang4*]Neqa [*er2*]Caa [*feng1sheng4*]VH11]V]VP

big-quantity and bountiful

'bountiful and of big quantity'

When lexical conjuncts are involved, the same principle is used. The priority is given to the predicate head of the sentence. Among possible argument roles, the nominal category is the default. An illustrative example can be found in (6).

(6) [[*wei4lan2 de tian1kong1*]NP [*yu3*]Caa[*zhu1qun2biao1han4*]S]S

aqua-blue DE sky and people ferocious

'That the sky being aqua blue and that the people being ferocious…'

### 3.3.2 Sisters Only

Following most current linguistic theory, argument roles and adjunct complements must be sisters of a lexical head. However, driven by our design criteria of minimal structural complexity, no same level iteration is allowed. Thus these arguments and adjuncts can be located by the straightforward definition of sisterhood: that they share the same mother-daughter relation with the head. The result is a flat structure.

### 3.3.3 Left First

This principle is designed to account for possible internal structure when there are more than two sisters without having to add on hierarchical complexity. Hence, the default interpretation of internal structure of multiple sisters is that the internal association starts from left to right.

## 4. Annotation Guidelines II: Structural Annotation of Thematic Information

A thematic relation contains a compact bundle of syntactic and semantic information. Although thematic relations are lexically encoded on a predicate, they can only be instantiated when that information is projected to phrasal arguments. In other words, the only empirical evidence for the existence of a thematic relation is a realized argument. However, a realized argument cannot by itself determine the thematic relation. The exact nature of the relation must be determined based on the lexical information from the predicate as well as checking of the compatibility of that realized argument. Since structural information alone cannot determine thematic relations, prototypical structural annotation, such as in the original Penn Treebank, does not include thematic roles since they contain non-structural information.

On the other hand, in theories where lexical heads drive the structural derivation / construction (e.g. ICG and HPSG and LFG), thematic relations are critical. Hence, we decided to encode realized thematic relations on each phrasal argument. The list of thematic relations encoded on the head predicate is consulted whenever a phrasal argument is constructed, and a contextually appropriate relation sanctioned by the lexical information is encoded. It is worth noting that in our account, we not only mark the thematic relations of a verbal predicate, but we also mark the thematic relations governed by a deverbal noun, among others. Also note that an argument of a preposition is marked as a placeholder DUMMY. This is because a preposition only governs an argument syntactically, while its thematic relation is determined by a higher verb.

(7) Thematic Roles: Classification and Inventory

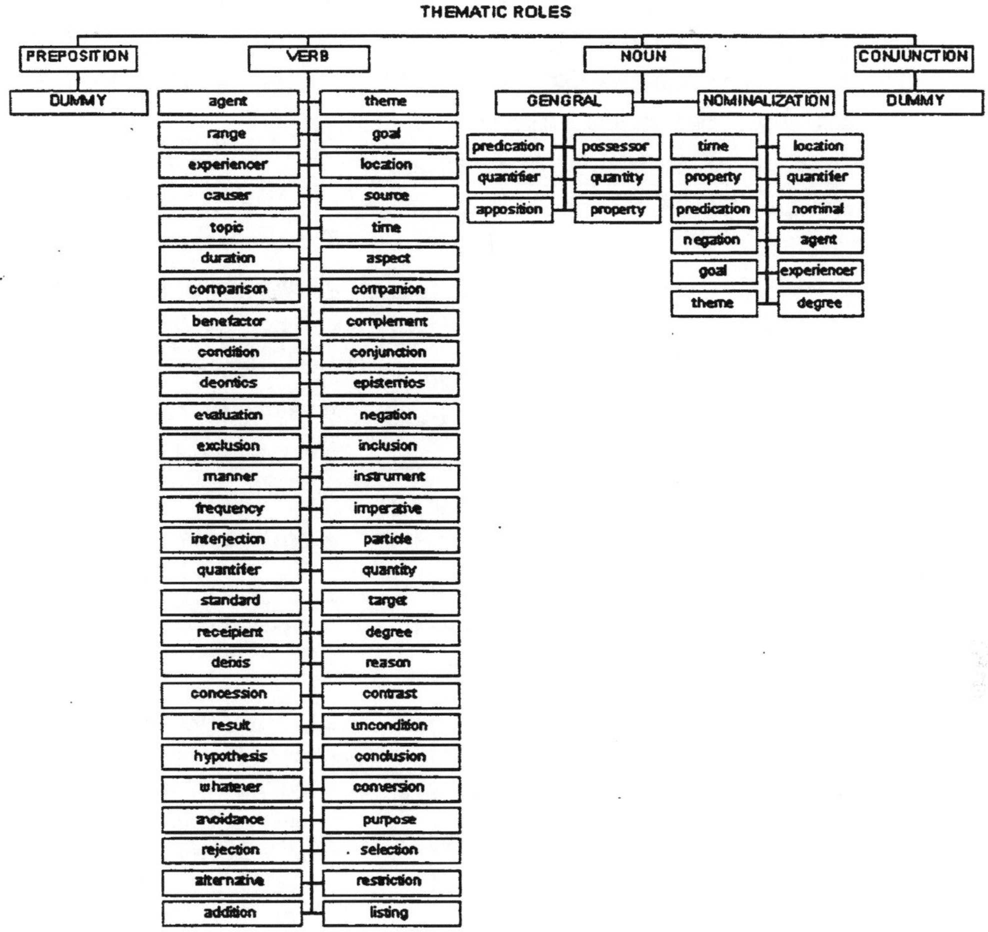


## 5. Current Status of the Sinica Treebank and On-line Interface

Following the above criteria and principles, we have already finished Sinica Treebank 1.0. It contains annotations of 38,725 Chinese structural trees containing 239,532 words. It covers subject areas that include politics, traveling, sports, finance, society, etc. This version of the Sinica Treebank will be released in the near future as soon as the licensing documents are cleared by the legal department of Academia Sinica. A small subset of it (1,000 sentences) is already available for researchers to download from the website *http://godel.iis.sinica.edu.tw/CKIP/trees1000.htm*. A searchable interface is also being developed and tested for researchers so that they can directly access the complete treebank information.

As an annotated corpus, one of the most important roles that a treebank can play is that it can serve as a shared source of data for linguistic, especially syntactic studies. Following the example of the successful Sinica Corpus, we have developed an on-line interface for extraction of grammatical information from the Sinica Treebank. Although the users that we have in mind are theoretical linguists who do not necessarily have computational background; we hope that non-linguists can also benefit from the ready availability of such grammatical information. And of course, computational linguists should be able to use this interface for quick references before going into a more in-depth study of the annotated corpus.

Currently, the beta site allows users specify a variety of conditions to search for structurally annotated sentences. Conditions can be specified in terms of keywords, grammatical tags (lexical or phrasal), thematic relations, or any boolean combination of the above elements. The search result can be presented as either annotated structure or simply the example sentences. Simply statistics, based on either straightforward frequency count or mutual information, are also available. For linguistically interesting information, such as the heads of various phrasal constructions, a user can simply look up the explicitly syntactic **Head** or semantic **head**; as well as **DUMMY** when it serves as a head placeholder. The website of this interface, as well as the general release of the Sinica Treebank 1.0, is scheduled to be announced at the second ACL workshop on Chinese Language Processing in October 2000.

## 6. Conclusion

The construction of the Sinica Treebank is only a first step towards application of structurally annotated corpora. Continuing expansion and correction will make this database an invaluable resource for linguistic and computational studies of Chinese.

## References


1.ABEILLE, Anne. 1999. Ed. Proceedings of *ATALA Workshop – Treebanks*. Paris, June 18-19, 1999. Univ. de Paris VII.

2.BOHMOVA, Alla and Eva Hajicova. 1999. How Much of the Underlying Syntactic Structure Can be Tagged Automatically? In Abeille (Ed). 1999.31-40.

3.CHEN, Feng-Yi, Pi-Fang Tsai, Keh-Jiann Chen, and Chu-Ren Huang. 2000. Sinica Treebank. [in Chinese] *Computational Linguistics and Chinese Language Processing*. 4.2.87-103.

4.CHEN, Keh-Jiann. 1996. A Model for Robust Chinese Parser. *Computational Linguistics and Chinese Language Processing*. 1.1.183-204.

5.CHEN, Keh-Jiann, Chu-Ren Huang. 1996. Information-based Case Grammar: A Unification-based Formalism for Parsing Chinese. In Journal of Chinese Linguistics Monograph Series No. 9. Chu-Ren Huang, Keh-Jiann Chen, and Benjamin K. T'sou Eds. *Readings in Chinese Natural Language Processing*. 23-45. Berkeley: JCL.

6.CHEN, Keh-Jiann, Chu-Ren Huang, Li-Ping Chang, Hui-Li Hsu. 1996.

Sinica Corpus: Design Methodology for Balanced Corpora. *Proceedings of the 11th Pacific Asia Conference on Language, Information, and Computation (PACLIC II)*. Seoul Korea. 167-176.

7.CHEN, Keh-Jiann and Shing-Huan Liu. 1992. Word Identification for Mandarin Chinese Sentences. *Proceedings of COLING*-92.101-105.

8.CHEN, Keh- Jiann, Shing-Huan Liu, Li-Ping Chang, Yeh-Hao Chin. 1994. A Practical Tagger for Chinese Corpora." *Proceedings of ROCLING VII*.111-126.

9.CHEN, Keh-Jiann, Chi-Ching Luo, Zhao-Ming Gao, Ming-Chung Chang, Feng-Yi Chen, and Chao-Ran Chen. 1999. The CKIP Chinese Treebank: Guidelines for Annotation. In Abeille (Ed). 1999.85-96.

10. CKIP (Chinese Knowledge Information Processing). 1993. The Categorical Analysis of Chinese. CKIP Technical Report 93-05. Nankang: Academia Sinica.

11. HUANG, Chu-Ren, Keh-Jiann Chen, Feng-Yi Chen, and Li-Li Chang. 1997. Segmentation Standard for Chinese Natural Language Processing. *Computational Linguistics and Chinese Language Processing*. 2.2.47-62

12. Lin, Fu-Wen. 1992. Some Reflections on the Thematic System of Information-based Case Grammar (ICG). CKIP Technical Report 92-01. Nankang: Academia Sinica.

13. Marcus, Mitch P., Beatrice Santorini, and M. A. Marcinkiewiicz. 1993. Building a Large Annotated Corpus of English: The Peen Treebank. Computational Linguistics. 19.2.313-330.

14. SAG, Ivan, Gerald Gazdar, Thomas Wasow, and Steven Weisler. 1985. Coordination and How to Distinguish Categories. Natural Language and Linguistic Theories. 117-171.

# Appendix

### 1. Lexical Categories

(1) NON-PREDCITIVE ADJVECTIVE: A
(2) CONJUNCTION: C
(3) ADVERB: D
(4) INTERJECTION: I
(5) NOUN: N
(6) DETERMINATIVES: Ne
(7) MEASURE WORD / CLASSIFIER: Nf
(8) POSTPOSITION WORD: Ng
(9) PRONOUN: Nh
(10) PREPOSITION: P
(11) PARTICLES: T
(12) VERB: V

### 2. Sample Sentence and Tree

那個挽髻的女人白髮之後

便不再理會庭前亭亭玉立的青草

*nage wanji de nyuren baifa zhihou bian buzai lihui*

that hair-style DE woman white-hair after then never pay-attention

*ting qian tingting yuli de qingcao*

courtyard front slender-ly standing-erect DE green-grass

'After her hair had turned white, that coiffured woman never paid any more attention to the nicely standing green grass in the front courtyard.'

S(agent:NP(quantifier:DM:那個| property:VP・的(head:VP(Head:VA4:挽髻) |Head:DE:的)|Head:Nab:女人)|time:GP (DUMMY:VP(Head:VH11:白髮)| Head: Ng:之後)|time:Dd:便|time:Dd:不再| Head: VC2:理會|goal:NP (property:VP・的(head: VP (location:NP(property:Ncb:庭| Head:Ncda:前)|Head:VH11:亭亭玉立)| Head:DE:的) | Head:Nab:青草))

# Enhancement of a Chinese Discourse Marker Tagger with C4.5

Benjamin K. T'sou[1], Tom B. Y. Lai[2], Samuel W. K. Chan[3], Weijun Gao[4], Xuegang Zhan[5]

[1 2 3]Language Information Sciences Research Centre
City University of Hong Kong
Tat Chee Avenue, Kowloon
Hong Kong SAR, China

Northeastern University, China

{[1]rlbtsou, [2]cttomlai}@uxmail.cityu.edu.hk, [3]swkchan@cs.cityu.edu.hk,
[4]wjgao@mail.neu.edu.cn, [5]zxg@ics.cs.neu.edu.cn

## Abstract

Discourse markers are complex discontinuous linguistic expressions which are used to explicitly signal the discourse structure of a text. This paper describes efforts to improve an automatic tagging system which identifies and classifies discourse markers in Chinese texts by applying machine learning (ML) to the disambiguation of discourse markers, as an integral part of automatic text summarization via rhetorical structure. Encouraging results are reported.

**Keywords**: discourse marker, Chinese corpus, rhetorical relation, automatic tagging, machine learning

## 1 Introduction

Discourse refers to any form of language-based communication involving multiple sentences or utterances. The most important forms of discourse of interest to Natural Language Processing (NLP) are text and dialogue. The function of discourse analysis is to divide a text into discourse segments, and to recognize and re-construct the discourse structure of the text as intended by its author.

Automatic text abstraction has received considerable attention (Paice 1990). Various systems have been developed (Chan et al. 2000). Ono et al. (1994), T'sou et al. (1992) and Marcu (1997) focus on discourse structure in summarization using the Rhetorical Structure Theory (RST, Mann and Thompson 1986). The theory has been exploited in a number of computational systems (e.g. Hovy 1993). The main idea is to build a discourse tree where each node of the tree represents an RST relation. Summarization is achieved by trimming unimportant sentences on the basis of the relative saliency or rhetorical relations.

The SIFAS (Syntactic Marker based Full-Text Abstraction System) system has been implemented to use discourse markers in the automatic summarization of Chinese (T'sou et al. 1999). In this paper, we report our efforts to improve the SIFAS tagging system by applying machine learning techniques to disambiguation of discourse markers. C4.5 (Quinlan, 1993) is used in our system.

## 2 Manual Tagging Process

To tag the discourse markers, the following coding scheme is designed to encode *Real* Discourse Markers (RDM) appearing in the SIFAS corpus (T'sou et al. 1998). We describe the $i^{th}$ discourse marker with a 7-tuple $RDM_i$:

$RDM_i$=< $DM_i$, $RR_i$, $RP_i$, $CT_i$, $MN_i$, $RN_i$, $OT_i$ >, where

$DM_i$ : the lexical item of the ***D**iscourse **M**arker*, or the value '*NULL*'.

$RR_i$ : the ***R**hetorical **R**elation* in which $DM_i$ is a constituent marker.

$RP_i$ : the ***R**elative **P**osition* of $DM_i$.

$CT_i$ : the ***C**onnection **T**ype* of $RR_i$.

$MN_i$ : the Discourse ***M**arker* Sequence ***N**umber*.

$RN_i$ : the Rhetorical ***R**elation* Sequence ***N**umber*.

$OT_i$ : the ***O**rder **T**ype* of $RR_i$. The value of $OT_i$ can be 1, -1 or 0, denoting respectively the normal order, reverse order or irrelevance of the premise-consequence ordering of $RR_i$.

For *apparent* discourse markers that do not function as a real discourse marker in a text, a different coding scheme is used to encode them. We describe the $i^{th}$ apparent discourse marker using a 3-Tuple $ADM_i$:

$ADM_i$=< $LI_i$, *, $SN_i$ >, where

$LI_i$ : the ***L**exical **I**tem* of the apparent discourse marker.

$SN_i$ : the ***S**equence **N**umber* of the apparent discourse marker.

In Chinese, discourse markers can be either words or phrases. To tag the SIFAS corpus, all discourse markers are organized into a discourse marker pair-rhetorical relation correspondence table. Part of the table is shown Table 1.

To construct an automatic tagging system, let us first examine the sequential steps in the tagging process of a human tagger.

S1. Written Chinese consists of running texts without word delimiters; the first step is is to segment the text into Chinese word sequences.

S2. On the basis of a discourse marker list, we identify those words in the text which appear on the list as Candidate Discourse Markers (CDMs).

S3. To winnow Real Discourse Markers (RDMs) and Apparent Discourse Markers (ADMs) from the CDMs, and encode the ADMs with a 3-tuple.

S4. To encode the RDM with a 7-tuple according to a Discourse Marker Pair-Rhetorical Relation correspondence table.

| Relat-ion | Front | Back | Con-nection Type | Order Type |
|---|---|---|---|---|
| Adver-sativity | | 可是 | Inter | 1 |
| Adver-sativity | | 可是 | Intra | 1 |
| Causa-lity | 因为 | 所以 | Intra | 1 |
| Causa-lity | 之所以 | | Intra | -1 |
| . | | | | |
| . | | | | |

**Table 1 Discourse Marker Pair-Rhetorical Relation Table**

## 3 Automatic Tagging Process

The identification of candidate discourse markers is based on a discourse marker list, which now contains 306 discourse markers plus a NULL marker. The markers are extracted from newspaper editorials of Hong Kong, Mainland China, Taiwan and Singapore. These markers constitute 480 distinct discontinuous pairs that correspond to 25 rhetorical relations. In actual usage, some discourse marker pairs designate multiple rhetorical relations according to context. Some pairs can represent both INTER-sentence and INTRA-sentence relations. Thus the correspondence between the discourse marker pairs and the rhetorical relations is not single-valued. Some discourse marker pairs correspond to more than one rhetorical relation or connection type. We have 504 correspondences between the discourse marker pairs and the rhetorical relations.

In practice, one discontinuous constituent member of a marker pair is often omitted. We use the NULL marker to indicate the omission. In the 504 correspondences, 244 of them are double constituent marker pairs, 260 are single constituent markers (i.e. One of the markers is NULL). And in the 244 double constituent markers, only 3 are not single-valued correspondences (one of which is an INTER/INTRA relation, and can easily be distinguished.). Thus the tagging of the 244 double constituent markers is basically a table searching process. But for the 260 single constituent markers, the identity of the NULL marker is often difficult to determine.

The SIFAS tagging system works in two modes: automatic and interactive (semi-automatic). The automatic tagging procedure is as follows:

1. Data preparation: Input data files are modified according to the required format.
2. Word segmentation: Because there are no delimiters between Chinese words in a text, words have to be extracted through a segmentation process.
3. CDM identification
4. Full-Marker RDM recognition
5. ADM identification (first pass, deterministic)
6. CDM feature extraction
7. ADM identification (2nd pass, via ML)
8. Tagging NULL-marker CDM pairs (via ML)
9. ADM and RDM sequencing, proof-reading, training data generation, and statistics

The following principles are adopted by the tagging algorithm to resolve ambiguity in the process of matching discontinuous discourse markers:

1. ***the principle of greediness***: When matching a pair of discourse markers for a rhetorical relation, priority is given to the first matched relation from the left.
2. ***the principle of locality***: When matching a pair of discourse markers for a rhetorical relation, priority is given to the relation where the distance between its constituent markers is shortest.
3. ***the principle of explicitness***: When matching a pair of discourse markers for a rhetorical relation, priority is given to the relation where both markers are explicitly presented.
4. ***the principle of superiority***: When matching a pair of discourse markers for a rhetorical relation, priority is given to the inter-sentence relation whose back discourse marker matched with the first word of a sentence.
5. ***the principle of Back-marker preference***: This is applicable only to rhetorical relations where either the front or the back marker is absent, or to a NULL marker. In such cases, priority is given to the relation with the back marker present.

Steps 1 to 6 and the five principles underlie the original naïve tagger of the SIFAS system (T'sou et al. 1998), which also contains the system framework.

# 4 Improvement

## 4.1 Problems

Many Chinese discourse markers have both discourse senses and alternate sentential senses in different context. For a human tagger, steps S3 and S4 in section 2 are not difficult because he/she can identify an ADM/RDM based on his/her text comprehension. However, for an automatic process, it is quite difficult to distinguish an ADM from an RDM if no syntactic/semantic information is available.

Another problem is the location of NULL-Marker described above. Our earlier statistics showed some characteristics in the distance measured by punctuation marks. Statistics from 80 tagged editorials show that most of the relations are INTRA-Sentence relations (about 93%), about 70% of the INTRA RDM pairs have NULL markers. Most of these RDM pairs are separated by ONE comma (62%). These statistics show the importance of the problems of positioning the NULL markers.

The naïve tagger partially solved the CDM discrimination and NULL marker location problems. Our experiment shows that about 45% of the ADMs can be correctly identified, and about 60% of the NULL markers can be correctly located one comma/period away from the current RDM. This leaves much room for improvement.

One solution is to add a few rules according to previous statistics. The original naïve tagger did not assume any knowledge of the statistics and behavioral patterns of discourse markers. From the error analysis, we extracted some additional rules to guide the classification and matching of the discourse markers. For example, one of the rules we extracted is:

> "A matching pair must be separated by at least two words or by punctuation marks". Using this rule, the following full marker matching error is avoided.

< 抓 紧 >< 实 施 >< 退 >< 耕 >< *还* ,conjunction,Front,Intra,5,5,1>< 林 >< *还* , conjunction, Back, Intra, 6,5,1><草>、<治理><水土流失><等><生态><建设>，<是,*,7><西部><地区><今后><<需要><着力><完成><的><重大><任务>。

Another solution is to use syntactic/semantic information through machine learning.

## 4.2 C4.5

Most empirical learning systems are given a set of pre-classified cases, each described by a vector of attribute values, and construct from them a mapping from attribute values to classes. C4.5 is one such system that learns decision-tree classifiers. It uses a divide-and-conquer approach to growing decision trees. The current version of C4.5 is C5.0 for Unix and See5 for Windows.

Let attributes be denoted $A=\{a_1, a_2, ..., a_m\}$, cases be denoted $D=\{d_1, d_2, ..., d_n\}$, and classes be denoted $C=\{c_1, c_2, ..., c_k\}$. For a set of cases $D$, a test $T_i$ is a split of $D$ based on attribute $a_i$. It splits $D$ into mutually exclusive subsets $D_1, D_2, ..., D_p$. These subsets of cases are single-class collections of cases.

If a test $T$ is chosen, the decision tree for $D$ consists of a node identifying the test $T$, and one branch for each possible subset $D_i$. For each subset $D_i$, a new test is then chosen for further split. If $D_i$ satisfies a stopping criterion, the tree for $D_i$ is a leaf associated with the most frequent class in $D_i$. One reason for stopping is that cases in $D_i$ belong to one class.

C4.5 uses ***arg max(gain(D,T))*** or ***arg max(gain ratio(D,T))*** to choose tests for split:

$$Info(D) = -\sum_{i=1}^{k} p(c_i, D) * \log 2(p(c_i, D))$$

$$Split(D,T) = -\sum_{i=1}^{p} \frac{|D_i|}{|D|} * \log 2(\frac{|D_i|}{|D|})$$

$$Gain(D,T) = Info(D) - \sum_{i=1}^{p} \frac{|D_i|}{|D|} * Info(D_i)$$

$$Gain\,ratio(D,T) = gain(D,T) / Split(D,T)$$

where, $p(c_i,D)$ denotes the proportion of cases in $D$ that belong to the $i^{th}$ class.

## 4.3 Application of C4.5

Since using semantic information requires a comprehensive thesaurus, which is unavailable at present, we only use syntactic information through machine learning.

The attributes used in the original SIFAS system include the candidate discourse marker itself, two words immediately to the left of the CDM, and two words immediately to the right of the CDM. The attribute names are F2, F1, CDM, B1, B2, respectively (T'sou et al, 1999). SIFAS only uses the Part Of Speech attribute of the neighboring words. This reflects to some degree the syntactic characteristics of the CDM.

To reflect the distance characteristics, we add two other attributes: the number of discourse delimiters (commas, semicolons for INTRA-sentence relation, periods and exclamation marks for INTER-sentence relation) before and after the current CDM, denoted Fcom and Bcom, respectively. For the location of the NULL marker, we still add an actual number of delimiters Acom.

The order of these attributes is: CDM, F1, F2, B1, B2, Fcom, Bcom Acom for Null marker location, and CDM, F1, F2, B1, B2, Fcom, Bcom, IsRDM for CDM classification, where IsRDM is a Boolean value.

The following are two examples of cases:

并且,?,q,a,a,7,1,1 for NULL marker location

包括,d,?,u,?,1,0,F for CDM classificati on

where "?" denotes that no corresponding word is at the position (beginning or end of sentence); a, d, q, and u are part-of-speech symbols in our segmentation dictionary, representing adjective, adverb, classifier, and auxiliary, respectively.

The following are two examples of the rules generated by the C4.5. The first is a CDM classification rule, and the other is a NULL marker location rule.

Rule 5: (11/1, lift 2.2)
CDM = 并
B1 = v
Fcom > 0
→ class T [0.846]

which can be explained as: if the word after the CDM "并" is a verb, and there is one comma in the sentence, before "并", then "并" is an RDM.

Rule 22: (1, lift 3.4)
B2 = p
Fcom > 1
→ class 2 [0.667]

which can be explained as: if the second word after the RDM is a preposition, and there is more then one commas before the current RDM, then the location of the NULL marker is two commas away from the RDM.

### 4.4 Objects in the SIFAS system

The objects in the new SIFAS tagging system are listed below.

1. Dictionary Editor: for the update of word segmentation dictionary and the rhetorical relation table.
2. Data Manager: for the modification of the input data (editorial texts) to conform with the required format.
3. Word Segmenter: for the segmentation of the original texts, and the recognition of CDMs.
4. RDM Tagger: The initial identification of RDMs is a table searching process. All those full-marker pairs are identified as rhetorical relations according to the principles described above. For those Null-marker pairs, the location of the Null maker is left to the rule interpreter.
5. ADM Tagger: The identification of ADMs is also a table searching process, because, without other syntactic/semantic information, the only way to identify ADMs from the CDMs is to find out that the CDM cannot form a valid pair with any other CDMs (including the NULL marker) to correspond to a rhetorical relation.
6. CDM Feature Extractor: For those untagged CDMs, the classification is carried out through C4.5. The Feature Extractor extracts syntactic information about the current CDM and send it to the Rule Interpreter (see below).
7. Rule Interpreter: C4.5 takes feature data file as the input to construct a classifier, and the rules formed are stored in an output file. The rule interpreter reads this output file and applies the rules to classify the CDMs. In our system, The Rule Interpreter functions as a NULL Marker Locator and a CDM classifier.
8. Sequencer: for the rearrangement of RDM and ADM order number. In the rearranging process, the Sequencer also extracts statistical information for analysis.
9. Interaction Recorder: for the recording of user interaction information for

statistics use.

10. Data Retriever: for data retrieval and browsing.

## 5 Evaluation

In order to evaluate the effectiveness of the tagging system in terms of the percentage of discourse markers that can be tagged correctly, we have chosen 80 tagged editorials from Ming Pao, a Chinese newspaper of Hong Kong, in the duration from December 1995 to January 1996 to form a training data set. Then we randomly selected 20 editorials from Mainland China and Hong Kong newspapers for the system to tag automatically, and then manually checked the results.

The total CDMs in the training data set is 4764, in which 2116 are RDMs and 2648 are ADMs. The distribution of INTER-sentence relations, INTRA-sentence relations, and NULL marker pairs is shown below.

| Total Relations | Inter-Sentence Relations | Intra-Sentence Relations | Relations with NULL marker pair |
|---|---|---|---|
| 1589 | 98 | 1491 | 1062 |
| 100% | 6.17% | 93.83% | 66.83% |

**Table 2 Distribution of INTER-/INTRA-sentence relations, and NULL marker pairs**

Our evaluation is based on counting the number of discourse markers that are correctly and incorrectly tagged.

The total CDMs in the test data set is 1134, in which 563 are RDMs and 571 are ADMs. The distribution of INTER-sentence relations, INTRA-sentence relations, and NULL marker pairs in the test data set is shown in Table 3.

| Total Relations | Inter-Sentence Relations | Intra-Sentence Relations | Relations with NULL marker pair |
|---|---|---|---|
| 424 | 23 | 401 | 285 |
| 100% | 5.42% | 94.58% | 67.22% |

**Table 3 Distribution of INTER-/INTRA-sentence relations, and NULL marker pairs in testing data set**

| Tagged Relations | Correctly tagged | NULL marker | Full marker | ADM/RDM | Other errors |
|---|---|---|---|---|---|
| 451 | 399 | 11 | 1 | 65 | 3 |

**Table 4 Test Results**

From the test results shown in Table 4, we can see that most of the errors are caused by the misclassification of the CDMs. An example of *Other errors* is shown below. The following sentence is from an editorial of People's Daily.

<我们><再次><重申>，<***NULL***,sufficiency,Front,Intra,0,81,1><一个中国><的><原则><不容><回避>，<不><承认><一个中国><的><原则>、<不><承认><台湾><是,*,80><中国><的><一部分>，<台湾海峡><***就***,sufficiency,Back,Intra,81,81,1<不会><有><持久><的><和平>，<两岸><关系><***就,*,82***><难以><改善>。

In the above sentence, the first "就" is matched with the NULL marker, but the second "就" is left as an ADM. This causes an "Other error" and an "ADM/RDM classification error".

The Gross Accuracy (GA) as defined in T'sou et al. (1999) is:

GA = correctly tagged discourse markers / total number of discourse markers = 95.38%

This greatly improves the performance compared with the original GA = 68.89%.

The overgeneration problem (tagged 415, actual 424) is caused by the mismatch of CDMs as RDM pairs, or by the misclassification of CDMs as RDMs. Following are two examples.

<如果,sufficiency,Front,Intra,54,54,1><我们><将,*,55><多元化><理解><成><谁><爱><说><什么><就,*,56><说><什么>，<他人><莫><能干><预>，<那,sufficiency,Back,Intra,57,54,1><就,*,58><好比><主张><在><现代><都市><中><可以><随地><便溺><而,*,59><他人><不得><干涉><一般>。

In this example, "如果" could have matched <将,*,55>, <就,*,56>, or <就,*,58>. Only the <将,*,55> and the <就,*,58> can be eliminated from the candidates according to the "simple rules" mentioned in section 4.1. The system has to choose from <就,*,56> and <那,*,57> to match with "如果". Luckily, the system has given a right choice here.

<一个中国><*是,conjunction,Front,Intra,46,46,1*><无可争辩><的><现实>，<NULL,conjunction,Front,Intra,0,49,1><一个中国><原则><*是,conjunction,Back,Intra,47,46,1*><包括,*,48><台湾><同胞><在内><的><绝大多数><中国人><的><共同><认识>，<也,conjunction,Back,Intra,49,49,1><得到><世界><上><绝大多数><国家><和><包括,*,50><联合国><在内><的><国际><组织><的><承认>。

The two "是" are misclassified as RDMs, and causes a mismatch of RDM pair. Such errors are difficult to avoid for an automatic system. Without further syntactic/semantic analysis, we can only hope for the ML algorithm to give us a solution from more training data.

## 6 Conclusion

In order to study discourse markers for use in the automatic summarization of Chinese text, we have designed and implemented the SIFAS system. In this paper, we have focused on the problems of NULL marker location and the classification of RDMs and ADMs. A study on applying machine learning techniques to discourse marker disambiguation is conducted. C4.5 is used to generate decision tree classifiers. Our results indicate that machine learning is an effective approach to improving the accuracy of discourse marker tagging. For interactive use of the system, if we set a threshold for the rule precision and only display those low precision rules for interactive selection, we can greatly speed up the semi-automatic tagging process.

## 7 References


Chan S., Lai T., Gao W. J. and T'sou B. K. (2000) "Mining Discourse Markers for Chinese Textual Summarization." In Proceedings of the Sixth Applied Natural Language Processing Conference and the North American Chapter of the Association for Computational Linguistics. Workshop on Automatic Summarization, Seattle, Washington, 29 April to 3 May, 2000.

Grosz B.J. and Sidner C. (1986) "Attention, Intention, and the Structure of Discourse," Computational Linguistics 12(3): 175-204.

Hirst G. (1981) "Discourse Oriented Anaphoral Resolution in Natural Language Understanding: A Review." Computational Linguistics 7(2): 85-98.

Hovy E. (1993) "Automated Discourse Generation using Discourse Structure Relations." Artificial Intelligence 63: 341-385.

Hwang C. H. and Schubert L. K. (1992) "Tense Trees as the 'Fine Structure' of Discourse." In Proc. 30th Annual Meeting, Assoc. for Computational Linguistics, pp. 232-240.

Lin H. L., T'sou B. K., H. C. Ho, Lai T., Lun C., C. K. Choi and C.Y. Kit. (1991) "Automatic Chinese Text Generation Based on Inference Trees." In Proc. of ROCLING Computational Linguistic Conference IV, Taipei, pp. 215-236.

Litman D. J. and Allen J. (1990) "Discourse Processing and Commonsense Plans." In Cohen et al.(ed.) Intentions in Communications, pp. 365-388.

Mann W. C. and Thompson S. A (1988) "Rhetorical Structure Theory: Towards a Functional Theory of Text Organization."

Text 8(3): 243-281.

Marcu D. (1997) "From Discourse Structures to Text Summaries." In Proceedings of the ACL/EACL'97 Workshop on Intelligent Scalable Text Summarization, Spain, pp. 82-88.

McKeown K. and Radev D. (1995) "Summaries of Multiple News Articles." In Proceedings of the 18th Annual International ACM SIGIR Conference on Research and Development in Information Retrieval, Seattle, pp. 74-82.

Ono K., Sumita K. and S. Miike. (1994) "Abstract Generation based on Rhetorical Structure Extraction." In Proceedings of International Conference on Computational Linguistics, Japan, pp. 344-348.

Paice C. D. (1990) "Constructing Literature Abstracts by Computer: Techniques and Prospects." Information Processing and Management 26(1): 171-186.

Quinlan J. Ross (1993) "C4.5 Programs for Machine Learning." San Mateo, CA: Morgan Kaufmann.

T'sou B. K., Ho H. C., Lai B. Y., Lun C. and Lin H. L. (1992) "A Knowledge-based Machine-aided System for Chinese Text Abstraction." In Proceedings of International Conference on Computational Linguistics, France, pp. 1039-1042.

T'sou B. K., Gao W. J., Lin H. L., Lai T. B. Y. and Ho H. C. (1999) "Tagging Discourse Markers: Towards a Corpus based Study of Discourse Marker Usage in Chinese Text" In Proceedings of the 18th International Conference on Computer Processing of Oriental Languages, March 1999, Japan, pp. 391-396.

T'sou B. K., Lin H. L., Ho H. C., Lai T. and Chan T. (1996) "Automated Chinese Full-text Abstraction Based on Rhetorical Structure Analysis." Computer Processing of Oriental Languages 10(2): 225-238.

Tsou, B.K., et al., 1998: 邹嘉彦, 连兴隆, 高维君, 黎邦洋, 何庆昌, "中文篇章中的关联词语及其引导的句子关系的自动标注", ICCIP'98, Beijing, Nov. 18-20, 1998.

# Statistically-Enhanced New Word Identification in a Rule-Based Chinese System

**Andi Wu**
Microsoft Research
One Microsoft Way
Redmond, WA 98052
Andiwu@microsoft.com

**Zixin Jiang**
Microsoft Research
One Microsoft Way
Redmond, WA 98052
jiangz@microsoft.com

## Abstract

This paper presents a mechanism of new word identification in Chinese text where probabilities are used to filter candidate character strings and to assign POS to the selected strings in a ruled-based system. This mechanism avoids the sparse data problem of pure statistical approaches and the over-generation problem of rule-based approaches. It improves parser coverage and provides a tool for the lexical acquisition of new words.

## 1 Introduction

In this paper, new words refer to newly coined words, occasional words and other rarely used words that are neither found in the dictionary of a natural language processing system nor recognized by the derivational rules or proper name identification rules of the system. Typical examples of such words are shown in the following sentences, with the new words underlined in bold.

有人要学好的东西，也有人要**拣拾**“垃圾”。
国安队只有胡建平**冷射**得手。
中国**女垒**获企业支持。
他们还将在一些城市举办世界杯奖杯真身**巡展**。
**维初**越野队的健将非常努力。
警方和刑事情报部门了解**球痞**们的活动。
这对美国人的肥胖症起了**助肥**作用。
他立即去附近一家**驾校**报了名。
邵逸夫**捐建**了此楼。
柔枝低低**弯垂**去**回吻**那多情的河水。
那是一杯色彩**鲜丽**的“鸡尾酒”
中国**健力宝**青年队旗开得胜。
西藏的**晒佛节**、**传昭**等也得到恢复。
他们突然一个个变成**生高马大**的“老美”。
女子在田径场上**争金夺银**。

The automatic identification of such words by a machine is a trivial task in languages where words are separated by spaces in written texts. In languages like Chinese, where no word boundary exists in written texts, this is by no means an easy job. In many cases the machine will not even realize that there is an unfound word in the sentence since most single Chinese characters can be words by themselves.

Purely statistical methods of word segmentation (e.g. de Marcken 1996, Sproat et al 1996, Tung and Lee 1994, Lin et al (1993), Chiang et al (1992), Lua, Huang et al, etc.) often fail to identify those words because of the sparse data problem, as the likelihood for those words to appear in the training texts is extremely low.

There are also hybrid approaches such as (Nie dt al 1995) where statistical approaches and heuristic rules are combined to identify new words. They generally perform better than purely statistical segmenters, but the new words they are able to recognize are usually proper names and other relatively frequent words. They require a reasonably big training corpus and the performance is often domain-specific depending on the training corpus used.

Many word segmenters ignore low-frequency new words and treat their component characters as independent words, since they are often of little significance in applications where the structure of sentences is not taken into consideration. For in-depth natural language understanding where full parsing is required, however, the identification of those words is critical, because a single unidentified word can cause a whole sentence to fail.

The new word identification mechanism to be presented here is used in a wide coverage Chinese parser that does full sentence analysis. It assumes the word segmentation process described in Wu and Jiang (1998). In this model, word segmentation, including unfound word identification, is not a stand-alone process, but an integral part of sentence analysis. The segmentation component provides a word lattice of the sentence that contains all the possible words, and the final disambiguation is achieved in the parsing process.

In what follows, we will discuss two hypotheses and their implementation. The first one concerns the selection of candidate strings and the second one concerns the assignment of parts of speech (POS) to those strings.

## 2 Selection of candidate strings

### 2.1 Hypothesis

Chinese used to be a monosyllabic language, with one-to-one correspondences between syllables, characters and words, but most words in modern Chinese, especially new words, consist of two or more characters. Of the 85,135 words in our system's dictionary, 9217 of them are monosyllabic, 47778 are disyllabic, 17094 are tri-syllabic, and the rest has four or more characters. Since hardly any new character is being added to the language, the unfound words we are trying to identify are almost always multiple character words. Therefore, if we find a sequence of single characters (not subsumed by any words) after the completion of basic word segmentation, derivational morphology and proper name identification, this sequence is very likely to be a new word. This basic intuition has been discussed in many papers, such as Tung and Lee (1994). Consider the following sentence.

(1) 维初男队中锋范建毅居然冷射得手。

This sentence contains two new words (not including the name 范建毅 which is recognized by the proper name identification mechanism) that are unknown to our system:

维初 (probably the abbreviated name of a junior high school)
冷射 (a word used in sports only but not in our dictionary)

Initial lexical processing based on dictionary lookup and proper name identification produces the following segmentation:

维 初 <u>男队</u> <u>中锋</u> <u>范建毅</u> <u>居然</u> 冷 射 <u>得手</u>

where 维初 and 冷射 are segmented into single characters. In this case, both single character-strings are the new words we want to find.

However, not every character sequence is a word in Chinese. Many such sequences are simply sequences of single-character words. Here is an example:

(2) 她回了国才会来看你。

After dictionary look up, we get

她 回 了 国 才 会 来 看 你

which is a sequence of 10 single characters. However, every character here is an independent word and there is no new word in the sentence. From this we see that, while most new words show up as a sequence of single characters, not every sequence of single characters forms a new word. The existence of a single-character string is the necessary but not sufficient condition for a new word. *Only those sequences of single characters where the characters are unlikely to be a sequence of independent words are good candidates for new words.*

### 2.2 Implementation

The hypothesis in the previous section can be implemented with the use of the Independent Word Probability (*IWP*), which can be a property of a single character or a string of characters.

#### 2.1.1 Defining IWP

Most Chinese characters can be used either as independent words or component parts of multiple character words. The IWP of a single character is the likelihood for this character to appear as an independent word in texts:

$$IWP(c) = \frac{N(Word(c))}{N(c)}$$

where *N(Word(c))* is the number of occurrences of a character as an independent word in the sentences of a given text corpus and *N(c)* is the total number of occurrence of this character in the same corpus. In our implementation, we computed the probability from a parsed corpus where we went through all the leaves of the trees, counting the occurrences of each character and the occurrences of each character as an independent word.

The parsed corpus we used contains about 5,000 sentences and was of course not big enough to contain every character in the Chinese language. This did not turn out to be a major problem, though. We find that, as long as all the frequently used single-character words are in the corpus, we can get good results, for what really matters is the *IWP* of this small set of frequent characters/words. These characters/words are bound to appear in any reasonably large collection of texts.

Once we have the *IWP* of individual characters (*IWP(c)*), we can compute the *IWP* of a character string (*IWP(s)*). *IWP(s)* is the probability of a sequence of two or more characters being a sequence of independent words. This is simply the joint probability of the *IWP(c)* of the component characters.

#### 2.1.2 Using IWP

With *IWP(c) and IWP(s)* defined , we then define a threshold *T* for *IWP*. A sequence *S* of two or more characters is considered a candidate for a new word only if its $IWP(s) < T$. When *IWP(s)* reaches *T*, the likelihood for the characters to be a sequence of independent words is too high and the string will not be considered to be a possible new word. In our implementation, the value of *T* is empirically determined. A lower *T* results in higher precision and lower recall while a higher *T* improves recall at the expense of precision. We tried different values and weighed recall against precision until we got the best performance. 维初 and 冷射 in Sentence (1) are identified as candidate dates because *IWP(s)*( 维初) = 8% and *IWP(s)*( 冷射) = 10% while the threshold is 15%. In our system, precision is not a big concern at this stage because the final filtering is done in the parsing process. We put recall first to ensure that the parser will have every word it needs. We also tried to increase precision, but not at the expense of recall.

## 3 POS Assignment

Once a character string is identified to be a candidate for new word, we must decide what syntactic category or POS to assign to this possible new word. This is required for sentence analysis where every word in the sentence must have at least one POS.

### 3.1. Hypothesis

Most multiple character words in Chinese have word-internal syntactic structures, which is roughly the POS sequence of the component characters (assuming each character has a POS or potential POS). A two-character verb, for example, can have a V-V, V-N, V-N or A(dv)-V internal structure. For a two-character string to be assigned the POS of verb, the POS/potential POS of its component characters must match one of those patterns. However, this matching alone is not the sufficient condition for POS assignment. Considering the fact that a single character can have more than one POS and a single POS sequence can correspond to the internal word structures of different parts of speech (V-N can be verb or a noun, for instance), simply assigning POS on the basis of word internal structure will result in massive over-generation and introduce too much noise into the parsing process. To prune away the unwanted guesses, we need more help from statistics.

When we examine the word formation process in Chinese, we find that new words are often modeled on existing words. Take the newly coined verb 冷射 as an example. Scanning our dictionary, we find that 冷 appears many times as the first character of a two-character verb, such as 冷冻, 冷凝, 冷笑, 冷藏, 冷轧, 冷敷, etc. Meanwhile, 射 appears many times as the second character of a two-character verb, such as 俯射, 反射, 平射, 折射, 斜射, 直射, etc. This leads us to the following hypothesis:

*A candidate character string for a new word is likely to have a given POS if the component characters of this string have appeared in the corresponding positions of many existing words with this POS.*

## 3.2. Implementation

To represent the likelihood for a character to appear in a given position of a word with a given POS and a given length, we assign probabilities of the following form to each character:

***P(Cat,Pos,Len)***

where Cat is the category/POS of a word, Pos is the position of the character in the word, and Len is the length (number of characters) of the word. The probability of a character appearing as the second character in a four-character verb, for instance, is represented as ***P(Verb,2,4)***.

### *3.1.1. Computing P(Cat,Pos,Len)*

There are many instantiations of ***P(Cat,Pos,Len)***, depending on the values of the three variables. In our implementation, we limited the values of *Cat* to Noun, Verb and Adjective, since they are the main open class categories and therefore the POSes of most new words. We also assume that most new words will have between 2 to 4 characters, thereby limiting the values of *Pos* to 1-4 and the values of *Len* to 2-4. Consequently each character will have 27 different kinds of probability values associated with it. We assign to each of them a 4-character name where the first character is always "P", the second the value of *Cat*, the third the value of *Pos*, and the fourth the value of *Len*. Here are some examples:

*Pn12* (the probability of appearing as the first character of a two-character noun)

*Pv22* (the probability of appearing as the second character of a two-character verb)

*Pa34* (the probability of appearing as the third character of a four-character adjective)

The values of those 27 kinds of probabilities are obtained by processing the 85,135 headwords in our dictionary. For each character in Chinese, we count the number of occurrences of this character in a given position of words with a given length and given category and then divide it by the total number of occurrences of this character in the headwords of the dictionary. For example,

$$Pv12(c) = \frac{N(v12(c))}{N(c)}$$

where *N(v12(c))* is the number of occurrences of a character in the first position of a two-character verb while *N(c)* is the total number of occurrences of this character in the dictionary headwords. Here are some of the values we get for the character射:

| | |
|---|---|
| *Pn12*(射) = 7% | *Pn22*(射) = 0% |
| *Pv12*(射) = 3% | *Pv22*(射) =24% |
| *Pv23*(射) = 39% | *Pa22*(射) =1% |

It is clear from those numbers that the character 射 tend to occur in the second position of two-character and three-character verbs.

### *3.1.2. Using P(Cat,Pos,Len)*

Once a character string is identified as a new word candidate, we will calculate the POS probabilities for the string. For each string, we will get *P(noun)*, *P(verb)* and *P(adj)* which are respectively the probabilities of this string being a noun, a verb or an adjective. They are the joint probabilities of the *P(Cat,Pos,Len)* of the component characters of this string. We then measure the outcome against a threshold. For a new word string to be assigned the syntactic category *Cat*, its *P(Cat)* must reach the threshold. The threshold for each *P(Cat )* is independently determined so that we do not favor a certain POS (e.g. Noun) simply because there are more nouns in the dictionary.

If a character string reaches the threshold of more than one *P(Cat)*, it will be assigned more than one syntactic category. A string that has both *P(noun)* and *P(verb)* reaching the threshold, for example, will have both a noun and a verb added to the word lattice. The ambiguity is then resolved in the parsing process. If a string passes the *IWP* test but fails the *P(Cat)* test, it will receive noun as its syntactic category. In other words, the default POS for a new word candidate is noun. This is what happened to 维初 in the Sentence (1). 维初 passed the *IWP* test, but failed each of the *P(Cat)* tests. As a result, it is made a noun by default. As we can see, this assignment is the correct one (at least in this particular sentence).

## 4. Results and Discussion

### 4.1. Increase in Parser Coverage

The new word identification mechanism discussed above has been part of our system for about 10 months. To find out how much contribution it makes to our parser coverage, we took 176,863 sentences that had been parsed successfully with the new word mechanism turned on and parsed them again with the new word mechanism turned off. When we did this test at the beginning of these 10 months, 37640 of those sentences failed to get a parse when the mechanism was turned off. In other words, 21.3% of the sentences were "saved" by this mechanism. At the end of the 10 months, however, only 7749 of those sentences failed because of the removal of the mechanism. At first sight, this seems to indicate that the new word mechanism is doing a much less satisfactory job than before. What actually happened is that many of the words that were identified by the mechanism 10 months ago, especially those that occur frequently, have been added to our dictionary. In the past 10 months, we have been using this mechanism both as a component of robust parsing and as a method of lexical acquisition whereby new entries are discovered from text corpora. This discovery procedure has helped us find many words that are found in none of the existing word lists we have access to.

### 4.2. Precision of Identification

Apart from its contribution to parser coverage, we can also evaluate the new word identification mechanism by looking at its precision. In our evaluation, we measured precision in two different ways.

In the first measurement, we compared the number of new words that are proposed by the guessing mechanism and the number of words that end up in successful parses. If we use *NWA* to stand for the number of new words that are added to the word lattice and *NWU* for the number of new words that appear in a parse tree, the precision rate will be *NWU / NWA*. Actual testing shows that this rate is about 56%. This means that the word guessing mechanism has over-guessed and added about twice as many words as we need. This is not a real problem in our system, however, because the final decision is made in the parsing process. The lexical component is only responsible for providing a word lattice of which one of the paths is correct. In the second measurement, we had a native speaker of Chinese go over all the new words that end up in successful parses and see how many of them sound like real words to her. This is a fairly subjective test but nonetheless meaningful one. It turns out that about 85% of the new words that "survived" the parsing process are real words.

We would also like to run a large-scale recall test on the mechanism, but found it to be impossible. To run such a test, we have to know how many unlisted new words actually exist in a corpus of texts. Since there is no automatic way of knowing it, we would have to let a human manually check the texts. This is too expensive to be feasible.

### 4.3. Contributions of Other Components

While the results shown above do give us some idea about how much contribution the new word identification mechanism makes to our system, it is actually very difficult to say precisely how much credit goes to this mechanism and how much to other components of the system. As we can see, the performance of this mechanism also depends on the following two factors:

(1) The word segmentation processes prior to the application of this mechanism. They include dictionary lookup, derivational morphology, proper name identification and the assembly of other items such as time, dates, monetary units, address, phone numbers, etc. These processes also group characters into words. Any improvement in those components will also improve the performance of the new word mechanism. If every word that "should" be found by

those processes has already been identified, the single-character sequences that remain after those processes will have a better chance of being real words.

(2) The parsing process that follows. As mentioned earlier, the lexical component of our system does not make a final decision on "wordhood". It provides a word lattice from which the syntactic parser is supposed to pick the correct path. In the case of new word identification, the word lattice will contain both the new words that are identified and the all the words/characters that are subsumed by the new words. A new word proposed in the word lattice will receive its official wordhood only when it becomes part of a successful parse. To recognize a new word correctly, the parser has to be smart enough to accept the good guesses and reject the bad guesses. This ability of the parser will imporve as the parser improves in general and a better parser will yield better final results in new word identification.

Generally speaking, the mechanisms using *IWP* and *P(Cat,Pos,Len)* provide the *internal* criteria for wordhood while word segmentation and parsing provide the *external* criteria. The internal criteria are statistically based whereas the external criteria are rule-based. Neither can do a good job on its own without the other. The approach we take here is not to be considered statistical natural language processing, but it does show that a rule-based system can be enhanced by some statistics. The statistics we need can be extracted from a very small corpus and a dictionary and they are not domain dependent. We have benefited from the mechanism in the analysis of many different kinds of texts.

## References


Chang, Jyun-Sheng, Shun-Der Chen, Sue-Jin Ker, Ying Chen and John S. Liu (1994) A multiple-corpus approach to recognition of proper names in Chinese texts, *Computer Processing of Chinese and Oriental Languages*, Vol. 8, No. 1 pp. 75-85.

Chen, Keh-Jiann and Shing-Huan Liu (1992). Word identification for Mandarin Chinese sentences, Proceedings of COLING-92, pp. 23-28.

Chiang, T. H., Y. C. Lin and K.Y. Su (1992). Statisitical models for word segmentation and unknown word resolution, *Proceedings of the 1992 R. O. C. Computational Linguistics Conference*, 121-146, Taiwan.

De Marcken, Carl (1996). *Unsupervised Language Acquisition*, Ph.D dissertation, MIT.

Lin, M. Y. , T. H. Chiang and K. Y. Su (1993) A prelimnary study on unknown word problem in Chinese word segmentation, *Proceedings of the 1993 R. O. C. Computational Linguistics Conference*, 119-137, Taiwan.

Lua, K T. Experiments on the use of bigram mutual information in Chinese natural language processing.

Nie, Jian Yun, et al. (1995) Unknown Word Detection and Segmentation of Chinese using Statistical and Heuristic Knowledge, Communications of COLIPS, vol 5, No. 1 &2, pp.47, Singapore.

Sproat, Richard, Chilin Shih, William Gale and Nancy Chang (1996). A stochastic finite-state word-segmentation algorithm for Chinese. *Computational Linguistics*, Volume 22, Number 3.

Tung, Cheng-Huang and Lee His-Jian (1994). Identification of unknown words from a corpus. *Computer Processing of Chinese and Oriental Languages*, Vol. 8 Supplement, pp. 131-145.

Wu, Andi and Zixin Jiang (1998) Word segmentation in sentence analysis, *Proceedings of the 1998 International Conference on Chinese Information Processing*, pp. 169-180.

Yeh, Ching-Long and His-Jian Lee (1991). Rule-based word identification for Mandarin Chinese sentences – a unification approach, *Computer Processing of Chinese and Oriental Languages*, Vol 5, No 2, Page 97-118.

# Comparing Lexicalized Treebank Grammars Extracted from Chinese, Korean, and English Corpora

**Fei Xia, Chung-hye Han, Martha Palmer, and Aravind Joshi**
University of Pennsylvania
Philadelphia PA 19104, USA
{fxia,chunghye,mpalmer,joshi}@linc.cis.upenn.edu

## Abstract

In this paper, we present a method for comparing Lexicalized Tree Adjoining Grammars extracted from annotated corpora for three languages: English, Chinese and Korean. This method makes it possible to do a quantitative comparison between the syntactic structures of each language, thereby providing a way of testing the Universal Grammar Hypothesis, the foundation of modern linguistic theories.

## 1 Introduction

The comparison of the grammars extracted from annotated corpora (i.e., Treebanks) is important on both theoretical and engineering grounds. Theoretically, it allows us to do a quantitative testing of the Universal Grammar Hypothesis. One of the major concerns in modern linguistics is to establish an explanatory basis for the similarities and variations among languages. The working assumption is that languages of the world share a set of universal linguistic principles and the apparent structural differences attested among languages can be explained as variation in the way the universal principles are instantiated. Comparison of the extracted syntactic trees allows us to quantitatively evaluate how similar the syntactic structures of different languages are. From an engineering perspective the extracted grammars and the links between the syntactic structures in the grammars are valuable resources for NLP applications, such as parsing, computational lexicon development, and machine translation (MT), to name a few.

In this paper we first briefly discuss some linguistic characteristics of English, Chinese, and Korean, and introduce the Treebanks for the three languages. We then describe a tool that extracts Lexicalized Tree Adjoining Grammars (LTAGs) from Treebanks and the results of its application to these three Treebanks. Next, we describe our methodology for automatic comparison of the extracted Treebank grammars, This consists primarily of matching syntactic structures (namely, templates and sub-templates) in each pair of Treebank grammars. The ability to perform this type of comparison for different languages has a definite positive impact on the possibility of sorting out the universal versus language-dependent features of languages. Therefore, our grammar extraction tool is not only an engineering tool of great value in improving the efficiency and accuracy of grammar development, but it is also very useful for investigating theoretical linguistics.

## 2 Three Languages and Three Treebanks

In this section, we briefly discuss some linguistic characteristics of English, Chinese, and Korean, and introduce the Treebanks for these languages.

### 2.1 Three Languages

These three languages belong to different language families: English is Germanic, Chinese is Sino-Tibetan, and Korean is Altaic (Comrie, 1987). There are several major differences between these languages. First, both English and Chinese have predominantly subject-verb-object (SVO) word order, whereas Korean has underlying SOV order. Second, the word order in Korean is freer than in English and Chinese in the sense that argument NPs are freely permutable (subject to certain discourse constraints). Third, Korean and Chinese freely allow subject and object deletion, but English does not. Fourth, Korean has richer inflectional morphology than English, whereas Chinese has little, if any, inflectional morphology.

## 2.2 Three Treebanks

The Treebanks that we used in this paper are the English Penn Treebank II (Marcus et al., 1993), the Chinese Penn Treebank (Xia et al., 2000b), and the Korean Penn Treebank (Chung-hye Han, 2000). The main parameters of these Treebanks are summarized in Table 1.[1] The tags in each tagset can be classified into one of four types: (1) syntactic tags for phrase-level annotation, (2) Part-Of-Speech (POS) tags for head-level annotation, (3) function tags for grammatical function annotation, and (4) empty category tags for dropped arguments, traces, and so on.

We chose these Treebanks because they all use phrase structure annotation and their annotation schemata are similar, which facilitates the comparison between the extracted Treebank grammars. Figure 1 shows an annotated sentence from the Penn English Treebank.

# 3 LTAGs and Extraction Algorithm

In this section, we give a brief introduction to the LTAG formalism and to a system named LexTract, which we build to extract LTAGs from Treebanks.

[1]The reason why the average sentence length for Korean is much shorter than those for English and Chinese is that a big portion of the corpus for Korean Treebank includes dialogues that contain many one-word replies, whereas English and Chinese corpora consist of newspaper articles.

```
((S (PP-LOC (IN at)
            (NP (NNP FNX))
   (NP-SBJ-1 (NNS underwriters))
    (ADVP (RB still))
    (VP (VBP draft)
        (NP (NNS policies))
        (S-MNR
          (NP-SBJ (-NONE- *-1))
          (VP (VBG using)
             (NP
               (NP (NN fountain) (NNS pens))
               (CC and)
               (NP (VBG blotting) (NN papers))))))))
```

Figure 1: An example from Penn English Treebank

## 3.1 LTAG formalism

LTAGs are based on the Tree Adjoining Grammar formalism developed by Joshi, Levy, and Takahashi (Joshi et al., 1975; Joshi and Schabes, 1997). The primitive elements of an LTAG are elementary trees (*etrees*). Each *etree* is associated with a lexical item (called the *anchor* of the tree) on its frontier. LTAGs possess many desirable properties, such as the Extended Domain of Locality, which allows the encapsulation of all arguments of the anchor associated with an *etree*. There are two types of *etrees*: initial trees and auxiliary trees. An auxiliary tree represents a recursive structure and has a unique leaf node, called the *foot* node, which has the same syntactic category as the root node. Leaf nodes other than anchor nodes and foot nodes are *substitution* nodes. *Etrees* are combined by two operations: substitution and adjunction. The resulting structure of the combined *etrees* is called a *derived tree*. The combination process is expressed as a *derivation tree*. Figure 2 shows the *etrees*, the derived tree, and the derivation tree for the sentence *underwriters still draft policies*. Foot and substitution nodes are marked by $*$, and $\downarrow$, respectively. The dashed and solid lines in the derivation tree are for adjunction and substitution operations, respectively.

## 3.2 The Form of Target Grammars

Without further constraints, the *etrees* in the target grammar (i.e., the grammar to be extracted by LexTract) could be of various shapes. LexTract recognizes three types of

| Language | corpus size (words) | average sentence length | # of POS tags | # of syntactic tags | # of function tags | # of empty category tags |
|---|---|---|---|---|---|---|
| English | 1,174K | 23.85 words | 36 | 26 | 20 | 12 |
| Chinese | 100K | 23.81 words | 34 | 25 | 26 | 7 |
| Korean | 30K | 10.52 words | 17 | 18 | 17 | 4 |

Table 1: Size of the Treebanks and the tagsets used in each Treebank

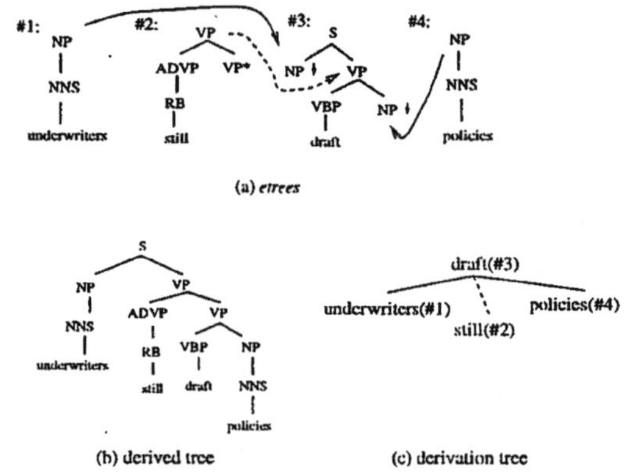


Figure 2: *Etrees*, derived tree, and derivation tree for *underwriters still draft policies*

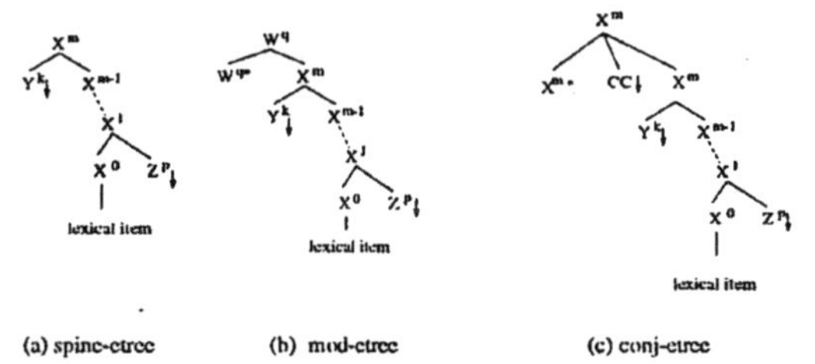


Figure 3: Three types of elementary trees in the target grammar

relation (namely, predicate-argument, modification, and coordination relations) between the anchor of an *etree* and other nodes in the *etree*, and imposes the constraint that all the *etrees* to be extracted should fall into exactly one of the three patterns in Figure 3.

- The spine-etrees for predicate-argument relations. $X^0$ is the head of $X^m$ and the anchor of the *etree*. The *etree* is formed by a spine $X^m \rightarrow X^{m-1} \rightarrow .. \rightarrow X^0$ and the arguments of $X^0$.

- The mod-etrees for modification relations. The root of the *etree* has two children, one is a foot node with the label $W^q$, and the other node $X^m$ is a modifier of the foot node. $X^m$ is further expanded into a spine-etree whose head $X^0$ is the anchor of the whole mod-etree.

- The conj-etrees for coordination relations. In a conj-etree, the children of the root are two conjoined constituents and a node for a coordination conjunction. One conjoined constituent is marked as the foot node, and the other is expanded into a spine-etree whose head is the anchor of the whole tree.

Spine-etrees are initial trees, whereas mod-etrees and conj-etrees are auxiliary trees.

### 3.3 Extraction algorithm

The core of LexTract is an extraction algorithm that takes a Treebank sentence such as the one in Figure 1 and Treebank-specific information provided by the user of LexTract, and produces a set of *etrees* as in Figure 4 and a derivation tree. We have described LexTract's architecture, its extraction algorithm, and its applications in (Xia, 1999; Xia et al., 2000a). Therefore, we shall not repeat them in this paper other than pointing out that LexTract is completely language-independent.

### 3.4 Experiments

The results of running LexTract on English, Chinese, and Korean Treebanks are shown in Table 2. *Templates* are *etrees* with the lexical items removed. For instance, #3, #6, and #9 in Figure 4 are three distinct *etrees* but they share the same *template*.

Figure 5 shows the log frequency of templates in the English Treebank and percentage of template tokens covered by template

| | template types | *etree* types | word types | *etree* types per word type | *etree* types per word token | CFG rules (unlexicalized) |
|---|---|---|---|---|---|---|
| Eng $G_1$ | 6926 | 131,397 | 49,206 | 2.67 | 34.68 | 1524 |
| Ch $G_2$ | 1140 | 21,125 | 10,772 | 1.96 | 9.13 | 515 |
| Kor $G_3$ | 634 | 9,787 | 6,747 | 1.45 | 2.76 | 177 |

Table 2: Grammars extracted from three Treebanks

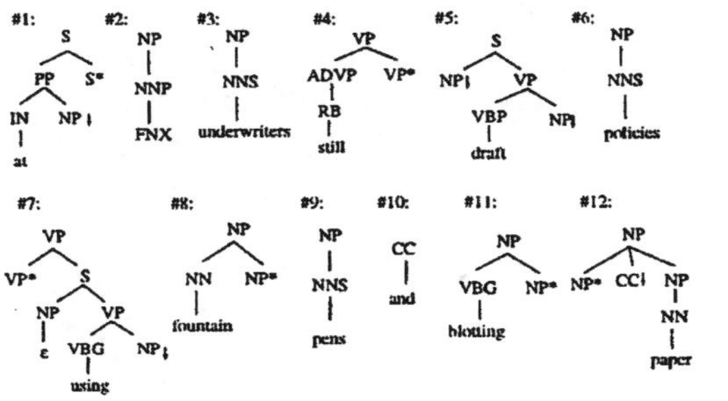

Figure 4: The extracted *etrees* from the fully bracketed *ttree*

types.[2] In both cases, template types are sorted according to their frequencies and plotted on the X-axis. The figure shows that a small subset of template types, which occurs very frequently in the Treebank and can be seen as the core of the Treebank grammar, covers the majority of template tokens in the Treebank. For instance, the most frequent template type covers 9.37% of the template tokens and the top 100 (500, 1000 and 1500, respectively) template types cover 87.1% (96.6%, 98.4% and 99.0%, respectively) of the tokens, whereas about half (3440) of the template types occur once, accounting for only 0.32% of template tokens in total.

## 4 Comparing Three Treebank Grammars

In this section, we describe our methodology for comparing Treebank grammars and the experimental results.

### 4.1 Methodology

To compare Treebank grammars, we need to ensure that the Treebank grammars are based on the same tagset. To achieve that, we first create a new tagset that includes all the tags

[2]If a template occurs $n$ times in the corpus, it is counted as one template type but $n$ template tokens.

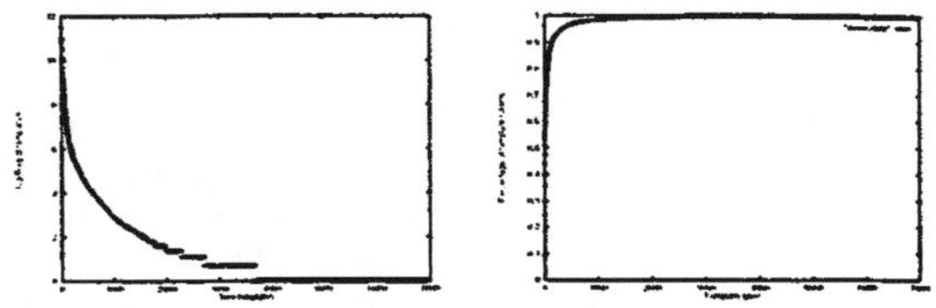

(a) Frequency (b) Coverage

Figure 5: *Etree* template types and template tokens in the Penn English Treebank
(X-axes: (a) and (b) template types
Y-axes: (a) log frequency of templates; (b) percentage of template token covered by template types)

from the three Treebanks. Then we merge some tags in this new tagset into a single tag. This step is necessary because certain distinctions among some tags in one language do not exist in another language. For example, the English Treebank has distinct tags for verbs in past tense, past participals, gerunds, and so on; however, no such distinction is morphologically marked in Chinese and, therefore, the Chinese Treebank uses the same tag for verbs regardless of the tense and aspect. To make the conversion straightforward for verbs, we use a single tag for verbs in the new tagset. Next, we replace the tags in the original Treebanks with the tags in the new tagset, and then re-run LexTract to build Treebank grammars from those Treebanks.

Now that the Treebank grammars are based on the same tagset, we can compare them according to the templates and sub-templates that appear in more than one Treebank — that is, given a pair of Treebank grammars, we first calculate how many templates occur in both grammars;[3] Next, we decompose

[3]Ideally, to get more accurate comparison results, we would like to compare *etrees*, rather than templates (which are non-lexicalized); however, comparing *etrees* requires bilingual parallel corpora, which we are cur-

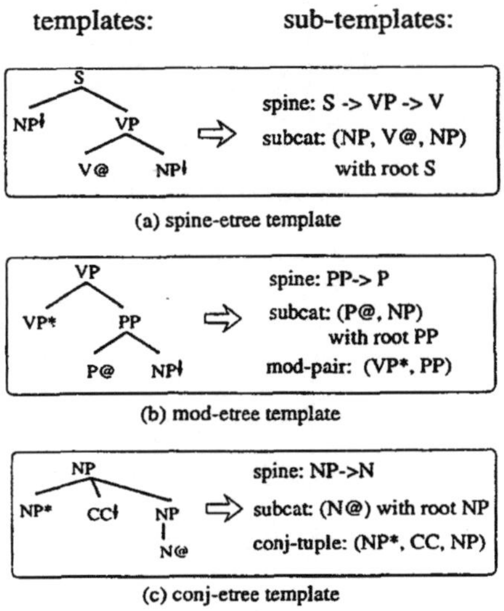


Figure 6: The decompositions of *etree* templates (In sub-templates, @ marks the anchor in subcategorization frame, * marks the modifiee in a modifier-modifiee pair.)

each template into a list of *sub-templates* (e.g., spines and subcategorization frames) and calculate how many of those sub-templates occur in both grammars. A template is decomposed as follows: A spine-etree template is decomposed into a spine and a subcategorization frame; a mod-etree template is decomposed into a spine, a subcategorization frame, and a modifier-modifiee pair; a conj-etree template is decomposed into a spine, a subcategorization frame, and a coordination tuple. Figure 6 shows examples of this decomposition for each type of template.

### 4.2 Experiments

After tags in original Treebanks being replaced with the tags in the new tagset, the numbers of templates in the new Treebank grammars decrease by about 50%, as shown in the second column of Table 3 (cf. the second column in Table 2). Table 3 also lists the numbers of sub-templates, such as spines and subcategorization frames, for each grammar.

Table 4 lists the numbers of template types shared by each pair of Treebank grammars and the percentage of the template tokens in each Treebank which are covered by these common template types. For example, there are 237 template types that appear in both English and Chinese Treebank grammars. These 237 template types account for 80.1% of template tokens in the English Treebank, and 81.5% of template tokens in the Chinese Treebank. The table shows that, although the number of matched templates are not very high, they are among the most frequent templates and they account for the majority of template tokens in the Treebanks. For instance, in the (Eng, Ch) pair, the 237 template types that appear in both grammars is only 7.5% of all the English template types, but they cover 80.1% of template tokens in the English Treebank. If we define the core grammar of a language as the set of the templates that occur very often in the Treebank, the data suggest that the majority of the core grammars are easily inter-mappable structures for these three languages.

If we compare sub-templates, rather than templates, in the Treebank grammars, the percentages of matched sub-template tokens (as in Table 5) are higher than the percentages of matched template tokens. This is because two distinct templates may share common sub-templates.

### 4.3 Unmatched templates

Our previous experiments (see Table 4) show that the percentages of unmatched template tokens in three Treebanks range from 16.0% to 43.8%, depending on the language pairs. Given a language pair, there are many possible reasons why a template appears in one Treebank grammar, but not in the other. We divide those unmatched templates into two categories: spuriously unmatched templates and truly unmatched templates.

**Spuriously unmatched templates** *Spuriously* unmatched templates are templates that either should have found a matched template in the other grammar or should not have been created by LexTract in the first place if the Treebanks were complete, uniformly annotated, and error-free. A spuriously unmatched template exists because of one of the

rently building.

| | *templates* | *subtemplates* | | | | |
|---|---|---|---|---|---|---|
| | | spines | subcat frames | mod-pairs | conj-tuples | total |
| Eng | 3139 | 500 | 541 | 332 | 53 | 1426 |
| Ch | 547 | 108 | 180 | 152 | 18 | 458 |
| Kor | 271 | 55 | 58 | 53 | 6 | 172 |

Table 3: Treebank grammars with the new tagset

| | | matched templates | templates with unique tags | other unmatched templates |
|---|---|---|---|---|
| (Eng,Ch) | type (#) | (237, 237) | (536, 99) | (2366, 211) |
| | token (%) | (80.1, 81.5) | (2.8, 12.3) | (17.1, 6.2) |
| (Eng, Kor) | type (#) | (83, 83) | (2075, 6) | (981, 182) |
| | token (%) | (57.7, 82.8) | (28.1, 0.1) | (14.2, 17.1) |
| (Ch, Kor) | type (#) | (59,59) | (324,6) | (164, 206) |
| | token (%) | (57.2, 84.0) | (29.4, 0.1) | (13.4, 16.0) |

Table 4: Comparisons of templates in three Treebank grammars

following reasons:

**(S1) Treebank size:** The template is linguistically sound in both languages, and, therefore, should belong to the grammars for these languages. However, the template appears in only one Treebank grammar because the other Treebank is too small to include such a template. Figure 7(S1) shows a template that is valid for both English and Chinese, but it appears only in the English Treebank, not in the Chinese Treebank.

**(S2) Annotation difference:** Treebanks may choose different annotations for the same constructions; consequentially, the templates for those constructions look different. Figure 7(S2) shows the templates used in English and Chinese for a VP such as *"surged 7 (dollars)"*. In the template for English, the *QP* projects to an NP, but in the template for Chinese, it does not.

**(S3) Treebank annotation error:** A template in a Treebank may result from annotation errors in that Treebank. If no corresponding mistakes are made in the other Treebank, the template in the first Treebank will not match any template in the second Treebank. For instance, in the English Treebank the word *about* in the sentence *About 5 people showed up* is often mis-tagged as a preposition, resulting in the template in Figure 7(S3). Not surprisingly, that template does not match any template in the Chinese Treebank.

**Truly unmatched templates** A *truly* unmatched template is a template that does not match any template in the other Treebank even if we assume both Treebanks are perfectly annotated. Here, we list three reasons why a truly unmatched template exist.

**(T1) Word order:** The word order determines the positions of arguments w.r.t. their heads, and the positions of modifiers w.r.t. their modifiees. If two languages have different word orders, their templates which include arguments of a head or a modifier are likely to look different. For example, Figure 8(T1) show the templates for transitive verbs in Chinese and Korean grammars. The templates do not match because of the different positions of the object of the verb.

**(T2) Unique tags:** For each pair of languages, some Part-of-speech tags and syntactic tags may appear in only one language. Therefore, the templates with those tags will not match any templates in the other language. For instance, in Korean the counterparts of preposition phrases in English and Chinese are noun phrases (with postpositions attaching to them, not preposition phrases); therefore, the templates with PP in Chinese,

| | | spines | subcat frames | mod-pairs | conj-tuples | total |
|---|---|---|---|---|---|---|
| (Eng,Ch) | type | (60,60) | (92, 92) | (83,83) | (11,11) | (246,246) |
| | token | (94.7,87.2) | (94.0, 86.3) | (82.6, 80.0) | (84.2, 99.1) | (91.4, 85.2) |
| (Eng, Kor) | type | (39, 39) | (40, 40) | (46, 46) | (1, 1) | (126,126) |
| | token | (70.3, 96.9) | (62.1, 96.6) | (56.8, 99.5) | (9.3, 52.3) | (63.4,97.3) |
| (Ch, Kor) | type | (28, 28) | (25,25) | (29,29) | (1, 1) | (83, 83) |
| | token | (74.2, 99.2) | (63.1, 98.1) | (60.2, 93.4) | (0.1, 0.4) | (66.1, 96.9) |

Table 5: Comparisons of sub-templates in three Treebank grammars

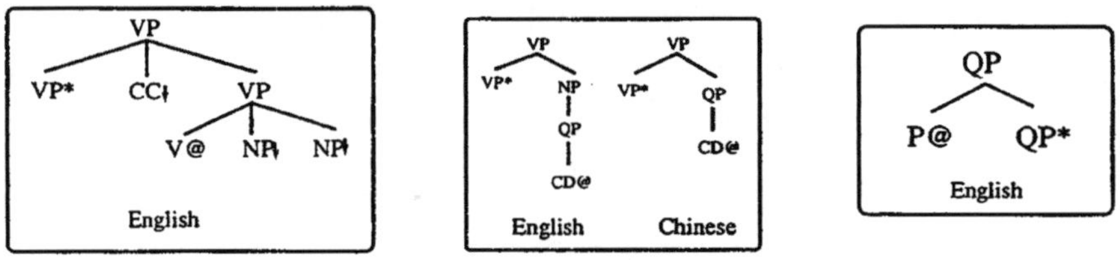


(S1) Treebank size (S2) annotation difference (S3) annotation error

Figure 7: Examples of spuriously unmatched templates

such as the left one in Figure 8(T2), do not match any template in Korean.

**(T3) Unique syntactic relations:** Some syntactic relations may be present in only one of the pair of languages being compared. For instance, the template in Figure 8(T3) is used for the sentence such as *"You should go," said John,* where the subject of the verb *said* appears after the verb. No such template exists in Chinese.

So far, we have listed six possible reasons for unmatched templates. Without manually examining all the unmatched templates, it is difficult to tell how many unmatched templates are caused by a particular reason. Nevertheless, these reasons help us to interpret the results in Table 4. For instance, the table shows that Korean grammars cover only 57.7% of template tokens in the English Treebank, and 57.2% in the Chinese Treebank, whereas the coverages for other language pairs are all above 80%. We suspect that this difference of coverage is mainly caused by (S1), (T1), and (T2). That is, first, Korean Treebank is much smaller than the English and the Chinese Treebanks, English and Chinese Treebanks may have many tree templates that simply was not found in the Korean Treebank; Second, English and Chinese are predominantly head-initial, whereas Korean is head-final, therefore, many templates in English and Chinese can not find matched templates in Korean because of the word order difference; Third, Korean does not have preposition phrases, causing all the templates in English and Chinese with PPs become unmatched. To measure the effect of the word order factor to the matching rate, we re-did the experiment in Section 4.2, but this time we ignored the word order — that is, we treat templates as unordered trees. The results are given in Table 6. Comparing this table with Table 4, we can clearly see that, the percentages of matched templates increase substantially for (Eng, Kor) and (Ch, Kor) when the word order is ignored. Notice that the matching percentage for (Eng, Ch) does not change as much because the word orders in English and Chinese are much similar than the orders in English and Korean.

## 5 Conclusion

We have presented a method of quantitatively comparing LTAGs extracted from Treebanks. Our experimental results show a high proportion of easily inter-mappable structures, giving a positive implications for Universal Grammar hypothesis, We have also described a number of reasons why a particular tem-

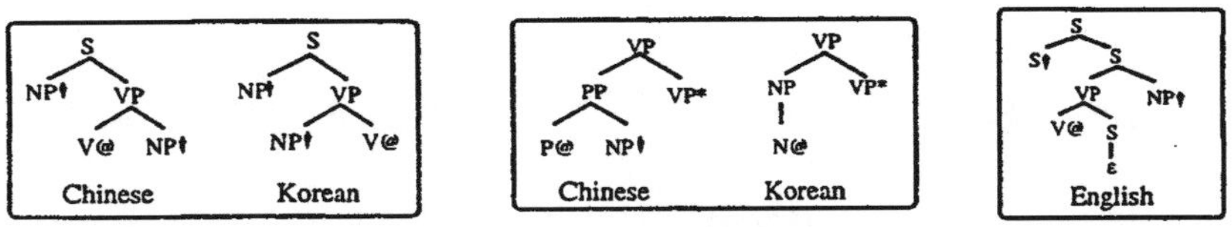


(T1) word order (T2) unique tags (T3) unique relation

Figure 8: Truly unmatched templates

| | | matched templates | tag mismatches | other mismatches |
|---|---|---|---|---|
| (Eng,Ch) | type | (334, 259) | (536, 99) | (2269, 189) |
| | token | (82.8, 82.2) | (2.8, 12.3) | (14.4, 5.5) |
| (Eng, Kor) | type | (222, 167) | (2075, 6) | (842, 98) |
| | token | (66.4, 92.4) | (28.1, 0.1) | (5.5, 7.5) |
| (Ch, Kor) | type | (126,125) | (324,6) | (97, 140) |
| | token | (68.3, 97.3) | (29.4, 0.1) | (2.3, 2.6) |

Table 6: Comparisons of templates w/o orders

plate does not match any template in other languages and tested the effect of word order on matching percentages.

There are two natural extensions of this work. First, running an alignment algorithm on parallel bracketed corpora to produce word-to-word mappings. Given such word-to-word mappings and our template matching algorithm, we can automatically create lexicalized *etree*-to-*etree* mappings, which can be used for semi-automatic transfer lexicon construction. Second, LexTract can build derivation trees for each sentence in the corpora. By comparing derivation trees for parallel sentences in two languages, instances of structural divergences (Dorr, 1993; Dorr, 1994; Palmer et al., 1998) can be automatically detected.

## References


Chung-hye Han. 2000. Bracketing Guidelines for the Penn Korean Treebank (draft). www.cis.upenn.edu/ xtag/korean.tag.

Bernard Comrie. 1987. *The World's Major Languages.* Oxford University Press, New York.

B. J. Dorr. 1993. *Machine Translation: a View from the Lexicon.* MIT Press, Boston, Mass.

B. J. Dorr. 1994. Machine translation divergences: a formal description and proposed solution. *Computational Linguistics*, 20(4):597–635.

Aravind Joshi and Yves Schabes. 1997. Tree Adjoining Grammars. In A. Salomma and G. Rosenberg, editors, *Handbook of Formal Languages and Automata.* Springer-Verlag, Herdelberg.

Aravind K. Joshi, L. Levy, and M. Takahashi. 1975. Tree Adjunct Grammars. *Journal of Computer and System Sciences.*

M. Marcus, B. Santorini, and M. A. Marcinkiewicz. 1993. Building a Large Annotated Corpus of English: the Penn Treebank. *Computational Linguistics.*

Martha Palmer, Owen Rambow, and Alexis Nasr. 1998. Rapid Prototyping of Domain-Specific Machine Translation System. In *Proc. of AMTA-1998*, Langhorne, PA.

Fei Xia, Martha Palmer, and Aravind Joshi. 2000a. A Uniform Method of Grammar Extraction and its Applications. In *Proc. of Joint SIGDAT Conference on Empirical Methods in Natural Language Processing and Very Large Corpora (EMNLP/VLC).*

Fei Xia, Martha Palmer, Nianwen Xue, Mary Ellen Okurowski, John Kovarik, Shizhe Huang, Tony Kroch, and Mitch Marcus. 2000b. Developing Guidelines and Ensuring Consistency for Chinese Text Annotation. In *Proc. of the 2nd International Conference on Language Resources and Evaluation (LREC-2000)*, Athens, Greece.

Fei Xia. 1999. Extracting Tree Adjoining Grammars from Bracketed Corpora. In *Proc. of 5th Natural Language Processing Pacific Rim Symposium (NLPRS-99)*, Beijing, China.

# The Research of Word Sense Disambiguation Method Based on Co-occurrence Frequency of Hownet†

Erhong Yang, Guoqing Zhang, and Yongkui Zhang
Dept of Computer Science, Shanxi University,
TaiYuan 030006, P. R. China
Email: zyk@sxu.edu.cn

## Abstract

Word sense disambiguation (WSD) is a difficult problem in natural language processing. In this paper, a sememe co-occurrence frequency based WSD method was introduced. In this method, Hownet was used as our information source , and a co-occurrence frequency database of sememes was constructed and then used for WSD. The experimental result showed that this method is successful.

## Keywords

word sense disambiguation, Hownet, sememe, co-occurrence

## 1. Introduction

Word sense disambiguation (WSD) is one of the most difficult problems in NLP. It is helpful and in some instances required for such applications as machine translation, information retrieval, content and thematic analysis, hypertext navigation and so on. The problem of WSD was first put forward in 1949. And then in the following decades researchers adopted many methods to solve the problem of automatic word sense disambiguation, including:1) AI-based method, 2) knowledge-based method and 3) corpus-based method.[1] Although some useful results have been got, the problem of word sense disambiguation is far from being solved.

The difficult of WSD is as follow: 1) Evaluation of word sense disambiguation systems is not yet standardized. 2) The potential for WSD varies by task. 3) Adequately large sense-tagged data sets are difficult to obtain. 4) The field has narrowed down approaches, but only a little. [2]

In this paper, we use a statistical based method to solve the problem of automatic word sense disambiguation.[3] In this method, a new knowledge base------Hownet[4,5] was use as knowledge resources. And instead of words, the sememes which are defined in Hownet were used to get the statistical figure. By doing this, the problem of data sparseness was solved to a large degree.

## 2. A Brief Introduction Of Hownet

Hownet is a knowledge base which was released recently on Internet. In Hownet, the concept which were represented by Chinese or English words were described and the relations between concepts and the attributes of concepts were revealed. In this paper, we use Chinese knowledge base, which is an important part of Hownet, as the resource of our disambiguation. The format of this file is as follow:

W_X =word
E_X = some examples of this word
G_X= the pos of this word
DEF= the definition of this word

† This research project is supported by a grant from Shanxi Natural Science Foundation of China

A important concept used in Hownet that we must introduce is sememe. In Hownet, sememes refer to some basic unit of senses. They are used to describe all the entries in Hownet and there are more than 1,500 sememe all together.

## 3. Sense Co-occurrence Frequency Database

It is well known that some words tend to co-occur frequently with some words than with others[6]. Similarly, some meaning of words tend to co-occur more often with some meaning of words than with others. If we can got the relations of word meanings quantitatively, it would have some help on word sense disambiguation. In Hownet, all words are defined with limited sememes and the combination of sememes is fixed. If we make statistic on the co-occurrence frequency of sememe so as to reflect the co-occurrence of words, the problem of data sparseness would be solved to a large degree. Based on the above thought, we built a sense co-occurrence frequency database to disambiguate word senses.

### 3.1 The Preprocessing Of Hownet

The Hownet we downloaded from Internet is in the form of plain text. It is not convenient for computer to use and it must been converted into a database. In the database, each lexical entry is converted into a record. The formalization description of the records is as follow:

<lexical entry> ::= <NO.><morphology><part-of-speech><definition>

Where NO. is the corresponding number of this lexical entry in Hownet. And the definition is composed of several sememes (short for SU) which were divided by comma. In addition, we have deleted the English sememes in order to saving space and speeding up the processing. Here are some examples after preprocessing:

| NO. | Morphology | Part-of-speech | definition |
|---|---|---|---|
| 21424 | 俭朴 | ADJ | 属性值,举止,俭,良 |
| 18888 | 坏 | ADJ | 属性值,好坏,坏,莠 |
| 18889 | 坏 | V | 损害 |
| 18887 | 坏 | V | 坏掉 |
| 18890 | 坏 | N | 念头,恶 |

### 3.2 The Creation Of Sememe Co-occurrence Frequency Database

The sememe co-occurrence frequency database is the basic of sense disambiguation. Now we will introduce it briefly.

The sememe co-occurrence frequency database is a table of two dimension. Each item corresponding to the co-occurrence frequency of a pair of sememes.

Before introducing the sememe co-occurrence frequency database, we gave the following definition:

**Definiton:** *suppose word W has m sense items in hownet, and the corresponding definition of each sense item is:* $y_{11}, y_{12}, \ldots, y_{1(n1)}$; $y_{21}, y_{22}, \ldots, y_{2(n2)}$; ...; $y_{m1}, y_{m2}, \ldots, y_{m(nm)}$ *respectively. We call* $\{y_{i1}, y_{i2}, \ldots, y_{i(ni)}\}$ *a sememe set of W(short for SS), and call* $\{\{y_{11}, y_{12}, \ldots, y_{1(n1)}\}, \{y_{21}, y_{22}, \ldots, y_{2(n2)}\}, \ldots, \{y_{m1}, y_{m2}, \ldots, y_{m(nm)}\}\}$ *the sememe expansion of W (short for SE).*

For example, in the above mentioned example, the word "俭朴" has only one sense item. The corresponding sememe set of this sense item is {属性值,举止,俭,良} and the sememe expansion of “俭朴” is {{属性值,举止,俭,良}}. The word “坏” has four sense items, and the corresponding sememe set of each item is {属性值,好坏,坏,莠}, {损害}, {坏掉} and {念头,恶} respectively. The sememe expansion of word “坏” is {{属性值,好坏,坏,莠}, {损害}, {坏掉}, {念头,恶}}。

When building the sememe co-occurrence frequency database, the corpus is segmented first and each word is tagged with its sememe expansion in Hownet. Then for each unique pair of words co-occurred in a sentence (here a sentence is a string of characters delimited by punctuations.), the co-occurrence data of sememes which belong to the definition of each words respectively were collect. When collecting co0occurrence data, we adopt a principle that every pair of word which co-occurred in a sentence should have equal contribution to the sememe co-occurrence data regardless of the number of sense items of this word and the length of the definition. Moreover, the contribution of a word should be evenly distributed between all the senses of a word and the contribution of a sense should been evenly distributed between all the sememe in a sense. The algorithm is as follow:

1.Initial each cell in the sememe co-occurrence frequency database(short for SCFD) with 0.

2.For each sentence S in training corpus, do 3-7.

3.For each word in sentense S, tag the sememe expansion to it.

4.For each unique pair of sememe expansion ($SE_i$, $SE_j$), do 5-7.

5.For each sememe $SU_{imp}$ in each sememe set $SS_{im}$ in $SE_i$, do 6-7.

6.For each sememe $SU_{jnq}$ in each sememe set $SS_{jn}$ in $SE_j$, do 7.

7.Increase the value of cell SCFD($SU_{imp}$, $SU_{jnq}$) and SCFD($SU_{jnq}$,$SU_{imp}$) by the product of w($SU_{imp}$) and w($SU_{jnq}$). Where w($SU_{xyz}$) is weight of $SU_{xyz}$ given by

$$W(SU_{xyz}) = \frac{1}{|SE_x| \times |SS_{xy}|}$$

It can be concluded from the above algorithm that the SCFD are symmetrical. In order to saving space and speeding up the processing, we only save those cells ($SU_i$,$SU_j$) that satisfying $SU_i \leqslant SU_j$.

### 3.3 The Sememe Co-occurrence Frequency Database Based Disambiguation Method

#### 3.3.1 The Sememe Co-occurrence Frequency Based Scoring Method

When disambiguate a polysemous word, we given the following equation as the score of a sense item of the polysemous word and the context containing this polysemous word. The context of the word is the sentence containing this word.

$$\begin{aligned} &score(S,C) \\ &= score(SS,C') - score(SS,GlobalSS) \end{aligned} \quad (1)$$

Where S is a sense item of polysemouse word W, C is the context containing W, SS is the corresponding sememe set of S, C' is the set of sememe expansion of words in C and GlobalSS is the sememe set that containing all of the sememe defined in Hownet.

$$score(SS,C') = \sum_{\forall SE \in C'} score(SS,SE') \Big/ |C'| \quad (2)$$

for any sememe set SS and sememe expansion set C'.

$$score(SS,SE') = \max_{SS' \in SE'} score(SS,SS') \quad (3)$$

for any sememe set SS and sememe expansion SE'.

$$score(SS,SS') = \sum_{\forall SU' \in SS'} score(SS,SU') \Big/ |SS'| \quad (4)$$

for any sememe set SS and SS'.

$$score(SS,SU') = \sum_{\forall SU \in SS} score(SU,SU') \Big/ |SS| \quad (5)$$

for any sememe set SS and sememe SU'.

$$score(SU,SU') = I(SU,SU') \quad (6)$$

for any sememe SU and SU'.

$$I(SU,SU') = \log_2 \frac{f(SU,SU') \cdot N^2}{g(SU) \cdot g(SU')} \quad (7)$$

Where f(SU,SU') is the co-occurrence frequency corresponding to sememe pair（SU, SU'） in SCFD. And for g(SU) and N, we have the following equation:

$$g(SU) = \sum_{\forall SU'} f(SU,SU') \quad (8)$$

$$N = \sum_{\forall SU, \forall SU'} f(SU,SU') \Big/ 2 \quad (9)$$

In equation (7), the mutual-information-like measure deviated from the stardard mutual-information measure by multiple a extra multiplicative factor N, this is because that the scale of the corpus is not large enough that the mutual-information of some sememes pairs would be negtive if it was not normalized by a extra multiplicative factor N. In equation (9), the sum of f(SU,SU') was divided by 2, this is because for each pair of sememes, $\sum_{\forall SU, \forall SU'} f(SU,SU')$ is increase by 2.

When disambiguation, we tag the sememe T that satisfying the following equation to polysemous word W.

$$T = \arg\max_{S} score(S,C) \quad (10)$$

### 3.3.2 The Creation Of Mutual Information Database

We have created a mutual information database according to (7),(8) and(9) Here is some examples:

The examples in table 1 have a high mutual information. The sememe pairs in this table have certain semantic relations. While the examples in table 2 have a low mutual information. And the sememe pairs in this table have no patency semantic relations.

Table 1: example of sememe pairs which have a high mutual information

| Sememe 1 | Sememe 2 | Mutual-Information | Sememe 1 | Sememe 2 | Mutual-Information |
|---|---|---|---|---|---|
| 赌博 | 寻欢 | 33.811057 | 表情 | 羞愧 | 27.418417 |
| 鼓吹 | 夸大 | 29.441937 | 昏迷 | 醒 | 27.234630 |
| 光洁度 | 摸 | 28.024560 | 味道 | 香 | 27.093292 |
| 跑 | 气喘 | 28.023521 | 慢待 | 漠 | 26.984521 |
| 使净 | 整理 | 27.571478 | 低植 | 蔬菜 | 26.710478 |

Table 2: example of sememe pairs which have a low mutual information

| Sememe 1 | Sememe 2 | Mutual-Information | Sememe 1 | Sememe 2 | Mutual-Information |
|---|---|---|---|---|---|
| 食品 | 政 | 8.693242 | 合作 | 末 | 9.171023 |
| 交往 | 医 | 8.754611 | 侧 | 液 | 9.357734 |
| 车 | 圆 | 8.793914 | 驱赶 | 正误 | 9.448947 |
| 合作 | 疾病 | 9.121846 | 程度 | 交换 | 9.528801 |
| 机构 | 疾病 | 9.150412 | 禽 | 主次 | 9.599495 |

It can been concluded from table 1 and table 2 that the mutual information can reflect the tightness of semantic relations.

## 4. Experiment And Analysis

We did the experiment on a corpus of 10,000 characters from People's Dialy.

Firstly, the corpus is segmented, and then the sememe co-occurrence frequecny database and mutual information database is created. In the mutual-information database, there is 709,496 data items corresponding to different sememes pairs. In order to speeding up the processing, the mutual-information database was sorted and indexed according to the first two bytes of each sememe pair. At last the experiment of disambiguation of some polysemous words was done. Here is two examples:

Example 1：全|省|两万四千|多|名|党政|干部|累计|处理|信访|案|十万|余|件|。

Example 2：这|是|香港|海关|今年|破获|的|第|一|宗|来自|内地|的|文物|走私|案。

We use the following euqation to access the accuracy ratio of disambiguation:

$$accuracy\quad ratio = \frac{the\ number of\ correctly tagged\ examples}{the\ total\ number of\ examples in\ testing\ set} \tag{11}$$

the experimental result is shown in table 4.

Table 3: Two examples that disambiguate using sememe co-occurrence frequency database

| The definition of word “案” | The score of sense items and the context of word “案” in example 1 | The score of sense items and the context of word “案” in example 2 |
|---|---|---|
| 文书 | 14.459068 | 8.659968 |
| 事情 | 9.817648 | 10.817648 |
| 事情 警 | 7.415986 | 12.415986 |
| 家具 放置 | -0.134779 | -0.134779 |
| 语文 提出 商讨 辩论 | -0.818518 | -0.818518 |
| 最大同现频率 | 14.459068 | 12.415986 |
| 排歧结果 | 文书 | 事情 警 |

Table 4: the experiment result

| | Total number of testing examples | The number of correctly tagged examples | Accurracy ratio |
|---|---|---|---|
| Close test | 100 | 75 | 75% |
| Open test | 100 | 71 | 71% |

The disambiguation method introduced above have the following charatristics:

(1) The problem of data spraseness is solved in a large degree.

(2) This disambiguation method avoids the laborious hand tagging of training corpus.

(3) This method can been easily applied to other kind of corpus.

## Reference

[1]. Nancy Ide, Jean Veronis, Introduction to the Special Issue on Word Sense Disambiguation: The State of the Art, Computational Linguistics, 1998, Volume 24, number 1, pp 1-40

[2]. Philip Resnik, David Yarowsky, A Perspective on Word Sense Disambiguation Methods and their

Evaluation, http://www.cs.jhu.edu/~yarowsky/pubs.html

[3]. Alpha K. Luk, Statistical Sense Disambiguation with Relatively Small Corpus Using Dictionary Definitions, 33rd Annual Meeting of the Association for Computational Linguistics,26-30 June, 1995, Massachusetts Institute of Technology, Cambridge, Massachusetts. USA, pp.181-188

[4]. 董振东, 语义关系的表达和知识系统的建造, 语言文字应用, 1998 年第 3 期, 总第 27 期, pp.76-82

[5]. 董振东, 知网，http://www.how-net.com.

[6]. Kenneth Ward Church, Word Association Norms, Mutual Information, and Lexicography, Computational Linguistics, 1990,Volume 16, Number 1, pp.22-29

# A trainable method for extracting Chinese entity names and their relations

Yimin Zhang & Zhou Joe F

Intel China Research Center
Kerry Center 6F1
No. 1 Guanghua Road, Chaoyang District
Beijing 100020, P.R. China

## Abstract

In this paper we propose a trainable method for extracting Chinese entity names and their relations. We view the entire problem as series of classification problems and employ memory-based learning (MBL) to resolve them. Preliminary results show that this method is efficient, flexible and promising to achieve better performance than other existing methods.

## 1. Introduction

Entity names and their relations form the main content of a document. By grasping the entity names and their relations from a document, we will be able to understand the document to some extent.

In the field of information extraction, much work has been done to automatically learn patterns [1] from training corpus in order to extract entity names and their relations from English documents. But for Chinese, researchers primarily use man-made rules and keyword sets to identify entity names [2]. Building rules is often complex, error-prone and time-consuming, and usually requires detailed knowledge of system internals. Some researchers also use statistical method [3], but the training needs lots of human annotated data and only local context information can be used. With this in the view, we have sought a more efficient and flexible trainable method to resolve this problem.

Section 2 first gives a general outline of the trainable method we have defined to extract Chinese entity names and their relations, then describes person name extraction, entity name classification and relation extraction in detail. Section 3 describes the preliminary experimental results of our method. Section 4 contains our remarks and discussion on possible extensions of the proposed work.

## 2. General Outline of the Method

We view the problem of Chinese entity names and their relations as a series of classification problems, such as person name boundary classification, entity name classification, noun phrase boundary classification and relation classification. If those classification problems are clarified, then we will be able to resolve the related extraction problem. For example, if we can correctly classify (or identify) the beginning or the ending boundaries of a person name appeared in a document, we will be able to extract the person name.

The process can be divided into two stages. The first stage is the learning process in which several classifiers are built from the training data. The second stage is the extracting process in which Chinese entity names and their relations are extracted using the classifiers learned. The learning algorithm used in the learning process is memory-based learning (MBL) [4]. MBL entails a classification based supervised learning approach. The approach has been named differently in a variety of contexts, such as similarity-based, example-based, analogical, case-based, instance-based, and lazy learning. We selected MBL as our learning algorithm because it suits well the domains with a large number of features from heterogeneous sources and can remember exceptional and low frequency cases that are useful to extrapolate from [5]. In addition, we can customize the learner using different weighting functions according to linguistic bias.

The main steps for the learning process are:

*Step 1:* Prepare training data in which all noun phrases, entity names and their relations are manually annotated.

*Step 2:* Segmenting, tagging, and partial parsing the training data.

*Step 3:* Extract the training sets (instance base) from the parsed training data. Four training sets are extracted for different tasks with each related to Chinese person names, entity names, noun phrases, or relations between entity names in the training data. The main features used in an example can be either local context features, e.g. dependency relation feature, or global context features, e.g. the features of a word in the whole document, or surface linguistic features, e.g. character feature and word feature, or deep linguistic features like semantic feature.

*Step 4:* Use MBL algorithm to obtain IG-Tree [4] for the four training sets. IG-Tree is a compressed representation of the training set that can be processed quickly in classification process. In our case, the resulted IG-Trees are PersonName-IG-Tree, EntityName-IG-Tree, NP-IG-Tree, and Relation-IG-Tree.

The main steps for extracting process are:

*Step 1:* Segmenting, tagging and partial parsing the input Chinese documents.

*Step 2:* Identify Chinese people names using PersonName-IG-Tree.

*Step 3:* Identify Chinese organization names using the same method as described in [2].

*Step 4:* Identify other entity names (location, time, number) using the same method as described in [2].

*Step 5:* Identify Chinese noun phrases (NP chunking) using NP-IG-Tree.

*Step 6:* Use entity names and noun phrases extracted to perform partial parsing again to fix the parsing errors.

*Step 7:* Use EntityName-IG-tree to classify the noun phrases extracted. This step will identify entity names that are missed in the previous steps.

*Step 8:* Use Relation-IG-Tree to identify relations between the extracted entity names.

For a better understanding of the algorithm, we will describe in detail the person name extraction, the entity name classification, and the relation extraction in the next subsection. Please note that we are not going to discuss NP chunking further since it is beyond the main theme of this paper.

## 2.1 Person Name extraction

Chinese person names can be divided into two categories, local Chinese person names that consist of Chinese surnames and given names and transliterated person names that are sound translations of foreign names. The length of a local person name ranges from 2 to 6 characters, while the length of a transliterated person name is unrestricted.

After segmentation, person names are usually divided into several words. The task is to extract the word sequences that are person name components. With this in view, we convert the person name extraction problem to an equivalent classification problem, i.e. classifying word sequences existing in the results of segmentation into two classes, namely Person-Name and Not-Person-Name.

To classify a word sequence we need to use a number of features.

(1) Word features: the beginning word/tag of the sequence, the ending word/tag of the sequence.

(2) Local context features: the n-th (n<=3) word/tag before/after the sequence; the verb before/after the sequence.

(3) Context dependency features: the dependency relations of the word sequence and the dependency relations of the first

word before/after the sequence. The main dependency relations include verb-object (the relation between a verb and its noun object), subject-verb (the relation between a verb and its subject), subject-adj (the relation between an adjective and its subject), adv-verb (the relation between a verb and its adverbial modifier), adv-adj (the relation between an adjective and its adverbial modifier), modifier-head (the relation between a noun and its modifier. In Chinese, the modifier can be adjective, noun, verb or other phrases).

The word features and local context features can be directly extracted from the parsing results of the training data. The extraction of dependency features needs more explanation. We employ the collocation information obtained from a large corpus [6] to help the Chinese partial parser do the parsing. In most cases, dependency relations can be taken directly from the parsing results. But, there are some instances that the parser does not function well resulting in flat parsing trees. Under these circumstances, we resort to some simple heuristics such as linear order for dependency relations, thus making our method robust enough to extract most of the dependency relations.

To make the learning process more efficient, we use Boolean features in the training set, so every feature described above is translated into several Boolean features. For example, for the feature 1th-Next-Word (the first word after the word sequence), its value is the top 500 words (ordered by frequency) that can appear after a person name. We translate it into 500 features with every feature name like 1th-Next-Word-XX in which XX is one of the 500 words. The feature value 1 means that the XX appear next to the word sequence in the instance. The translated examples have about several thousands of Boolean features, which will be a big challenge for machine learning algorithms like C4.5 and CN2, but for MBL this is not a big problem. Furthermore, we use sparse array representation to make the storage requirement much lower.

For every word sequence in the training data that meets with one of the following three requirements, we extract that word sequence, including its class and all its features described above:

(1) Begin with a surname, plus 1 or 2 characters.

(2) Begin with two surnames, plus 1 or 2 characters.

(3) Begin with a character included in the first character set of transliterated person names (extracted from training data), plus several characters. The name may not surpass a normal word (that is included in a list of 5000 most frequently used Chinese words), because these normal words rarely occurred in a transliterated name.

For example, if in the training data, three words "W1 W2 W3" are annotated as a person name, then we will extract a Person-Name "W1 W2 W3" and Not-Person-Name "W1 W2".

After all the examples are extracted from the training data, they are fed to MBL Learner to get the PersonName-IG-Tree.

In the extracting process, we do the same as in the learning process to extract all examples, but the class of every example is unknown to us in advance. With the PersonName-IG-Tree, we can derive the class of every example, and then all word sequences classified as PersonName are extracted.

When a person name appears more than once in a document, we can rely on cache mechanism, similar to those described in [2], to solve ambiguous cases. For example, a person name "李文" appears more than once in a document. We first erroneously extract "李文亲" from a sentence "集团总裁李文亲率一个大型代表团造访中国", then correctly extract "李文" from another sentence "李文来华考察". Now "李文亲" and "李文" are both in the cache, the cache mechanism will be able to correct the first error based on the heuristics that, if an extracted person name is a substring of another extracted person name and they do not appear in one sentence, then only the substring is the correct person name.

To better understand the process of extracting person names, we describe a few intuitive examples below.

(1) Sample 1

The sentence: "总经理李少华认为"

The segmentation result: "总经理 李 少 华 认为".

Here both "李少华" and "李少" are person name candidates for extraction. Because no dependency relations are found for the next word "华" and most training examples with this feature are classified as Not-Person-Name in training data, so "李少" is also classified as Not-Person-Name. Both the previous word "总经理" and the next word "认为" are positive evidences that make it certain that ""李少华" should be classified as a person name, therefore our algorithm correctly extracted it from this sentence.

(2) Sample 2

The sentence: "记者看到一张通知"

The segmentation result: "记者 看到 一 张 通知".

Our algorithm correctly classified "张通知" as not a person name. The reason is that in the training data all word sequences whose previous word is "一" is a not a person name.

These examples show that our method performs disambiguation well thanks to the MBL learner's capability of catching exceptions.

## 2.2 Entity Name Classification

The task of entity name classification is to classify the given noun phrases into several categories, such as organization name, product name, location, etc., as well as person names that are missed in the previous extraction.

In addition to the features used in person name extraction, more features are needed. Some of these features are equivalent to the features used in Crystal [8], such as subject-auxiliary-noun, e.g. the relation between "联想公司" and "公司" in the sentence "联想公司是一家著名的计算机公司". Some features are specific to Chinese. Semantic features are also included to make the learned classifier more powerful. The semantic features of a word can be taken from a widely used Chinese thesaurus [7] that classifies Chinese words into 12 broad categories, 94 middle categories, and 1428 small categories. There are about 70 thousands words in the thesaurus.

Unlike other inductive learning systems in the field of information extraction, such as Crystal, we use a general machine learning algorithm to do the learning. The most relevant earlier work is the experiment described in [8] using the machine learning algorithm C4.5. Though their experiment showed that the performance of C4.5 based method was comparable to Crystal, they abandoned this method due to the time complexity of C4.5 when dealing with large number of features. MBL is similar to C4.5 in that both are general machine learning algorithms. Their differences lie in that MBL is a lazy learning algorithm that keeps all training data in memory and only abstracts at classification time by extrapolating a class from the most similar items in memory, therefore, its time complexity is much lower than C4.5, especially when training data contains large number of features and examples. Actually, in Soderland's analysis [8], MBL's time complexity is only slightly greater than that of Crystal. Though the instance-based algorithm like MBL may require large memory, the advanced hardware technology available today can overcome this problem. A sparse vector representation will also lower the memory requirement. Taken all these into consideration, MBL is well suited for entity name extraction and relation extraction. Furthermore, the simple instance representation and weight function make

MBL-based method more flexible and extensible. Any useful features can be added to the system without any modification to the algorithm. In Crystal, however, adding more features may affect the correctness of weight function used in finding similar examples. Our method can employ global features, i.e. features beyond the sentence level. We treat a NP and all its occurrences (including its anaphorical references) in one text as one single example and all context words that are in some dependency relations to this NP as this example's features. Thus, we can resolve more complicated cases than Crystal. For example, if a NP is in subj-verb relation with verb “说” , it can be a person name or an organization name. But, if we know all verbs that have subj-verb relations with this NP, then we will know the exact class this NP belongs to.

The steps for entity name classification are similar to the steps in person name extraction. Our method is quite impressive in that it can learn a lot of context features to classify the entity names, e.g. it correctly classifies "启明" in "启明的父亲" (Qiming's father) as a person name. Such a person name cannot be recognized in person name extraction because it does not begin with a surname or first character of transliterated person names.

## 2.3 Relation extraction

This task is to identify relation classes between entity names. Our current classes include employee-of, location-of, product-of, and no-relation. The relations we can extract are by no means restricted to this set. We can expand the set if training data are provided.

The features for this task include features used in Soderland's experiment [8]. These features are equivalent to the syntactic-lexical or syntactic-semantic constraints used in Crystal. The feature name begins with the name of the syntax position (SUBJ, OBJ, PP-OBJ etc.), followed by the name of the constraint and the actual term or class name. For example, "联想总裁" in the subject position would include the features:

SUBJ-Terms-联想
SUBJ-Terms-总裁
SUBJ-Mod-Terms-联想 // the terms in the modifier of the subject
SUBJ-Head-Terms-总裁
SUB-Classes-Employee // the semantic categories of the subject
SUB-Mod-Classes-Organization
SUB-Head-Classes-Organization

More features are introduced in our method, such as the linear order of entity names, the word(s) between the entity names, the relative position of the entity names (in one sentence or in neighboring sentences), etc. These features will make our method more robust than Crystal.

For every two related entity names in the training data, we identify a training example and extract it. After all the examples are extracted from the training data, they are fed to MBL Learner to get the Relation-IG-Tree.

In the extracting process, we do the same as in the learning process to extract all pairs of entity names. Then using the Relation-IG-Tree, we can derive the relation between every pair of entity names.

To better understand the process of relation extraction, we describe a couple of examples below.

(1) Sample 1

The input text: 浪潮集团作为国内著名的IT 硬件设备制造商，…

In the entity extraction, we have extracted "浪潮集团" as a company name and "IT硬件设备" as a product name. In the training data, some training examples have similar sentence patterns, e.g. "Company Name (作为/是) ...Product Name 制造商", and most of the time there are product-of relation between the two entity names. Based on this evidence, a product-of relation can be identified between "浪潮集团" and "IT硬件设备".

(2) Sample 2

The input text: 吴士宏再度成为媒体关注的焦点。不过，这次她是以TCL集团副总裁兼信息产业公司总经理的身份。

In the entity extraction, we have extracted "吴士宏" as a person name and "TCL集团" as a company name. Now we want to test if these two entity names have an employee-of relation. As can be seen in the training data, if a person name and a company name appear in neighboring sentences, and no other person names and company names are found in between, they tend to have a employee-of relation. Based on this evidence, an employee-of relation can be identified between "吴士宏" and "TCL集团". Current systems, such as Crystal, would find it difficult to resolve because these two entity names appear in different sentences.

## 3. System Evaluation

To test our method we prepare a manually annotated corpus comprised of about 200 business news. All the entity names (about 500 person names and 300 organization names), noun phrases, and relations (i.e. employee-of, product-of, location-of) in the corpus were manually annotated. Ten pairs of training set and testing set were randomly selected from the corpus with each set equivalent to half size of the entire corpus. We ran our learning and extracting processes on all the data sets and calculated the mean recall and precision rates. The results are showed in Table. 1.

Table 1: Evaluation for extracting Chinese entity names and their relations

| | Recall | Precision |
|---|---|---|
| Person Name | 86.3% | 83.2% |
| Organization Name | 73.4% | 89.3% |
| Employee-Of | 75.6% | 92.3% |
| Product-Of | 56.2% | 87.1% |
| Location-Of | 67.2% | 75.6% |

As can been seen, our performance in person name and organization name extraction is comparable to other systems [2,3] considering the relatively small size of the training corpus. Based on our survey, our work on extracting entity relations is unprecedented for Chinese, therefore we are unable to establish a benchmark. But, the extraction of emloyee-of relation looks quite good. Detailed analysis reveals that our method can handle well some instances where co-reference resolution is needed because we introduced cross-sentence features. The method did poorly on product-of relation extraction due to the errors in noun phrases chunking. With a better NP chunking module, the performance can be improved.

## 4. Conclusion

In this paper we presented a trainable method for extracting Chinese entity names and their relations. The method provides a unified framework based on MBL. Our preliminary experiment demonstrates that this trainable method is efficient and flexible. Any linguistic features, either surface or deep, can be easily added into the system. Preliminary experiments have shown that our performance is comparable to or better than other existing trainable methods, such as HMM and Crystal. Our work, however, is still in its preliminary stage. More thorough evaluation is required using larger testing corpora. Some algorithmic extensions are also expected so as to improve the performance, including automatic feature selection, coreference resolution, etc.

### *Reference*


[1] S. Soderland, D. Fisher, J. Aseltine, and W. Lehnert. CRYSTAL: Inducing a conceptual dictionary. In Proceedings of the Fourteenth International Joint Conference on Artificial Intelligence, Montreal, Canada, August 1995.

[2] H.-H. Chen, Y.-W. Ding, S.-C. Tsai, G.-W. Bian, Description of the NTU System used for MET-2, Message Understanding Conference

Proceedings(MUC-7), Washington, DC. Available at http://www.muc.saic.com /proceedings/muc_7_proceedings/ntumet2.pdf. 1998.

[3] Shihong Yu, Shuanhu Bai and Paul Wu , Description of the Kent Ridge Digital Labs System Used for MUC-7, Message Understanding Conference Proceedings, Washington, DC. Available at http://www.muc.saic.com/proceedings/muc_7_proceedings/kent_ridge.pdf. 1998.

[4] Walter Daelemans, Jakub Zavrel, Ko van der Sloot, and Antal van den Bosch. TiMBL: Tilburg Memory Based Learner, version 3.0, Reference Guide Reference: ILK Technical Report 00-01. Available at http://ilk.kub.nl/~ilk/papers/ilk0001.ps.gz., 2000.

[5] Walter Daelemans, Antal van den Bosch, Jakub Zavrel, Jorn Veenstra, Sabine Buchholz, and Bertjan Busser. Rapid development of NLP modules with memory-based learning, In Proceedings of ELSNET in Wonderland, pp. 105-113. Utrecht: ELSNET, 1998.

[6] D. Lin. Extracting Collocations from Text Corpora. First Workshop on Computational Terminology, Montreal, Canada, August, 1998.

[7] Mei Jiaju, 《Tong Yi Ci Ci Lin》 (Chinese), Shanghai Dictionary Publishing Press, Shanghai, 1983.

[8] S. Soderland. "CRYSTAL: Learning Domain-specific Text Analysis Rules", Technical Report, Center for Intelligent Information Retrieval, University of Massachusetts, Available from http://www-nlp.cs.umass.edu/ciir-pubs/te-43.pdf, 1996.

# Statistics Based Hybrid Approach to Chinese Base Phrase Identification

Tie-jun ZHAO, Mu-yun YANG, Fang LIU, Jian-min YAO, Hao YU

Department of Computer Science and Engineering, Harbin Institute of Technology
{tjzaho, ymy, liufang, james, yu}@mtlab.hit.edu.cn

**ABSTRACT**

This paper extends the base noun phrase(BNP) identification into a research on Chinese base phrase identification. After briefly introducing some basic concepts on Chinese base phrase, this paper presents a statistics based hybrid model for identifying 7 types of Chinese base phrases in view. Experiments show the efficiency of the proposed method in simplifying sentence structure. Significance of the research lies in it provides a solid foundation for the Chinese parser.

**Keywords:** Chinese base phrase identification, parsing, statistical model

## 1 Introduction

Decomposing syntactic analysis into several phases so as to decrease its difficulty is a new stream in NLP research. The successful POS tagging has encouraged researchers to explore further possibility for resolving sub-problems in parsing(Zhou, et al, 1999). The typical examples are the recognition of BaseNP in English and Chinese.

In English BNP (base noun phrase) is defined as simple and non-nesting noun phrases, i.e. noun phrases that do not contain other noun phrase descendants (Church, 1988). After that researches on BNP identification reports promising results for such task in English. Observing that the Chinese BNP is different form English, (Zhao & Huang, 1999) puts forward the definition of Chinese BNP in terms of combination of determinative modifier and head noun. According to them a BNP in Chinese can be recursively defined as:

*BaseNP ::= Determinative modifier + Noun | Nominalized verb(NV)*
*Determinative modifier ::= Adjective | Differentiable Adjective(DA) | Verb | Noun | Location | String | Numeral + Classifier*

Inspired by these researches, we extend the concept of BNP to Base Phrase in Chinese. It is based on such knowledge that there are many structures, not only NP, in which the trivial components closely attach to their central words and constitute a basic phrase in a Chinese sentence. Obviously, resolving all these base phrases will greatly benefit Chinese parser by reliving it from some pre-processing (though non-trivial) and enable it focus on the most subtle syntactic structures.

Since the whole system of Chinese base phrase is still under discussing, this paper just presents some tentative research achievements on statistics based hybrid model to Chinese base phrase identification. For the 7 types we considered at present, our algorithm turns out promising results and smoothes the way for a better Chinese parser.

## 2 Statistics Based Hybrid Approach to Chinese Base Phrase Identification

### 2.1 Concepts and Definitions

In addition to BNP, constituents of many local structure in Chinese centers around a core word with certain fixed POS sequences. Therefore their identification is slightly different from parsing in that it bears relatively simple phenomenon. Like BNP identification, identification of these phenomena before parsing will provide a simpler sequence for parser, and thus deserves a separate research.

Currently, we are considering 7 Chinese base phrases in our research, namely base adjective phrase(BADJP), base adverbial phrase (BADVP), base noun phrase (BNP), base temporal phrase (BTN), base location phrase (BNS), base verb phrase (BVP) and base quantity phrase (BMP) . Though theoretically definitions for these base phrases are still unavailable, Appendix I lists the preliminary illustrations for them in BNF format (necessary account for POS annotation can also be found)..

To frame the identification of Chinese base phrases, we further develop the following concepts:

**Definition 1**: Chinese based phrases are recognized as atomic parts of a sentence beyond words that posses certain functions and meanings. A base phrase may consist of words or other base phrases, but its constituents, in turn, should not contain any base phrases.

**Definition 2**: Base phrase tag is the token representing the syntactic function of the phrase. At present, base tag either falls in one of the 7 Chinese base phrases we are considering or not:

*Phrase-Tag ::= BADJP | BADVP | BNP | BTN | BNS | BVP | BMP | NULL*

**Definition 3**: Boundary tag denotes the possible relative position of a word to a base phrase. A boundary tag for a given word is either L( left boundary of a base phrase), R( right boundary of a ), I(inside a base phrase) or O(outside the base phrase).

## 2.2 Duple Based HMM Parser

Based on above definitions, we could, in view of Wojciech's proposal [Wojciech and Thorsten, 1998], interpret the parsing of Chinese base phrases as the following:

Suppose the input as a sequence of POS annotations $T=(t_0,\ldots\ldots,t_n)$ . The task is to find *RC*, a most possible sequence of duples formed by base phrase tags and boundary tags, among the POS sequence *T*.

$$RC=(\langle r_0,c_0\rangle,\ldots\ldots,\langle r_n,c_n\rangle),$$

in which $r_i$ $(1<i<=n)$ indicates the boundary tags, $c_i$ represents the base phrase tags.

To go along with the POS tagger developed previously by us, we first think of preserving HMM (hidden Markov Model) for parsing Chinese base phrases. Thus the following formula is usually at hand:

$$\overline{RC} = \arg\max p(RC \mid T) = \arg\max \frac{p(RC) * p(T \mid RC)}{p(T)}$$

For a given sequence of *T*, this formula can be transformed into:

$$\overline{RC} = \arg\max\ p(RC \mid T) = \arg\max\ p(RC) * p(T \mid RC)$$

Essentially this model could be established through bigram or tri-gram statistical training by a annotated corpus. In practice, we just build our model from 10,000 manual annotated sentences with common bi-gram training:

$$p(RC) = \prod_{i=1}^{n} p(RC_i \mid RC_{i-1})$$

$$p(T \mid RC) = \prod_{i=1}^{n} p(T_i \mid RC_i)$$

In realization, a Viterbi algorithm is adopted to search the best path. An open test on additional 1000 sentences is performed to check its accuracy. Results are shown in Table1(note precision is calculated by word).

| | Precision for R | Precision for C | Precision for Both R and C |
|---|---|---|---|
| Close Test | 85.7% | 87.5% | 79.0% |
| Open Test | 82.4% | 85.1% | 74.7% |

Table 1. Results for Duple Based HMM

## 2.3 Triple Based MM Exploiting Linguistic Information

Although results shown in Table 1 is encouraging enough for research purposes, it is still lies a long way for practical Chinese parser we are aiming at. Reasons for errors may be account by too coarse-grained information provided by RC. Observing the fact that the Chinese base phrase occurs more frequently with some fixed patterns, i.e. some frozen POS chains, we decide to improved our previous model by emphasizing the contribution given by POS information.

Adding *t* denoting POS in the duple (r,

c), we develop a triple in the form of (t,r,c) for the calculation of a node. Naturally, the new model is changed into a MM (Markov model) as:

$$\overline{TRC} = \arg\max\ p(TRC)$$

$$= \arg\max \prod_{i=1}^{n} p(TRC_i \mid TRC_{i-1})$$

To train this model, we still using a bi-gram model. Applying the same corpus and tests described above, we got the performance of triple based MM identifier for Chinese base phrases (see Table 2).

| | Precision for R | Precision for C | Precision for Both R and C |
|---|---|---|---|
| Close Test | 89.2% | 91.5% | 84.6% |
| Open Test | 88.4% | 89.9% | 83% |

Table 2. Result for Triple Based MM

## 2.4 Further Improvement Through TBED Learning

Like other statistical models, the above model, whether duple based or triple based, both seem to reach an accuracy ceiling after enlarging training set to 12, 000 or so. To cover the remaining accuracy, we apply the transformation-based error driven (TBED) learning strategy described in [Brill, 1992] to acquired desired rules.

In our module, some initial rules are first designed as compensation of statistical model. Applying these rules will cause new mistakes as well as make correct identifications. Then the module will compare the processed texts with training sentences, generate new rules according to pre-defined actions and update its rule bank after evaluation (see Fig 1.).

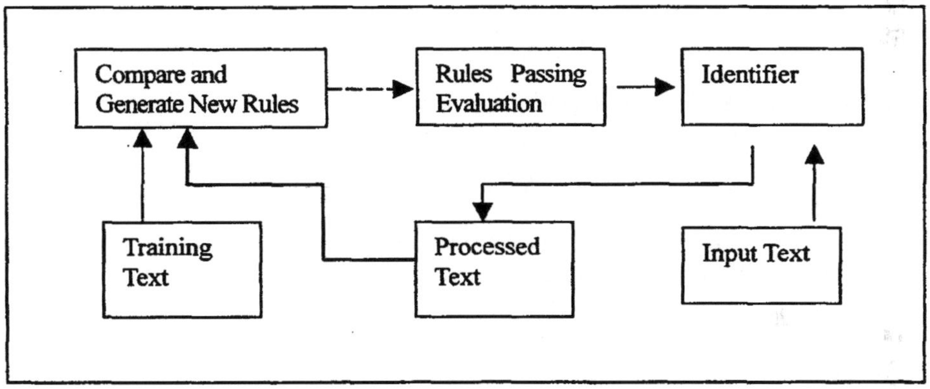


Figure 1. TBED Learning Module

The dotted line in fig 2. will stop functioning if pre-set accuracy is reached by the identifier for the Chinese base phrase. Evaluation of new rules is based on an greedy algorithm: only rule with max contribution (max correction and min error) will be added. Design of rule generation (pre-defined actions) is similar to those described in [Brill, 1992].

Table 3 shows a significant improvement after applying rules obtained through TBED learner. It is also the final performance of the proposed Chinese base phrase identification model.

| | Precision for R | Precision for C | Precision for Both R and C |
|---|---|---|---|
| Close | 91.2% | 92.8% | 89% |
| Open | 90.4% | 91.1% | 87.1% |

Table 3. Results after TBED Module

## 3 Conclusions and Discussions

We have accomplished preliminary experiments on identification of various types of base phrases defined in this paper. The data shown in last section prove that our method generates satisfactory results for

Chinese base phrase identification. The overall process of our method is outlined the following figure.

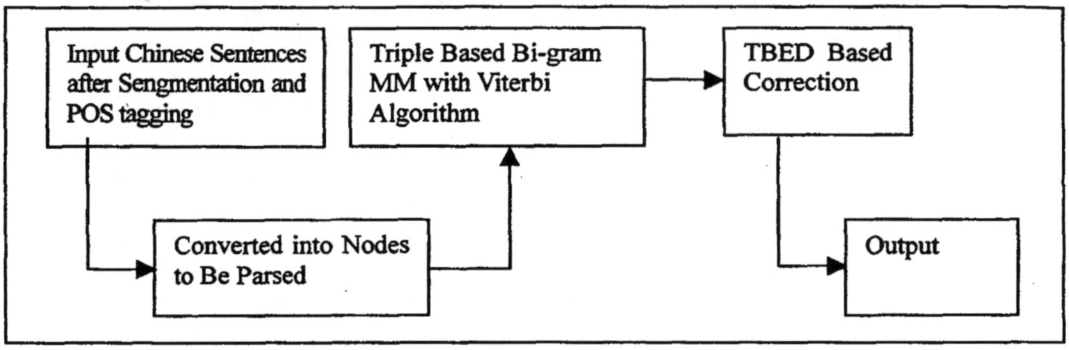


Fig 2. Processing of Chinese Based Phrase Identification

However, the 7 types Chinese base phrases we have proposed are far from perfection. Even what we have proposed for the 7 phrases is still under test. Further improvement will focus on two aspects: one is to discuss and add new base phrase for a broader coverage; the other is to define, theoretically or empirically, the Chinese base phrases with more strict constraints. Of course, new techniques to improved the accuracy of statistical model are the constant aim of our research.

To sum up, Chinese base phrase identification will reduce complexity of a Chinese parser. The successful identification of the 7 base phrases clearly simplifies the structure of the sentence. We expect that the research described in this paper will lay a solid foundation for a high-accuracy Chinese parser.

**Reference**

[Church, 1988] K. Church, A stochastic parts program and noun phrase parser for unrestricted text, In: Proc. of Second Conference on Applied Natural Language Processing, 1988

[Wojciech and Thorsten, 1998] Wojciech Skut and Thorsten Brants, Chunk Tagger, Statistical Recongnition of Noun Phrases, In ESSLLI-98 Workshop on Automated Acquisition of Syntax and Parsing, Saarbrvcken, 1998.

[Zhao & Huang, 1999] Zhao Jun and Huang Chang-Ning, The model for Chinese baseNP structure analysis, Chinese J. Computer, 22(2): pp141-146

[Zhou, et al, 1999] Zhou Qiang, Sun Mao-Song, Huang Chang-Ning, Chunk parsing scheme for Chinese sentences, Chinese J. Computer, 22(11): pp1159-1165

**Appendix** Illustration of 7 Chinese Base Phrases in BNF

The patterns listed here are far from complete (even for the 7 phrases themselves). Theoretical definition is beyond this paper and what we provide here is actually stage results of expert observation and linguistic abstraction.

**BADJP** ::= $d^+$+a | d+BADJP | $a^+$ | a+BADJP | BADVP+a | BADVP+BADJP

**BADVP** ::= a+usdi(地) | d+usdi | vg+usdi | BADJP+usdi | BADVP+usdi | BMP+usdi

**BMP** ::= $m^+$ | $m^+$+$q^+$ | m+q+m | d+m+q | f+m+q | r+m+q | $BMP^+$

**BNP** ::= a+n | a+usde(的)+n | a+usde+BNP | a+BNP | b+n | b+usde+n | b+usde+BNP | b+BNP | d+usde+n | f+n | f+usde+n | f+BNP | m+n | m+BNP | $n^+$ | n+usde+n | n+usde+BNP | n+usde+BMP | n+BNP | q+n | q+BNP | r+a+n | r+m+n | r+n | r+usde+n | r+usde+BNP | r+BNP | s+n | s+usde+n | s+usde+BNP | t+n | t+usde+n | t+usde+BNP | vg+usde+n | vg+usde+BNP | BADJP+n | BADJP+usde+n | BADJP+usde+BNP | BADJP+BNP | BMP+n | BMP+usde+n | BMP+usde+BNP | BMP+BNP | BNP+n | BNP+usde+n | BNP+usde+BNP | BNP+usde+BMP | BNP+BNP | BNS+usde+n | BNS+usde+BNP | BNS+BNP | BTN+usde+n | BTN+usde+BNP | BVP+usde+n | BVP+usde+BNP

**BNS** ::= a+nd | m+nd | n+s | r+nd | n+usde+f | n+usde+nd | n+usde+s | n+usde+BNS | $nd^+$ | r+usde+nd | r+usde+s | s+usde+nd | s+usde+BNS | BNP BNS | $BNS^+$

**BTN** ::= a+t | m+t | r+t | $t^+$ | t+usde+t | BMP+t | BTN+t | BNP+usde+t

**BVP** ::= a+vg | d+vg | vg+d+a | vg+d+vq | vg+d+vb | vg+usdf(得)+a | vg+usdf+d | vg+usdf+vq | vg+usdf+u | vg+usdf+BADJP | vg+ut | vg+vb | vg+ut+vq | vq+vg | vq+BVP | vz+vg | vz+BVP | BADJP+vg | BADVP+vg | BADVP+BVP | BVP+ut | BVP+vq | BVP+BVP

| Symbol | Part-Of-Speech | Examples |
|---|---|---|
| a | Adjective | 漂亮(beautiful), 浪漫(romantic) |
| d | Adverb | 很(very), 依然(still) |
| f | Temporal/spacial position word | 中(in), 上(on), 之间(between) |
| m | numeral | 一(one), 二(two), 三(three) |
| n | noun | 人民(people), 西红柿(tomato), 计算机(computer) |
| nd | Name of place | 北京(Beijing), 哈尔滨(Harbin), 纽约(New York) |
| q | classifier | 群(flock), 个(NULL) |
| r | pronoun | 你(you), 我(I, me), 他(he, him) |
| s | location noun | 附近(around), 室外(outside) |
| t | time noun | 昨天(yesterday), 七月(July) |
| ut | tense auxiliary | 着,了,过(NULL) |
| vb | Complemental verb | 完,住(NULL) |
| vg | common verb | 知道(know), 渴望(long for) |
| vq | directional verb | 出,下来(NULL) |
| vz | modal verb | 可以(can), 应该(should) |

Table for POS symbols used in Appendix

# A Block-Based Robust Dependency Parser for Unrestricted Chinese Text[1]

**Ming Zhou**
Microsoft Research China,
Sigma Centre, 49#, Zhichun Road,
100080, Beijing, China
mingzhou@microsoft.com

**Abstract**

Although substantial efforts have been made to parse Chinese, very few have been practically used due to incapability of handling unrestricted texts. This paper realizes a practical system for Chinese parsing by using a hybrid model of phrase structure partial parsing and dependency parsing. This system showed good performance and high robustness in parsing unrestricted texts and has been applied in a successful machine translation product.

## Introduction

Substantial efforts have been made to parse western languages such as English, and many powerful computational models have been proposed (Gazdar, et al, 1987, Tomita, M, 1986). However, very limited work has been done with Chinese. This is mainly due to the fact that the structure of the Chinese language is quite different from English. Therefore the computational model in processing English may not be directly applied to the Chinese language. Lin-Shan Lee et al (1991) proposed a Chinese natural language processing system with special consideration of some typical phenomena of Chinese. Jinye Zhou et al (1986) presented a deterministic Chinese parsing methodology using formal semantics to combine syntactic and semantic analysis. However, most of the proposed approaches were realized on small-scale lexicon and rule base (usually thousands words and tens or hundreds rules). It is still an open issue whether these models will work on real texts containing various ungrammatical phenomena. A parser capable of handling real text should have not only large lexicon and big rule base, but also high robustness in coping with different kinds of ungrammatical phenomena. Therefore, it is important to design a grammar scheme which not only is capable of representing the unique grammar structures which are different with English, but also qualified of handling unrestricted text.

Phrase structure scheme is usually used in English parsing models to represent sentence structures, but it is not convenient and not strong enough to express Chinese sentence by phrase structure in some occasions. For examples:

Sentence-1 我们请她喝啤酒。

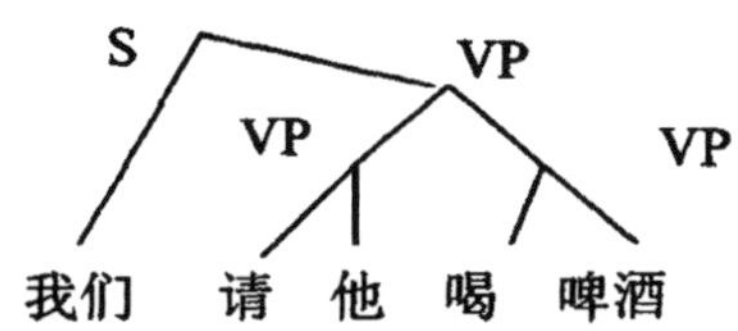


Fig. 1 phrase structure

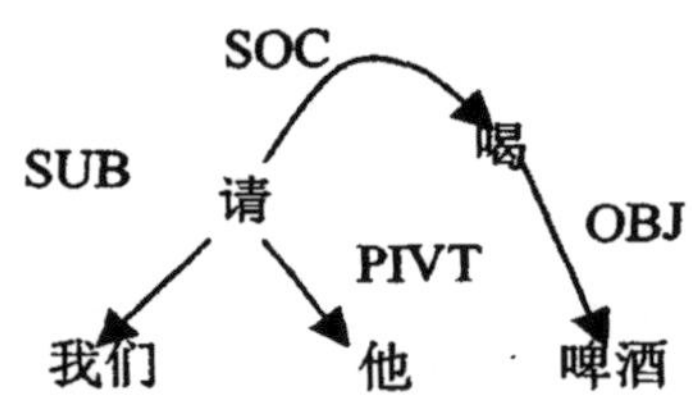


Fig.2 dependency structure

[1] This work was mainly done while the author visited Kodensha Ltd, Japan during 1996-1999

Sentence-1 is a pivot sentence(兼语句), i.e., “她” is not only the object of “请” but also the subject of ”喝”. But this phrase structure cannot indicate the relations clearly as shown in Fig.1. However, the grammar structure is clarified if it is represented in dependency structure (Fig. 2). Therefore, it is believed that dependency grammar scheme is more suitable than phrase structure to represent Chinese structures (Zhou, Huang, 1994). However, traditional Dependency grammar realizes the dependency relations between any of two specific words, then numerous word based dependency knowledge should be constructed, this is a time-consuming task. Fortunately, knowledge for phrase structure parsing has been accumulated for Chinese for many years and it should be re-used to compensate the lack of knowledge of word-based dependency parsing. Therefore, to combine the advantages of phrase structure parsing and dependency parsing, we propose a new parsing strategy, called “block-based dependency parsing”.

A “block” means a basic component of sentence, for example, there are six blocks for sentence 1:

[我们][请][她][喝][啤酒][。]

Another example:
Sentence 2: 昨天上午我们请她的全班同学喝了一箱啤酒]。
Blocks:[昨天上午] [我们] [请] [她的全班同学] [喝了] [一箱啤酒][。]

A block represents an information unit in communications. For example, in Chinese-Japanese machine translation, translations of the members within a block in a Chinese sentence usually are in a same blocks in the Japanese translation. Furthermore, it is clear to represent block with phrase structure, while it is rather complicated with dependency structure.

This block-based dependency parsing process works like follows. For an input sentence, basic components of sentence, i.e., “blocks” are first identified by an ATN-like partial parsing procedure, which produces a clear skeleton of the sentence structure. In our phrase structure analysis, we don’t try to deduce the whole sentence into root S, instead, we only try to get the components, namely blocks. This partial parsing strategy guarantees high robustness. Then dependency parsing is applied in order to build dependency relations among blocks. The dependency parsing skips ungrammatical portions it encounters. This strategy confines ungrammatical portion and avoids errors to be propagated globally. By partial parsing and skip strategy, this parser can handle long, complicated, or even faulty sentences. The experiments show that this parser is very robust and powerful. A parser constructed based on this approach has been developed, with 220,000 words, 5,000 part-of-speech tagging rules, over 1,000 block parsing rules and 300 dependency parsing rules. This parser has been applied in a Chinese-Japanese machine translation product (Zhou, 1999). To the author’s knowledge, this parser is one of the largest scale Chinese parser ever implemented in the world.

The outline of this paper is as follows. In section 1, we present our special solution to part-of-speech tagging which significantly affects the Chinese parsing. Section 2 describes in details the block-based dependency parsing approach. We then explain the dependency parsing algorithm in section 3. The experiment and its analysis are given in section 4. The conclusion is given in section 5.

## 1 Rule-based part-of-speech tagging

The Chinese language has many special syntactic phenomena substantially different from English (Chao, 1981; Huang, 1982, Wu and Hou, 1982). One of the biggest problems is that there is no morphological change for a verb, whether the verb functions as the predicate, subject, object, or modifier of a noun. For instance:

我们要进一步加大打击力度。（[打击V力度N] NP）

西部开发是今后五十年的主要目标（[西部N开发V] NP）

Chinese linguistics literature insists that those words are verbs, and should be marked as “V”, regardless of what context they are in. In this sense, there will be phrase structure rules for noun phrase like:

NP->N+V

NP->V+N

However, there must be some rules for VP, S like:

S->N+V

VP->V+N

Therefore the conflict of rules becomes very serious. It means that part-of-speech information in Chinese is too weak to support Chinese syntactical analysis. To solve this problem, we propose that in the part-of-speech tagging stage, the real grammar features of this kind of words are determined directly as N, instead of V. To do this, we describe all possible word category information for a word in the lexicon, for example：

努力　V/ N/F/A
//V: verb; N: noun; F: adverb; A: adjective

A set of rules with comprehensive context constraints is designed to determine the specific part-of-speech of a word in a context. For example:

1. X(N|R)+努力(V|N|F|A) + X(V*)->努力(F) + X(V)
2. 的+努力(V|N|F|A) + X(没有)->的+努力(N) + X(N)
3. 的+努力(V|N|F|A) + X(V|N)->的+努力(A) + X(N)
4. 正在+努力(V|N|F|A) + X(~V)->正在+努力(V)

X(N|R): a word X, whose word category may includes N,R, or others.
R: Pronoun;
*: any part-of-speeches;
V* having V category;
~V having no V category;

It is ideal if we have a large corpus which has been tagged with thins kind of word category information, so that we can obtain tagging rules or obtained n-gram model by training. However, at present, we can't find a Chinese corpus tagged with this kind of part-of-speech information as the training data. We had to write the part-of-speech disambiguation rules manually. Currently, over 5,000 linguistics rules have been designed.

## 2 Block-based Chinese dependency analysis

As indicated in Fig. 3, block-based dependency analysis consists of four modules, i.e., word segmentation, part-of-speech tagging, block analysis and dependency analysis. A bi-directional heuristic longest matching method is applied to decide the optimal word sequence. A set of manually compiled linguistic rules is applied to decide the optimal word category sequence. In a partial parsing process, first, local structures (such as duplication, prefix and suffix) are identified by a set of word formation rules, and proper names are identified by a set of construction rules. This kind of local structures are called meta-blocks. Then frame structures (DP), which have paired starting word and ending word , such as "在"…. "时", "从"…. "中" etc are identified, but its internal structure analysis is delayed. Then ATN network is used to identify the basic blocks, called level-1 blocks (these blocks don't contain IP, LP and DP). Then we use a set of heuristic rules to identify the boundaries of IP and LP. Then ATN network will use again to identify the complicated blocks, called level-2 blocks, which may contain LP, DP, IP as its components. Then a sequence of blocks obtained is then transported to dependency parser, which will generate dependency relations among blocks. After that, we will recursively parse the internal parts of IP,

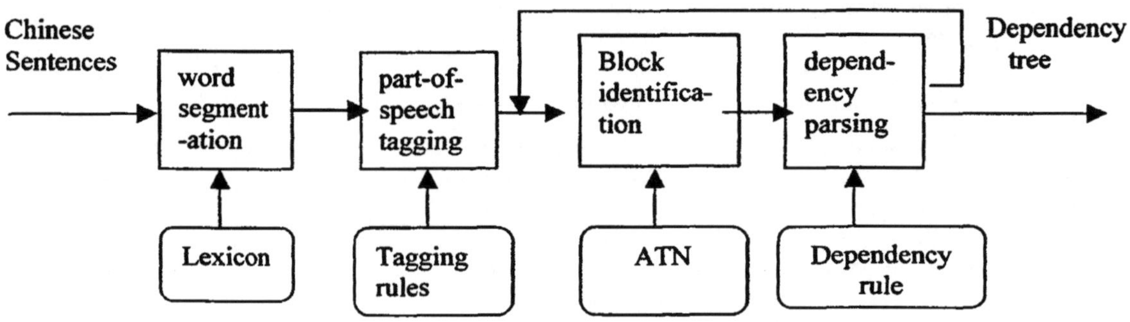


Fig. 3 Configuration of the block-based dependency parser

LP and DP to get its inner blocks and dependency relations.

We define 11 kinds of blocks as explained below.

| | | |
|---|---|---|
| NP | Noun phrase | 我的书 |
| UP | Digital phrase | 14560,三千二百 |
| UG | Digital-classifier phrase | 五斤,六十米 |
| NTL | Phrase expressing the period of time | 三十年, 60 个月 |
| NTP | Phrase expressing the exact time | 一九八九年三月 |
| AP | Adjective phrase | 美丽大方 |
| FP | Adverb phrase | 勤奋刻苦地（学习英语） |
| VP | Verb phrase | 学习研究 |
| IP | Preposition phrase | 为人民服务 |
| LP | Post-position phrase | 仓库里 |
| DP | Frame structure | 为公司的利益起见,在打击盗版方面 |

Table 1 Blocks defined in the system

Except PP, LP and DP, each kind of block is defined by a set of rules in the form of phrase structure rule. All of these rules combined with syntactic and semantic constraints are implemented as an ATN network (Allen, 1995).

We also define 17 kinds of dependency relations for Chinese as shown in table 2.

| | | |
|---|---|---|
| 1 | SUB | Subject(主语) |
| 2 | OBJ1 | Indirect-object间接宾语) |
| 3 | OBJ2 | Direct object(直接宾语) |
| 4 | COMP | Complement(补语) |
| 4 | NUM | Amount(数量关系) |
| 5 | TOP | Topic(主题) |
| 6 | ADVN | Near adverbs（副词状语） |
| 7 | ADVF | Far adverbs（介词短语、方位短语、框式结构状语） |
| 8 | QT | miscellaneous before verbs (动词之前的闲杂成分) |
| 10 | HT | miscellaneous after verbs(动词之后的闲杂成分) |
| 11 | PUNC | Punctuation mark(标点符号) |
| 12 | PIVT | Pivot(兼語) |
| 13 | SOC | Pivot-complement(兼語补语) |
| 14 | VAA | Series of verbs after(向后连续动作) |
| 15 | VAB | Series of verbs before(向前连续动作) |
| 16 | G | 能愿动词接续关系 |
| 17 | LOG | Logical relation between sentences(假设、因果) |

Table 2 Dependency relations used in the system

For an Input: S= $w_1, w_2, \cdots, w_n$, the expected parse result includes two parts as described below:

① T : a set of sub-trees, each sub-tree represents a block.

$$T=\{T_1,T_2,T_3.....T_n\ \}$$

② D: a set of 3-tuple in the form of {governor, dependant, dependency-relation}, which represents dependency relations between blocks.

$$D=\{<gov_1,dep_1,rela_1>,<gov_2,dep_2,rela_2>,\ldots <gov_m,dep_m,rela_m>\}$$

**Algorithm 1: The block-based parsing algorithm**

1) Identification DP by matching the starting word and ending word;
2) Identification of meta-blocks by bottom-up analysis;
3) Identification of NP, UP, UG, NTL, NTP, AP, FP, VP of level 1 by bottom-up analysis;
4) Identification LP, PP by looking for left boundary for LP and right boundary for IP, by using a set of Chinese linguistic rules;
5) Identification of NP, UP, UG, NTL, NTP, AP, FP, VP of level 2 by bottom-up analysis;
6) Dependency parsing with the blocks identified;
7) For blocks LP, DP and LP, recursively do 1 thorough 6.

In the following, we will illustrate the parsing process with an example.

Sentence 3: 实行不实行质量管理对中小运输企业提高经营水平来说非常重要。

**(1)Word Segmentation & Part-of-speech tagging**

/实行 V/不 F/实行 V/*质量 N/管理 N*/对 I/中小 A/运输 N/企业 N/提高 V/*经营 N/水平 N*/来说 L/非常 F/重要 A/。 P/

**(2) Meta-blocks identification**

[/实行 V/不 F/实行 V/]VP

**(3) Frame structure identification**

[对 I/中小 A/运输 N/企业 N/提高 V/*经营 N/水平 N*/来说 L/]DP

**(4) Block identification**

block1: [/实行 V/不 F/实行 V/]VP

block2:[*质量 N/管理 N/*]NP
block3: [对 I/中小 A/运输 N/企业 N/提高 V/*经营N/水平* N/来说 L/]DP
block4: [非常 F/重要 A/]AP
block5: [。 P/]

**(5)Predicate Identification**

Block4 is determined as the predicate.

**(6) Dependency parsing**

(block2, block1, OBJ1)
(block3, block4, ADVF)
(block1, block4, SUB)
(block5, bolck4, PUNC)

**(7)Repeat the above parsing process to analyze the internal structure of DP, IP and LP**

Analyze block3 recursively (The detailed process is omitted).

Lots of efforts have been made to parse languages into phrase structure, and many powerful computational models have been proposed (Gazdar, *et al,* 1987, Tomita, M, 1986*)*. We build up an ATN like network to identify these blocks. Since the ATN approaches can be found in the literatures (Allen, 1995), we will not describe this algorithm in details here. In the next section, we will focus on a new efficient algorithm for Chinese dependency parsing.

## 3 Dependency analysis

Text For an Input: S=$block_1, block_2, \cdots, block_n$, the dependency parsing will generate a set of 3-tuple in the form of {governor, dependant, dependency-relation}, which represents dependency relations between blocks in the given sentence.

$$\{<gov_1, dep_1, rela_1>, <gov_2, dep_2, rela_2>, \ldots <gov_m, dep_m, rela_m>\}$$

**Algorithm 2: The dependency parsing**

1) Count the number of block qualifying of acting as a predicate, denoted as *s*. These kind of blocks are called "predicate candidates".
2) Decide the predicate from these s blocks, denoted as $block_i$
3) If *s*=0, return; //need not analysis;
4) For any case of S, S=1,2,... (S>0), do dependency parsing respectively;

A sentence may contain *s* predicate candidates. For each case, we defined a detailed analysis algorithm. Up to now, the parser is designed to have ability to treat with sentences containing up to 7 predicate candidates. In case a sentence has more than 7 predicate candidates, it will be partitioned into two parts, and then doing analysis in turn.

Suppose the predicate block is $block_i$, the number of "predicate candidates" is denoted as *s*. We explain the dependency parsing by the following two simple cases.

**Case 1: s=1**

- For all $block_k$ before $block_i$, builds dependency relations of ($block_k, block_i$,SUB),($block_k, block_i$,ADV), ($block_k, block_i$,G), ($block_k, block_i$,TOP);
- For all $block_k$ after $block_i$, builds dependency relations of ($block_k, block_i$,COMP),($block_k, block_i$,OBJ1), ($block_k, block_i$,OBJ2), etc.

**Case 2: s=2,** Let's say the another predicate candidate is $block_j$

- For all $block_k$ before $block_i$, builds dependency relations of ($block_k, block_i$,SUB), ($block_k, block_i$,ADV), ($block_k, block_i$,G), ($block_k, block_i$,TOP);
- For all $block_k$ after $block_j$, builds dependency relations of ($block_k$, $block_j$,COMP), ($block_k$, $block_j$,OBJ1), ($block_k, block_j$,OBJ2), etc.
- For blocks between $block_i$ and $block_j$, Conducts detailed analysis based on the verb categories of $block_i$ and $block_j$
- Determines the dependency relation between $block_i$ and $block_j$

## 4 Experiments

A parsing system was implemented and extensive experiments have been performed. The system is written in C and tested on Pentium PC. A total of over 1,000 phrase structure rules and over 3,00 dependency rules were used for block-based parsing. We built a large lexicon of 220,000 word entries, with word category information and necessary syntactical and semantic features. This approach has been incorporated as Chinese parsing model in a successful commercial Chinese-Japanese machine translation system J-Beijing (Zhou, 1999).

This system accepts Chinese text and output the parsing result for each sentence. Each input sentence is defined as a word string ending with period, comma, question mark, semicolon, exclamation mark.

We evaluated the parsing result with two corpus: ① "primary school textbook of Singapore"(新加坡小学课本), a corpus consists of single sentences of modern Chinese, including 1842 sentences, which not only covers most Chinese sentence types, but also includes various of morphological phenomena, such as word duplication, affix, suffix, etc. ② Some news articles collected from People's Daily(1998,1999,2000). The sentences are real text, so there are lots of unknown words (mainly proper nouns), long sentences, complicated sentences, ellipsis, etc. The evaluation results are listed in table 3.

| Test corpus | #sentence | Average sentence length (words) | Analysis precision |
|---|---|---|---|
| Primary school textbook, Singapore | 1842 | 7.34 | 90.4% |
| People's Daily | 1400 | 14.52 | 67.7% |

Table 3 Evaluation result

Although this model has produced satisfactory initial results, some natural difficulties for the Chinese language still remain, such that further improvement is highly desired. Through mistake analysis, we found that some of main issues affecting the system performance seriously, as is listed below.

**1) Word segmentation**

- 将来

  /克林顿/总统/将来/上海/。/

  /克林顿/总统/将/来/上海/。/

"将来" can not only function as single word, but also function as two words with totally different meaning.

**2) Part-of-speech tagging**

(1,我,R) (2,对,I) (3,你,R) (4,为,I) *(5,发展,N)* (6,中俄关系,N) (7,所,E) (8,作,V) (9,的,E) *(10,积极,F) (11,努力,F)* (12,表示,V,P) (13,高度,N) (14,赞赏,V,C) (15,, ,P)

**3) Compound noun**

- 研究工作

  /我们/正在/研究/工作/

  /这个/研究工作/十分/重要/

- 研究过程

  /我们/正在/研究/过程/参数/

  /在/这个/研究/过程/中/,/

Since compound nouns cannot exhaustively numerated, errors will be inevitable.

**4) Identification of proper noun**

(1,江主席,N) (2,电贺,V,P) *(3,普,A) (4,京,N)* (5,当选,V,C) (6,俄,N) (7,联邦,N) (8,总统,N)

**5) Syntactical ambiguity**

(1,祝愿,V,P) (2,中俄,N) (3,两国,N) (4,世代,N) *(5,做,V,C) (6,好,A,□) (6,邻居,N)* (7,好,A) (8,伙伴,N) (9,好,A) (10,朋友,N) (11,。 ,P)

For pattern of "V+A+N", there are usually two kinds of reduction methods:

[[V+A]vp+N] *做好/邻居*

[V+[A+N]np] *做/好邻居*

All of these problems need further improvements in the future.

## Conclusion

In this paper, a practical Chinese parser is presented. The block-based dependency parsing strategy is a novel integration of phrase structure partial approach and dependency parsing approach. The partial parsing approach and dependency parsing approach can cope with ungrammatical or faulty, or complicated sentences, therefore making the system highly robust. Furthermore, our top-down strategy of identifying the Chinese special structures such as frame structures, preposition structures, post-preposition structures produces a simplified sentence skeleton, thereby improving the efficiency of parsing.

Although this model has shown satisfactory initial results, some natural difficulties for the Chinese language still remain, and further work will be needed. We currently determine the word category by a set of linguistics rules compiled by human which limits the precision of identification precision. Therefore, other approaches such as statistical approach or some kind of hybrid approach will be adopted in the future. In addition, new methods in handling ambiguous word segmentation, proper noun and compound noun identification, block analysis, predicate identification and dependency analysis will be studied.

**Acknowledgements**

Our thanks go to Dr. Kai-Fu Lee and Prof. Changning Huang of Microsoft Research China for their valuable suggestions. Also thanks all the members of Chinese-Japanese MT group of Kodensha for their great efforts in testing the parsing system and improving the dictionary.

**References**

Gazdar, G.,Franz.,A., Osborne, K., and Evans, R. (1987), Natural Language Processing in the 1980s.", CSLI, Stanford University.

Tomita, M. (1986). Efficient Parsing for Natural Language: A Fast Algorithm for Practical Systems, Boston: Kluwer.

Jinye Zhou, Shi-kuo Chang (1986), A Methodology for Deterministic Chinese Parsing, Computer Processing of Chinese & Oriental Languages, Vol. 2, No. 3 May 1986.

Lin-Shan Lee, Lee-Feng Chien, Longj-ji Lin, James Huang, K.-J. Chen (1991), An Efficient Natural Language Processing System Specially Designed for the Chinese Language, Computational Linguistics, Vol.17, No. 4, 1991

M. Zhou (1999), J-Beijing Chinese-Japanese Machine Translation System, Proceedings of JSCL, 312-319, Beijing, 1-3, Nov, 1999

Jingcun Wu, Xuechao Hou, Modern Chinese Syntactical Analysis, Beijing University Press, 1982.

Zhengsheng Luo, Changjian Sun, Cai Sun (1995), An Approach to the Recognition of predicated in the automatic analysis of Chinese sentence patterns, Advances and applications on Computational Linguistics, Tsinghua University Press

Chao, Y.R. (1968). A Grammar of Spoken Chinese, Berkeley, CA: University of California Press

M. Zhou, C.N.Huang, (1994) An Efficient Syntactic Tagging Toll for Corpora. Proc. COLING 94, Kyoto, pp. 945-955.

Huang, J. (1982). Logical relations in Chinese and the theory of grammar, Doctoral dissertation, Massachusetts Institute of Technology, Cambridge, MA.

# Annotating information structures in Chinese texts using HowNet

**GAN Kok Wee**
**Department of Computer Science,**
**Hong Kong University of Science and Technology, Clear Water Bay,**
**Kowloon, Hong Kong.**
**gankw@cs.ust.hk**

**WONG Ping Wai**
**Department of Computer Science,**
**Hong Kong University of Science and Technology, Clear Water Bay,**
**Kowloon, Hong Kong.**
**wongpw@cs.ust.hk**

## Abstract

**This paper reported our work on annotating Chinese texts with information structures derived from HowNet. An information structure consists of two components: HowNet definitions and dependency relations. It is the unit of representation of the meaning of texts. This work is part of a multi-sentential approach to Chinese text understanding. An overview of HowNet and information structure are described in this paper.**

## 1 Introduction

Corpora are essential resources to any research in language engineering. For Chinese, efforts in building large corpora started in the 90s. For instance, the PH corpus of 4 million Chinese characters with word boundary information was released in 1993 (Guo, 1993). The first version of the Sinica corpus of two millions words marked with word boundaries and parts-of-speech was released in 1995 (CKIP, 1995). In 1996, a small corpus of 5266 distinct words (inclusive of punctuation marks) with a total occurrence frequency of 51870 was released (Yu et al., 1996). This corpus was derived from the Singapore Primary School Chinese Language Textbooks. It contained information on word boundaries, parts-of-speech and also syntactic structures. In 2000, two additional bracketed corpora have just been announced. The first one, the Chinese Penn Treebank, includes 100-thousand words (Xia et al., 2000). The second one, the Sinica Treebank, which is derived from the Sinica corpus, contains 38,725 sentences with 1000 of them released to the public[1] (CKIP, 2000).

The historical development of Chinese corpus construction has shown a consensus in incorporating more powerful linguistic structures into corpora. As noted by Marcus (1997), the more powerful linguistic structures will help in improving the accuracy of parsing. This is especially true to isolating language such as Chinese. However, there is very little work on annotating corpora with semantic information. To the best of our knowledge, there is only one report of this kind. The work by Lua[2] annotated 340,000 words with semantic class information as defined in a thesaurus of synonyms (Mei, 1983). With the release of HowNet[3], a bilingual general knowledge base, Gan and Tham (1999) reported the first corpus of 30,000 words that was annotated with the general knowledge structure defined in HowNet. This paper reported an extension of the work in Gan and Tham (1999) on the annotation of information structures in Chinese texts. In Section 2, an overview of HowNet is provided. Information structure and an illustration will be given in Section 3.

## 2 An Overview of HowNet

HowNet is a bilingual general knowledge-base describing relations between concepts and relations between the attributes of concepts. The latest version covers over 65,000 concepts in

---

[1] **http://godel.iis.sinica.edu.tw/CKIP/trees1000.htm**

[2] **http://www.cslp.com.nus.edu/sg/cslp/**

[3] **http://www.HowNet.com (Dong Zhendong, Dong Qiang; HowNet)**

Chinese and close to 75,000 English equivalents. The relations include hyponymy, synonymy, antonymy, meronymy, attribute-host, material-product, converse, dynamic role and concept cooccurrence. The philosophy behind the design of HowNet is its ontological view that all physical and non-physical matters undergo a continual process of motion and change in a specific space and time. The motion and change are usually reflected by a change in state that in turn, is manifested by a change in value of some attributes. The top-most level of classification in HowNet thus includes: entity, event, attribute and attribute value. It is important to point out that the classification is derived in a bottom-up manner. First, a set of sememes, the most basic set of semantic units that are non-decomposable, is extracted from about 6,000 Chinese characters. This is feasible because each Chinese character is monosyllabic and they are meaning-bearing. Similar sememes are grouped. The coverage of the set of sememes is tested against polysyllabic concepts to identify additional sememes. Eventually, a total of over 1,400 sememes are found and they are organized hierarchically. This is a closed set from which all concepts are defined. The bottom-up approach takes advantage of the fact that all concepts, either current or new, can be expressed using a combination of one or more existing Chinese characters. It is yet to find a new concept that has to resort to the creation of a new Chinese character. Therefore, by deriving the set of sememes in a bottom-up fashion, it is believed that the set of sememes is stable and robust enough to describe all kinds of concepts, whether current or new. The fact that HowNet has verified this thesis over 65,000 concepts is a good proof of its robustness.

## 2.1 Types of Relation

The definition of a concept in HowNet expresses one or more of the following relations.

### *2.1.1 Dynamic Role*

There are a total of 71 dynamic roles defined in HowNet. Dynamic role resembles case role in case grammar (Fillmore, 1968). However, it differs from case role in that it is concerned with all probable actants of an event and the roles they play in the event. The issue of whether these actants can be realized grammatically is not its concern. For example,

> Concept(1): 吃齋 (be a vegetarian for religious reasons)
> DEF=eat|吃, patient=vegetable|蔬菜, religion|宗教

At the syntactic level, "吃齋" is an intransitive verb. According to case grammar, it has only one case role: ***agent***. However, for this word, the ***patient*** is self-contained in its constituent (i.e. "齋" ). HowNet specifies this explicitly and indicates the category (*'vegetable'*[4]) of prototypical concepts which fills up this role.

Another distinguishing feature of dynamic role is its use in defining concepts of '*entity*' class.

> Concept(2): 毛筆 (writing brush)
> DEF=PenInk|筆墨, *write|寫

Through the use of the "*" pointer, the above definition states that the concept being defined (毛筆) is the instrument of the event type 寫 '*write*'.

HowNet also uses dynamic role to specify the attributes that a concept contains. For example,

> Concept(3): 突如其來 (arise suddenly)
> DEF=happen|發生, manner=sudden|驟

The definition of concept (3) specifies that the manner of the event is *'sudden'*.

### *2.1.2 Hyponymy Relation*

The '*event*' and '*entity*' classes in HowNet are organized in a hierarchical manner. The parent class is a hypernym of its children classes. Details of the organization are available from the HowNet site and are therefore omitted here.

### *2.1.3 Meronymy Relation*

Meronymy relation is expressed through the

[4] **We use single-quote and italic to mark sememes in HowNet.**

pointer “%”. For example,

Concept (4): 中央處理器 (CPU)
DEF=part|部件, %computer|電腦, heart|心

The class of the concept “中央處理器” is ‘part’. It is a part of the class ‘computer’. The function of the part “中央處理器” is the ‘heart’ of the whole ‘computer’.

### *2.1.4 Material-Product Relation*

Material-product relation is expressed through the pointer “?”. For example,

Concept (5): 毛線 (knitting wool)
DEF=material|材料, ?clothing|衣物

“毛線” belongs to the class ‘material’. It is a material for the product ‘clothing’.

### *2.1.5 Attribute-Host Relation*

Attribute-host relation is expressed by the pointer “&”. For example,

Concept (6): 面子 (face)
DEF=attribute|屬性, reputation|名聲, &human|人, &organization|組織

“面子” is an attribute; in particular, it is about the attribute ‘reputation’. The hosts could be ‘human’ as well as ‘organization’.

### *2.1.6 Concept Co-occurrence Relation*

Some concept typically co-occurs with certain concept. For example,

Concept (7): 不法之徒 (lawless person)
DEF=human|人, fierce|暴, crime|罪, #police|警, undesired|莠

The typical context where the concept “不法之徒” is used involves the concept ‘police’. This type of relation is expressed by the pointer “#”.

## 3 Information Structures

Dong (2000) uses the example “毒品走私集團” (Narcotic drugs smuggling group) to illustrate what information structure is. Describing the structure of this phrase at the syntactic level, such as the analysis of Penn Treebank (Xue, 1999: 72-77), only reveals that it is a noun phrase with the head of “集團” modified by a relative clause “毒品走私” which involves operator movement. At the semantic level of description, we would indicate that “集團” (group) is the ***agent*** of the event “走私” (smuggle) and “毒品” (Narcotic drugs) is the ***patient*** of “走私” (smuggle). The informaton structure of this example consists of two parts, the dependency relations and the HowNet definitions. The descriptions are as follows:

Dependency relations: 毒品[patient]←走私←[agent]集團

Definitions: 毒品: medicine|藥物, ?addictive|嗜好物
走私: transport|運送, manner=secret|秘, crime|罪
集團: community|團體

In this example, the descriptions specify that a ‘*community*’ is an ***agent*** involved in a ‘*transport*’ event transporting the ***patient*** ‘*medicine*’. Furthermore, the ‘*transport*’ event is a ‘*crime*’ and the manner is ‘*secret*’. The ‘*medicine*’ is a material of ‘*addictive*’ products. The arrow between two concepts is a dependency connection with the concept pointed to by the arrow denoting the dependent and the concept at the other end as the governor. The name of the dependency relation is enclosed in a square bracket and it could appear at either the dependent or the governor side.

Currently, over 60 types of information structure have been defined. The pattern of information structure is specified in the following format: (sememe) [DRel] → [DRel] (sememe), where *DRel* means the name of a dependency relation. For the dependency relation to apply, the governor and the dependent must satisfy the requirement of the sememes. Table 1 shows a subset of the information structures. Information structures are derived in a bottom-up fashion from analysing the mechanisms used in the composition of words. This approach is based on the insight that mechanisms used in word formation are also applicable to phrase and sentence construction in Chinese. For example, the type "(時間|time) [時間|time] ← (事件|event)" applies to the formation of the following units at various levels of linguistic structure:

| | |
|---|---|
| word level: | "午←睡" (afternoon nap) |
| phrase level: | "暑期←補習" (summer study) |
| sentence level: | "長期←商品短缺" (long-time shortage of commodities) |
| | "1999年12月9日星期四←發生洩漏" (leaking occurs on Thursday, December 9, 1999) |

In the process of annotating the corpus, the coverage of information structure types at the phrase and sentence levels was evaluated and missing types are added. The new types arise mainly due to function words. For example, the type "(modality|語氣) [modality|語氣] ← (事件|event)" is due to the use of function words such as "務必" (must) and "應該" (must). These are words expressing the attitude of the speaker of an utterance towards an event.

## 3.1 An example

We annotated a subset of the Sinica corpus (version 3.0) of 30,000 words with information structures. The corpus includes 103 newspaper texts covering the crime domain. The annotation has been completed and is currently under verification. We expect to release the corpus and the annotation guideline at the end of this year. An example of our annotation is shown below and its information structures are shown in Figure 1 at the end of this paper. The difference between this work and the work reported in Gan and Tham (1999) lies in the addition of the dependency relations into the annotation.

(1) 台南 縣 新化 警分局
Tainan county Xinhua police branch

刑事組 小 隊長
criminal group junior captain

林文政 昨天 下午
Lin Wenzheng yesterday afternoon

舉 槍 自戕 後 ，[5]
raise gun suicide after,

"After Lin Wenzheng, a junior captain with the Criminal Investigation Department of the Xinhua police branch of Tainan county, committed suicide by shooting himself yesterday afternoon,"

The hierarchical structure in Figure 1 is another way to represent the relation between governor and dependent, as illustrated in Figure 2. C1 immediately dominates C2, indicating that C1 is the governor and C2 the dependent. The relation between them is either R1 or R2. R1 is located at the same level as C1 and R2 is located at the same level as C2. These two possibilities could also be represented linearly as shown in (2).

| Concept | Relation | Concept |
|---|---|---|
| C1 | R1 | |
| | R2 | C2 |

**Figure 2: Relations between concepts**

(2) C1 [R1] → [R2] C2

R2 between the two concepts C1 and C2 should be read as "C2 is the R2 of C1". For example, "下午" (afternoon) is the ***time*** of "舉" (raise). R1 between C1 and C2 should be interpreted as "C1 is the R1 of C2". For example, the "time" between "後" (after) and "自戕" (suicide) should be interpreted as "後" is the ***time*** of "自戕".

The HowNet definitions of the concepts in (1) are provided in Table 2:

**[5] A string of Chinese characters ending with a punctuation mark is regarded as a unit for information structure annotation.**

**Table 2: An example of HowNet definitions**

<table>
<tr><th>Concept</th><th>Definition</th></tr>
<tr><td>台南</td><td>place|地方，city|市，ProperName|專，(China|中國)</td></tr>
<tr><td>縣</td><td>place|地方</td></tr>
<tr><td>新化</td><td>place|地方, ProperName|專, (Taiwan|台灣)</td></tr>
<tr><td>警分局</td><td>institution|機構, police|警, branch|支</td></tr>
<tr><td>刑事組</td><td>part|部件，%institution|機構，police|警</td></tr>
<tr><td>小</td><td>aValue|屬性值，importance|主次，secondary|次</td></tr>
<tr><td>隊長</td><td>human|人, #occupution|職位, official|官</td></tr>
<tr><td>林文政</td><td>human|人, ProperName|專</td></tr>
<tr><td>昨天</td><td>time|時間, past|昔, day|日</td></tr>
<tr><td>下午</td><td>time|時間, afternoon|午</td></tr>
<tr><td>舉</td><td>lift|提升</td></tr>
<tr><td>槍</td><td>weapon|武器, *firing|射擊</td></tr>
<tr><td>自戕</td><td>suicide|自殺</td></tr>
<tr><td>後</td><td>time|時間, future|將</td></tr>
<tr><td>，</td><td>{punc|標點}</td></tr>
</table>

The structures in Figure 1 and Table 2 reveal the following information:

(a) example (1) is about the time after a *'suicide'* event;

(b) preceding the 'suicide' event is the event *'raise'*;

(c) the ***time*** of the *'raise'* event is "昨天下午", the ***agent*** is "林文政" and the ***patient*** is a *'weapon'*;

(d) the *'occupation'* of "林文政" is "隊長" which is an *'official'* of *'secondary'* importance and "林文政" belongs to the *'institution'* "警分局刑事組";

(e) the location of the *'institution'* "警分局刑事組" is at "台南縣新化".

This kind of representation enables a computer to analyse texts at a deeper level of understanding. As an English and Chinese bilingual common-sense knowledge system, HowNet can contribute much to better text understanding and machine translation (Dong 1999).

# 4 Conclusion

The work reported here constitutes part of our efforts to develop a new strategy for Chinese text understanding. The strategy was proposed by Dong (1999). It starts with tagging each concept with the most probable HowNet definitions. The second step is to determine the information structures as described in this paper. The last step is to recover the implicit information structures from the surface information structures based on two additional knowledge sources: (i) relations between the event types as defined in HowNet; and (ii) rules governing the interplay of dynamic roles between event types. For example, the *'suicide'* event in example (1) does not mention its agent directly. The means of committing *'suicide'* by *'firing'* is also implicit. The recovery of this information will be the main issues to be resolved at the final stage. In parallel with our annotation effort, we are also working on developing automatic algorithms for the disambiguation of HowNet definitions and the identification of information structures. The creation of the two additional knowledge bases will be our future plan.


# Acknowledgements

This work was supported by the Hong Kong Research Grant Council. We would also like to thank Dong Zhendong. Without his advice, this work would not be possible.


# References


CKIP (1995) *中央研究院平衡語料庫的內容與說明, 技術報告95-02* [Technical Report no. 95-02, the content and illustration of Sinica corpus of Academia Sinica]. Institue of Information Science, Academia Sinica.

Dong, Zhendong (1999) *Bigger Context and Better Understanding – Expectation on Future MT Technology*. In "Proceedings of Intenational Conference on Machine Translation & Computer Language Information Processing", 26-28 June 1999, Beijing, China, pp. 17-25.

Dong Zhendong (2000) *中文信息結構模式* [The pattern of Chinese information structure], ms.

Fillmore C. J. (1968) *The case for case*. In "Universals in Linguistic Theory", E. Bach, R. Harms, eds., New York, Holt, Rinehart and Winston.

Gan, Kok-Wee and Wai-Mun Tham (1999) *基於知網的常識知識標註* [General Knowledge Annotation Based on HowNet], Computational Linguistics and Chinese Language Processing, vol. 4, 2, pp. 39-86.

Guo, Jin (1993) PH: A Chinese corpus. Communications of COLIPS, 3/1, pp. 45-48.

Marcus, Mitch (1997) Invited speech at the 5th Workshop on Very Large Corpora.

Mei, Jiaju, Yiming Lan, Yunqi Gao, Yongxiang Ying (1983) *同義詞詞林* [A Dictionary of Synonyms], Shanghai Cishu Chubanshe.

Xia, Fei, Martha Palmer, Nianwen Xue, Mary Ellen Okurowski, John Kovarik, Fu-Dong Chiou, Shizhe Huang, Tony Kroch and Mitch Marcus (2000) *Developing Guidelines and Ensuring Consistency for Chinese Text Annotation.* In "Proceedings of the second International Conference on Language Resources and Evaluation" (LREC-2000), Athens, Greece.

Xue, Nianwen, Fei Xia, Shizhe Huang, Anthony Kroch (1999) *The Bracketing Guidelines for the Penn Chinese Treebank (Draff II)*, http://www.upenn.edu/ctb/.

Yu, Shiwen, Qiang Zhou, Wei Zhang, Yunyun Zhang, Weidong Zhan, Baobao Chang, Zhifang Sui (1996) *Word segmented and POS tagged 12 volumes of Singapore Chinese primary school text.* Communications of COLIPS, 6(1), pp. 41.

**Table 1: A subset of information structures**

**Information structures of Coordination**

| | Type | SYN_S | Dependent | R2 | | Head | Example |
|---|---|---|---|---|---|---|---|
| 1 | Entity | N←N | Entity | [coordinate] | ← | Entity | 花-草，花-卉，禽-獸，風-浪，姓-名，官-兵，師-生，師-徒，部-委，飯-菜，夫-婦 |
| | | N←N | Part | [coordinate] | ← | Part | 皮-肉，骨-肉，手-腳，科-室，委-辦，章-節 |
| 2 | Attribute Value | A←A | Attribute Value | [coordinate] | ← | Attribute Value | 鮮-嫩，白-淨，富-強，窮-困，清-新，老-弱，物美-價廉，天真-活潑，年富-力強 |
| 3 | Event | V←V | Event | [coordinate] | ← | Event | 領-養，醫-護，醫-患，調-控，調-研，教-學，餐-飲，哭-喊，哭-訴，生-死，存-亡 |

**Information structures of Patient**

| | Type | SYN_S | Head | R1 | | R2 | Dependent | Example |
|---|---|---|---|---|---|---|---|---|
| 1 | Head initial | V→N | Event | | → | [patient] | Thing | 吃-飯，賣-國，理-髮，染-髮，害-人，害-己，殺-敵，輸-血，侵-權，侵-華 |
| | | V→N | Event, Act, Pass | | → | [patient] | Time | 度-日，過-年，過-冬，過-夜，越-冬，享-年，共度-難關，度過-難關 |
| | | V→N | Event | | → | [patient] | Event | 深化-改革，改善-供應，加強-管理，加強-領導，加強-團結，加強-學習 |
| | | V→N | Event, Act | | → | [patient] | Attribute Value | 刪-繁，就-簡，去-舊，增-新，吐-故，納-新，獎-勤，罰-懶，反-腐，倡-廉 |

| | Type | SYN_S | Dependent | R2 | | R1 | Head | Example |
|---|---|---|---|---|---|---|---|---|
| 2 | Head final | V←N | Event, Act | | ← | [patient] | Thing | 僱-員，選-手，囚-犯，囚-徒，愛-人，棄-嬰，棄-婦，使-女，遺-言，遺-願 |
| | | V←N | Event | | ← | [patient] | Thing | 獵-物，產-物，造-物，建築-物，產-品，制-品，廢-品，批-語，製成-品，半成-品 |
| | | N←V | Thing/ Part | [patient] | ← | | Event, Act | 蔬-食，貨-運，客-運，水-污染，文物-走私，毒品-走私，貨物-運輸，旅客-運輸 |

## Figure 1: A Graphical View of Information Structures

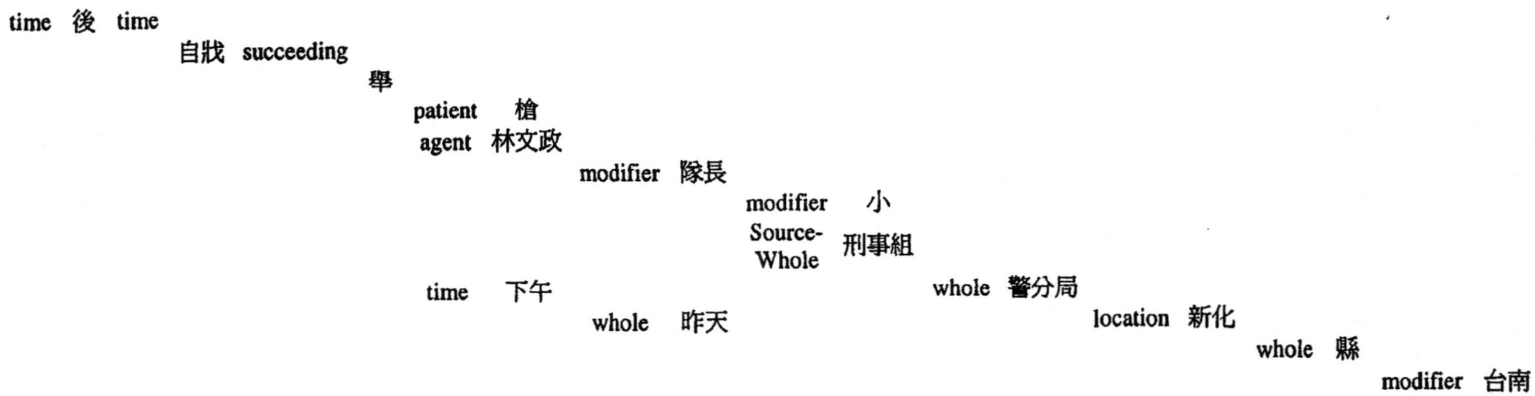

# Machine Learning Methods for Chinese Web Page Categorization

**Ji He[1], Ah-Hwee Tan[2] and Chew-Lim Tan[1]**
[1]School of Computing, National University of Singapore
10 Kent Ridge Crescent, Singapore 119260
{heji,tancl}@comp.nus.edu.sg
[2]Kent Ridge Digital Labs
21 Heng Mui Keng Terrace, Singapore 119613
ahhwee@krdl.org.sg

## Abstract

This paper reports our evaluation of *k* Nearest Neighbor (kNN), Support Vector Machines (SVM), and Adaptive Resonance Associative Map (ARAM) on Chinese web page classification. Benchmark experiments based on a Chinese web corpus showed that their predictive performance were roughly comparable although ARAM and kNN slightly outperformed SVM in small categories. In addition, inserting rules into ARAM helped to improve performance, especially for small well-defined categories.

## 1 Introduction

Text categorization refers to the task of automatically assigning one or multiple predefined category labels to free text documents. Whereas an extensive range of methods has been applied to English text categorization, relatively few have been benchmarked for Chinese text categorization. Typical approaches to Chinese text categorization, such as Naive Bayes (NB) (Zhu, 1987), Vector Space Model (VSM) (Zou et al., 1998; Zou et al., 1999) and Linear List Square Fit (LLSF) (Cao et al., 1999; Yang, 1994), have well studied theoretical basis derived from the information retrieval research, but are not known to be the best classifiers (Yang and Liu, 1999; Yang, 1999). In addition, there is a lack of publicly available Chinese corpus for evaluating Chinese text categorization systems.

This paper reports our applications of three statistical machine learning methods, namely *k* Nearest Neighbor system (kNN) (Dasarathy, 1991), Support Vector Machines (SVM) (Cortes and Vapnik, 1995), and Adaptive Resonance Associative Map (ARAM) (Tan, 1995) to Chinese web page categorization. kNN and SVM have been reported as the top performing methods for English text categorization (Yang and Liu, 1999). ARAM belongs to a popularly known family of predictive self-organizing neural networks which until recently has not been used for document classification. The trio has been evaluated based on a Chinese corpus consisting of news articles extracted from People's Daily (He et al., 2000). This article reports the experiments of a much more challenging task in classifying Chinese web pages. The Chinese web corpus was created by downloading from various Chinese web sites covering a wide variety of topics. There is a great diversity among the web pages in terms of document length, style, and content. The objectives of our experiments are two-folded. First, we examine and compare the capabilities of these methods in learning categorization knowledge from real-life web documents. Second, we investigate if incorporating domain knowledge derived from the category description can enhance ARAM's predictive performance.

The rest of this article is organized as follows. Section 2 describes our choice of the feature selection and extraction methods. Section 3 gives a summary of the kNN and SVM, and presents the less familiar ARAM algorithm in more details. Section 4 presents our evaluation paradigm and reports the experimental results.

## 2 Feature Selection and Extraction

A pre-requisite of text categorization is to extract a suitable feature representation of the documents. Typically, word stems are suggested as the representation units by information retrieval research. However, unlike English and other Indo-European languages, Chinese text does not have a natural delimiter between words. As a consequence, word segmentation is a major issue in Chinese document processing. Chinese word segmentation methods have been extensively discussed in the literature. Unfortunately perfect precision and disambiguation cannot be reached. As a result, the inherent errors caused by word segmentation always remains as a problem in Chinese information processing.

In our experiments, a word-class bi-gram model is adopted to segment each training document into a set of tokens. The lexicon used by the segmentation model contains 64,000 words in 1,006 classes. High precision segmentation is not the focus of our work. Instead we aim to compare different classifier's performance on noisy document set as long as the errors caused by word segmentation are reasonably low.

To select keyword features for classification, $\chi$ (CHI) statistics is adopted as the ranking metric in our experiments. A prior study on several well-known corpora including Reuters-21578 and OHSUMED has proven that CHI statistics generally outperforms other feature ranking measures, such as term strength (TS), document frequency (DF), mutual information (MI), and information gain (IG) (Yang and J.P, 1997).

During keyword extraction, the document is first segmented and converted into a keyword frequency vector $(tf_1, tf_2, \ldots, tf_M)$, where $tf_i$ is the in-document term frequency of keyword $w_i$, and $M$ is the number of the keyword features selected. A term weighting method based on *inverse document frequency* (IDF) (Salton, 1988) and the L1-normalization are then applied on the frequency vector to produce the keyword feature vector

$$\mathbf{x} = \frac{(x_1, x_2, \ldots, x_M)}{\max\{x_i\}}, \quad (1)$$

in which $x_i$ is computed by

$$x_i = (1 + \log_2 tf_i) \log_2 \frac{n}{n_i}, \quad (2)$$

where $n$ is the number of documents in the whole training set, and $n_i$ is the number of training documents in which the keyword $w_i$ occurs at least once.

## 3 The Classifiers

### 3.1 $k$ Nearest Neighbor

$k$ Nearest Neighbor (kNN) is a traditional statistical pattern recognition algorithm (Dasarathy, 1991). It has been studied extensively for text categorization (Yang and Liu, 1999). In essence, kNN makes the prediction based on the $k$ training patterns that are closest to the unseen (test) pattern, according to a distance metric. The distance metric that measures the similarity between two normalized patterns can be either a simple L1-distance function or a L2-distance function, such as the plain Euclidean distance defined by

$$D(\mathbf{a}, \mathbf{b}) = \sqrt{\sum_i (a_i - b_i)^2}. \quad (3)$$

The class assignment to the test pattern is based on the class assignment of the closest $k$ training patterns. A commonly used method is to label the test pattern with the class that has the most instances among the $k$ nearest neighbors. Specifically, the class index $y(x)$ assigned to the test pattern $\mathbf{x}$ is given by

$$y(x) = \text{argmax}_i\{n(\mathbf{d}_j, c_i) | \mathbf{d}_j \in kNN\}, \quad (4)$$

where $n(\mathbf{d}_j, c_i)$ is the number of training pattern $\mathbf{d}_j$ in the $k$ nearest neighbor set that are associated with class $c_i$.

The drawback of kNN is the difficulty in deciding a optimal $k$ value. Typically it has to be determined through conducting a series of experiments using different values.

### 3.2 Support Vector Machines

Support Vector Machines (SVM) is a relatively new class of machine learning techniques first introduced by Vapnik (Cortes and Vapnik, 1995). Based on the *structural risk minimization* principle from the computational learning theory, SVM seeks a decision surface to separate the training data points into two classes and makes decisions based on the *support vectors* that are selected as the only effective elements from the training set.

Given a set of linearly separable points $S = \{\mathbf{x}_i \in \mathbf{R}^n | i = 1, 2, \ldots, N\}$, each point $\mathbf{x}_i$ belongs to one of the two classes, labeled as $y_i \in \{-1, +1\}$. A *separating hyper-plane* divides $S$ into two sides, each side containing points with the same class label only. The *separating hyper-plane* can be identified by the pair $(\mathbf{w}, b)$ that satisfies

$$\begin{aligned} &\mathbf{w} \cdot \mathbf{x} + b = 0 \\ \text{and} \quad &y_i(\mathbf{w} \cdot \mathbf{x}_i + b) \geq 1 \end{aligned} \tag{5}$$

for $i = 1, 2, \ldots, N$; where the dot product operation $\cdot$ is defined by

$$\mathbf{w} \cdot \mathbf{x} = \sum_i w_i x_i \tag{6}$$

for vectors $\mathbf{w}$ and $\mathbf{x}$. Thus the goal of the SVM learning is to find the *optimal separating hyper-plane* (*OSH*) that has the maximal margin to both sides. This can be formularized as:

$$\begin{aligned} \text{minimize} \quad & \tfrac{1}{2}\mathbf{w} \cdot \mathbf{w} \\ \text{subject to} \quad & y_i(\mathbf{w} \cdot \mathbf{x}_i + b) \geq 1 \end{aligned} \tag{7}$$

The points that are closest to the *OSH* are termed *support vectors* (Fig. 1).

The SVM problem can be extended to linearly non-separable case and non-linear case. Various quadratic programming algorithms have been proposed and extensively studied to solve the SVM problem (Cortes and Vapnik, 1995; Joachims, 1998; Joachims, 1999).

During classification, SVM makes decision based on the *OSH* instead of the whole training set. It simply finds out on which side of the *OSH* the test pattern is located.

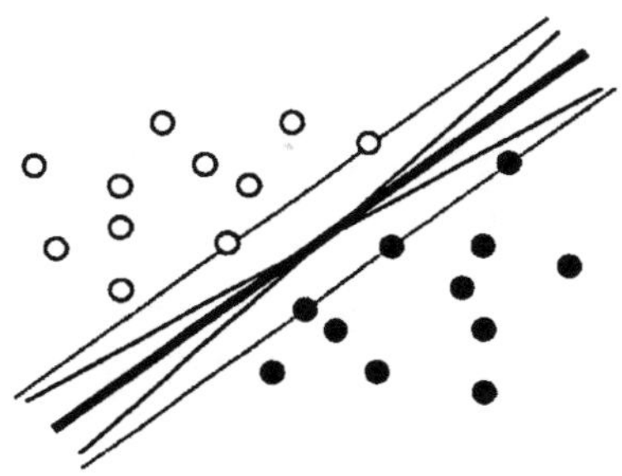

Figure 1: *Separating hyperplanes* (the set of solid lines), *optimal separating hyperplane* (the bold solid line), and *support vectors* (data points on the dashed lines). The dashed lines identify the max margin.

This property makes SVM highly competitive, compared with other traditional pattern recognition methods, in terms of computational efficiency and predictive accuracy (Yang and Liu, 1999).

In recent years, Joachims has done much research on the application of SVM to text categorization (Joachims, 1998). His $SVM^{light}$ system published via http://www-ai.cs.uni-dortmund.de/FORSCHUNG/VERFAHREN/SVM_LIGHT/svm_light.eng.html is used in our benchmark experiments.

### 3.3 Adaptive Resonance Associative Map

Adaptive Resonance Associative Map (ARAM) is a class of predictive self-organizing neural networks that performs incremental supervised learning of recognition categories (pattern classes) and multidimensional maps of patterns. An ARAM system can be visualized as two overlapping Adaptive Resonance Theory (ART) modules consisting of two input fields $F_1^a$ and $F_1^b$ with an $F_2$ category field (Tan, 1995; Tan, 1997) (Fig. 2). For classification problems, the $F_1^a$ field serves as the input field containing the document feature vector and the $F_1^b$ field serves as the output field containing the class prediction vector. The $F_2$ field contains the activities of the recognition categories that are used to encode the patterns.

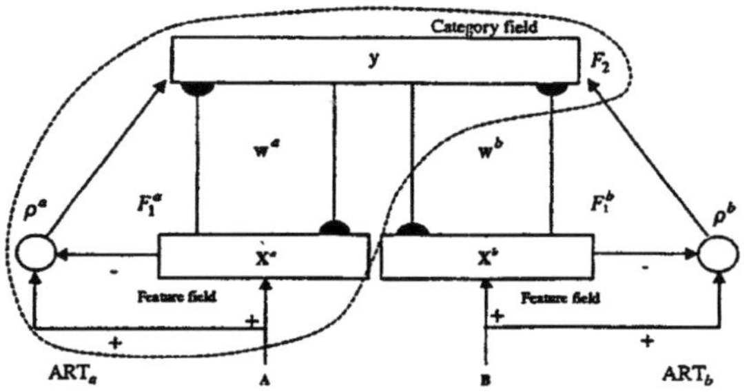


Figure 2: The Adaptive Resonance Associative Map architecture

When performing classification tasks, ARAM formulates recognition categories of input patterns, and associates each category with its respective prediction. During learning, given an input pattern (document feature) presented at the $F_1^a$ input layer and an output pattern (known class label) presented at the $F_1^b$ output field, the category field $F_2$ selects a winner that receives the largest overall input. The winning node selected in $F_2$ then triggers a top-down priming on $F_1^a$ and $F_1^b$, monitored by separate reset mechanisms. Code stabilization is ensured by restricting encoding to states where resonance are reached in both modules. By synchronizing the unsupervised categorization of two pattern sets, ARAM learns supervised mapping between the pattern sets. Due to the code stabilization mechanism, fast learning in a real-time environment is feasible.

The knowledge that ARAM discovers during learning is compatible with IF-THEN rule-based presentation. Specifically, each node in the $F_2$ field represents a recognition category associating the $F_1^a$ patterns with the $F_1^b$ output vectors. Learned weight vectors, one for each $F_2$ node, constitute a set of rules that link antecedents to consequences. At any point during the incremental learning process, the system architecture can be translated into a compact set of rules. Similarly, domain knowledge in the form of IF-THEN rules can be inserted into ARAM architecture.

The ART modules used in ARAM can be ART 1, which categorizes binary patterns, or analog ART modules such as ART 2, ART 2-A, and fuzzy ART, which categorize both binary and analog patterns. The fuzzy ARAM (Tan, 1995) algorithm based on fuzzy ART (Carpenter et al., 1991) is introduced below.

**Parameters:** Fuzzy ARAM dynamics are determined by the choice parameters $\alpha_a > 0$ and $\alpha_b > 0$; the learning rates $\beta_a \in [0,1]$ and $\beta_b \in [0,1]$; the vigilance parameters $\rho_a \in [0,1]$ and $\rho_b \in [0,1]$; and the contribution parameter $\gamma \in [0,1]$.

**Weight vectors:** Each $F_2$ category node $j$ is associated with two adaptive weight templates $\mathbf{w}_j^a$ and $\mathbf{w}_j^b$. Initially, all category nodes are uncommitted and all weights equal ones. After a category node is selected for encoding, it becomes *committed*.

**Category choice:** Given the $F_1^a$ and $F_1^b$ input vectors $\mathbf{A}$ and $\mathbf{B}$, for each $F_2$ node $j$, the choice function $T_j$ is defined by

$$T_j = \gamma \frac{|\mathbf{A} \wedge \mathbf{w}_j^a|}{\alpha_a + |\mathbf{w}_j^a|} + (1-\gamma)\frac{|\mathbf{B} \wedge \mathbf{w}_j^b|}{\alpha_b + |\mathbf{w}_j^b|}, \quad (8)$$

where the fuzzy AND operation $\wedge$ is defined by

$$(\mathbf{p} \wedge \mathbf{q})_i \equiv min(p_i, q_i), \quad (9)$$

and where the norm $|.|$ is defined by

$$|\mathbf{p}| \equiv \sum_i p_i \quad (10)$$

for vectors $\mathbf{p}$ and $\mathbf{q}$.

The system is said to make a choice when at most one $F_2$ node can become active. The choice is indexed at $J$ where

$$T_J = \max\{T_j : \text{for all } F_2 \text{ node } j\}. \quad (11)$$

When a category choice is made at node $J$, $y_J = 1$; and $y_j = 0$ for all $j \neq J$.

**Resonance or reset:** Resonance occurs if the *match functions*, $m_J^a$ and $m_J^b$, meet the vigilance criteria in their respective modules:

$$m_J^a = \frac{|\mathbf{A} \wedge \mathbf{w}_J^a|}{|\mathbf{A}|} \geq \rho_a \quad (12)$$

and

$$m_J^b = \frac{|\mathbf{B} \wedge \mathbf{w}_J^b|}{|\mathbf{B}|} \geq \rho_b. \quad (13)$$

Learning then ensues, as defined below. If any of the vigilance constraints is violated, mismatch reset occurs in which the value of the choice function $T_J$ is set to 0 for the duration of the input presentation. The search process repeats to select another new index $J$ until resonance is achieved.

**Learning:** Once the search ends, the weight vectors $\mathbf{w}_J^a$ and $\mathbf{w}_J^b$ are updated according to the equations

$$\mathbf{w}_J^{a(\text{new})} = (1-\beta_a)\mathbf{w}_J^{a(\text{old})} + \beta_a(\mathbf{A} \wedge \mathbf{w}_J^{a(\text{old})}) \tag{14}$$

and

$$\mathbf{w}_J^{b(\text{new})} = (1-\beta_b)\mathbf{w}_J^{b(\text{old})} + \beta_b(\mathbf{B} \wedge \mathbf{w}_J^{b(\text{old})}) \tag{15}$$

respectively. *Fast learning* corresponds to setting $\beta_a = \beta_b = 1$ for committed nodes.

**Classification:** During classification, using the choice rule, only the $F_2$ node $J$ that receives maximal $F_1^a \rightarrow F_2$ input $T_j$ predicts $\text{ART}_b$ output. In simulations,

$$y_j = \begin{cases} 1 & \text{if } j = J \text{ where } T_J > T_k \\ & \text{for all } k \neq J \\ 0 & \text{otherwise.} \end{cases} \tag{16}$$

The $F_1^b$ activity vector $\mathbf{x}^b$ is given by

$$\mathbf{x}^b = \sum_j \mathbf{w}_j^b y_j = \mathbf{w}_J^b. \tag{17}$$

The output prediction vector $\mathbf{B}$ is then given by

$$\mathbf{B} \equiv (b_1, b_2, \ldots b_N) = \mathbf{x}^b \tag{18}$$

where $b_i$ indicates the likelihood or confidence of assigning a pattern to category $i$.

**Rule insertion:** Rule insertion proceeds in two phases. The first phase parses the rules for keyword features. When a new keyword is encountered, it is added to a keyword feature table containing keywords obtained through automatic feature selection from training documents. Based on the keyword feature table, the second phase of rule insertion translates each rule into a M-dimensional vector **a** and a N-dimensional vector **b**, where $M$ is the total number of features in the keyword feature table and $N$ is the number of categories. Given a rule of the following format,

IF $x_1, x_2, \ldots, x_m$
THEN $y_1, y_2, \ldots, y_n$

where $x_1, \ldots, x_m$ are antecedents and $y_1, \ldots, y_n$ are consequences, the algorithm derives a pair of vectors **a** and **b** such that for each index $i = 1, \ldots, M$,

$$a_i = \begin{cases} 1 & \text{if } w_i = x_j \text{ for some } j \in \{1, \ldots, m\} \\ 0 & \text{otherwise} \end{cases} \tag{19}$$

where $w_i$ is the $i^{th}$ entry in the keyword feature table; and for each index $i = 1, \ldots, N$,

$$b_i = \begin{cases} 1 & \text{if } w_i = y_j \text{ for some } j \in \{1, \ldots, n\} \\ 0 & \text{otherwise} \end{cases} \tag{20}$$

where $w_i$ is the class label of the category $i$.

The vector pairs derived from the rules are then used as training patterns to initialize a ARAM network. During rule insertion, the vigilance parameters $\rho_a$ and $\rho_b$ are each set to 1 to ensure that only identical attribute vectors are grouped into one recognition category. Contradictory symbolic rules are detected during rule insertion when identical input attribute vectors are associated with distinct output attribute vectors.

## 4 Empirical Evaluation

### 4.1 The Chinese Web Corpus

The Chinese web corpus, collected in-house, consists of web pages downloaded from various Chinese web sites covering a wide variety of topics. Our experiments are based on a subset of the corpus consisting of 8 top-level categories and over 6,000 documents. For each category, we conduct binary classification experiments in which we tag the current category as the positive category and the other seven categories as the negative categories. The corpus is further partitioned into training and testing data such that the number of the training documents is at least 2.5 times of that of the testing documents (Table 1).

Table 1: The eight top-level categories in the Chinese web corpus, and the training and test samples by category.

| Category | Description | Train | Test |
|---|---|---|---|
| *Art* | Topic regarding literature, art | 325 | 102 |
| *Belief* | Philosophy and religious beliefs | 131 | 40 |
| *Biz* | Business | 2647 | 727 |
| *Edu* | Education | 205 | 77 |
| *IT* | Computer and internet informatics | 1085 | 309 |
| *Joy* | Online fresh, interesting info | 636 | 216 |
| *Med* | Medical care related web sites | 155 | 57 |
| *Sci* | Various kinds of science | 119 | 39 |

Table 2: A sample set of 19 rules generated based on the accompanied description of the Chinese web categories.

| | | |
|---|---|---|
| *Art* | :- | 国画 (Chinese painting) |
| *Belief* | :- | 祷告 (pray) 法师 (rabbi) |
| *Biz* | :- | 促销 (promotion) 房地产 (real estate) 客户 (client) |
| *Edu* | :- | 本科 (undergraduate) 导师 (supervisor) 校园 (campus) |
| *IT* | :- | 版本 (version) 病毒 (virus) 防火墙 (firewall) 程式 (program) |
| *Joy* | :- | 灯谜 (lantern riddle) |
| *Med* | :- | 保健 (health care) 处方 (prescription) 法医学 (medical jurisprudence) |
| *Sci* | :- | 超自然 (supernaturalism) 高技术 (high technology) |

### 4.2 Experiment Paradigm

kNN experiments used the plain Euclidean distance defined by equation (3) as the similarity measure. On each pattern set containing a varying number of documents, different values of $k$ ranging from 1 to 29 were tested and the best results were recorded. Only odd $k$ were used to ensure that a prediction can always be made.

SVM experiments used the default built-in inductive SVM parameter set in $SVM^{light}$, which is described in detail on the web site and elsewhere (Joachims, 1999).

ARAM experiments employed a standard set of parameter values of fuzzy ARAM. In addition, using a voting strategy, 5 ARAM systems were trained using the same set of patterns in different orders of presentation and were combined to yield a final prediction vector.

To derive domain theory on web page classification, a varying number (ranging from 10 to 30) of training documents from each category were reviewed. A set of domain knowledge consists of 56 rules with about one to 10 rules for each category was generated. Only positive rules that link keyword antecedents to positive category consequences were included (Table 2).

### 4.3 Performance Measures

Our experiments adopt the most commonly used performance measures, including the *recall*, *precision*, and $F_1$ measures. *Recall* ($R$) is the percentage of the documents for a given category that are classified correctly. *Precision* ($P$) is the percentage of the predicted documents for a given category that are classified correctly. $F_1$ rating is one of the commonly used measures to combine $R$ and $P$ into a single rating, defined as

$$F_1 = \frac{2RP}{(R+P)}. \tag{21}$$

These scores are calculated for a series of binary classification experiments, one for each category. Micro-averaged scores and macro-averaged scores on the whole corpus are then produced across the experiments. With micro-averaging, the performance measures are produced across the documents by adding up all the documents counts across the different tests, and calculating using these summed values. With macro-averaging, each category is assigned with the same weight and performance measures are calculated across the categories. It is understandable that micro-averaged scores and macro-averaged scores reflect a classifier's performance on large categories and small categories respectively (Yang and Liu, 1999).

Table 3: Predictive performance of the four classifiers on the Chinese web corpus.

| | kNN | | | SVM | | |
|---|---|---|---|---|---|---|
| Category | $P$ | $R$ | $F_1$ | $P$ | $R$ | $F_1$ |
| *Art* | .795 | .304 | .440 | .398 | .402 | .400 |
| *Belief* | .773 | .425 | .548 | .556 | .500 | .526 |
| *Biz* | .724 | .689 | .706 | .692 | .703 | .698 |
| *Edu* | .380 | .351 | .365 | .602 | .074 | .180 |
| *IT* | .309 | .333 | .321 | .394 | .307 | .345 |
| *Joy* | .381 | .236 | .291 | .462 | .255 | .328 |
| *Med* | .833 | .351 | .494 | .330 | .544 | .411 |
| *Sci* | .625 | .128 | .213 | .137 | .179 | .156 |
| Micro-ave. | .584 | .482 | .528 | .523 | .521 | .522 |
| Macro-ave. | .600 | .352 | .422 | .384 | .454 | .380 |

| | ARAM | | | ARAM w/rules | | |
|---|---|---|---|---|---|---|
| Category | $P$ | $R$ | $F_1$ | $P$ | $R$ | $F_1$ |
| *Art* | .653 | .461 | .540 | .706 | .471 | **.565** |
| *Belief* | .750 | .750 | .750 | .714 | .750 | .732 |
| *Biz* | .742 | .622 | .677 | .745 | .604 | .667 |
| *Edu* | .421 | .312 | .358 | .420 | .273 | .331 |
| *IT* | .444 | .259 | .327 | .437 | .291 | **.350** |
| *Joy* | .600 | .208 | .309 | .618 | .194 | .296 |
| *Med* | .421 | .421 | .421 | .448 | .456 | **.452** |
| *Sci* | .292 | .179 | .222 | .409 | .231 | **.295** |
| Micro-ave. | .619 | .453 | .523 | .628 | .450 | **.524** |
| Macro-ave. | .540 | .402 | .451 | .562 | .409 | **.461** |

### 4.4 Results and Discussions

Table 3 summarizes the three classifier's performances on the test corpus in terms of *precision*, *recall*, and $F_1$ measures. The micro-averaged scores produced by the trio, which were predominantly determined by the classifiers' performance on the large categories (such as *Biz*, *IT*, and *Joy*), were roughly comparable. Among the three, kNN seemed to be marginally better than SVM and ARAM. Inserting rules into ARAM did not have a significant impact. This showed that domain knowledge was not very useful for categories that already have a large number of training examples. The differences in the macro-averaged scores produced by the three classifiers, however, were much more significant. The macro-averaged $F_1$ score obtained by ARAM was noticeably better than that of kNN, which in turn was higher than that of SVM. This indicates that ARAM (and kNN) tends to outperform SVM in small categories that have a smaller number of training patterns.

We are particularly interested in the classifier's learning ability on small categories. In certain applications, such as personalized content delivery, a large pre-labeled training corpus may not be available. Therefore, a classifier's ability of learning from a small training pattern set is a major concern. The different approaches adopted by these three classifiers in learning categorization knowledge are best seen in the light of the distinct learning peculiarities they exhibit on the small training sets.

kNN is a lazy learning method in the sense that it does not carry out any off-line learning to generate a particular category knowledge representation. Instead, kNN performs on-line scoring to find the training patterns that are nearest to a test pattern and makes the decision based on the statistical presumption that patterns in the same category have similar feature representations. The presumption is basically true to most pattern instances. Thus kNN exhibits a relatively stable performance across small and large categories.

SVM identifies *optimal separating hyperplane* (*OSH*) across the training data points and makes classification decisions based on the representative data instances (known as *support vectors*). Compared with kNN, SVM is more computationally efficient during classification for large-scale training sets. However, the *OSH* generated using small training sets may not be very representative, especially when the training patterns are sparsely distributed and there is a relatively narrow margin between the positive and negative patterns. In our experiments on small training sets including *Art*, *Belief*, *Edu*, and *Sci*, SVM's performance were generally lower than those of kNN and ARAM.

ARAM generates recognition categories from the input training patterns. The incrementally learned rules abstract the major representations of the training patterns and eliminate minor inconsistencies in the data patterns. During classifying, it works in a similar fashion as kNN. The major difference is that ARAM uses the learned recognition categories as the similarity-scoring unit whereas kNN uses the raw in-processed training patterns as the distance-scoring unit. It follows that ARAM is notably more scalable than kNN by its pattern abstraction capability and therefore is more suitable for handling very large data sets.

The overall improvement in predictive performance obtained by inserting rules into ARAM is also of particular interest to us. ARAM's performance was more likely to be improved by rule insertion in categories that are well defined and have relatively fewer numbers of training patterns. As long as a user is able to abstract the category knowledge into certain specific rule representation, domain knowledge could complement the limited knowledge acquired through a small training set quite effectively.

## Acknowledgements

We would like to thank our colleagues, Jian Su and Guo-Dong Zhou, for providing the Chinese segmentation software and Fon-Lin Lai for his valuable suggestions in designing the experiment system. In addition, we thank T. Joachims at the University of Dortmund for making $SVM^{light}$ available.

## References

Suqing Cao, Fuhu Zeng, and Huanguang Cao. 1999. A mathematical model for automatic Chinese text categorization. *Journal of the China Society for Scientific and Technical Information [in Chinese]*, 1999(1).

G.A. Carpenter, S. Grossberg, and D.B. Rosen. 1991. Fuzzy ART: Fast stable learning and categorization of analog patterns by an adaptive resonance system. *Neural Networks*, 4:759–771.

C. Cortes and V. Vapnik. 1995. Support vector networks. *Machine learning*, 20:273–297.

Belur V. Dasarathy. 1991. *Nearest Neighbor (NN) Norms: NN Pattern Classification Techniques*. IEEE Computer Society Press, Las Alamitos, California.

Ji He, A.-H. Tan, and Chew-Lim Tan. 2000. A comparative study on Chinese text categorization methods. In *PRICAI'2000 International Workshop on Text and Web Mining*, Melbourne, August.

T. Joachims. 1998. Text categorization with support vector machines: Learning with many relevant features. In *Proceedings of the European Conference on Machine Learning*, Springer.

T. Joachims. 1999. *Making large-Scales SVM learning Pracical. Advances in Kernel Methods - Support Vector Learning*. B. Scholkopf, C. Burges and A. Smola (ed.), MIT Press.

Salton. 1988. Term weighting approaches in automatic text retrieval. *Information Processing and Management*, 24(5):513–523.

A.-H. Tan. 1995. Adaptive resonance associative map. *Neural Networks*, 8(3):437–446.

A.-H. Tan. 1997. Cascade ARTMAP: Integrating neural computation and symbolic knowledge processing. *IEEE Transactions on Neural Networks*, 8(2):237–235.

Y. Yang and Pedersen J.P. 1997. A comparative study on feature selection in text categorization. In *the Fourteenth International Conference on Machine Learning (ICML'97)*, pages 412–420.

Y. Yang and X. Liu. 1999. A re-examination of text categorization methods. In *22nd Annual International ACM SIGIR Conference on Research and Development in Information Retrieval (SIGIR'99)*, pages 42–49.

Y. Yang. 1994. Expert network: Effective and efficient learning from human decisions in text categorization and retrieval. In *17th Annual International ACM SIGIR Conference on Research and Development in Information Retrieval (SIGIR'94)*.

Y. Yang. 1999. An evaluation of statistical approaches to text categorization. *Journal of Information Retrieval*, 1(1/2):67–88.

Lanjuan Zhu. 1987. The theory and experiments on automatic Chinese documents classification. *Journal of the China Society for Scientific and Technical Information [in Chinese]*, 1987(6).

Tao Zou, Ji-Cheng Wang, Yuan Huang, and Fu-Yan Zhang. 1998. The design and implementation of an automatic Chinese documents classification system. *Journal for Chinese Information [in Chinese]*, 1998(2).

Tao Zou, Yuan Huang, and Fuyan Zhang. 1999. Technology of information mining on WWW. *Journal of the China Society for Scientific and Technical Information [in Chinese]*, 1999(4).

# Semantic Annotation of Chinese Phrases Using Recursive-Graph

**Ji Donghong**
Kent Ridge Digital Labs,
Singapore, 119613
dhji@krdl.org.sg

## Abstract

In this paper, we propose a recursive graph based scheme for semantic annotation of Chinese phrases. Compared with others, this scheme can fully differentiate those Chinese phrases that comprise the same content words but hold different meanings due to their different word order or some involved function words, and capture the hierarchical conceptual structure of Chinese phrases, which underlies their main semantic information. We also give the guidelines for annotating various commonly used types of Chinese phrases.

## 1 Introduction

Semantically annotated linguistic data are important resources for natural language processing, and have been used in many NLP areas, e.g., parsing, word sense disambiguation, co-reference resolution and information extraction, etc. But due to huge efforts needed in building them and general difficulties in dealing with semantic information, such resources are scarcely seen for most languages including Chinese, if not all.

In this paper, we focus on Chinese phrases and present a recursive graph based scheme for their semantic annotation. Compared with the same task for sentences, it only involves a relatively small data set and simple semantic information but has potential generality and application.

As a specific semantic annotation task, two problems should be made clear at first. One is at which goal the annotation is aimed. In our case, the goal is established to be to help disclose the correspondence between linguistic forms and meaning, which is also the primary goal in both traditional linguistic research (Chomsky, 1968) and natural language understanding (Allen, 1995).

The other problem is whether the annotation can significantly contribute to the established goal. In our case, the answer is of course positive. First, the phrases themselves are a specific kind of linguistic forms, thus their semantic annotation directly provides the correspondence between them and their meanings. Second, by some kinds of analogy rules, these annotated phrases can be examples for deriving the correspondence between new phrases and their meanings. Third, as compared with western languages, Chinese language has a specific feature that its sentences form in roughly the same way as its phrases (Zhu, 1982), which shows that by some kinds of combinatory rules, the mapping between sentences and their meanings can also be determined based on the examples.

The remainder of this paper is organised as the following. In section 2, we describe the motivation of introducing recursive graph. In section 3, we formally define what is a recursive graph. In section 4, we specify how commonly used types of Chinese phrases are annotated using recursive graph. In section 5, we give the conclusion and discuss some future work.

## 2 Motivation

In general, semantic annotation of linguistic forms is to associate with them their semantic information being represented in some formal languages or diagrams. With the semantic information involved varying, the formal languages or diagrams may be different.

One commonly used diagram for semantic annotation of linguistic forms is dependent tree, in which the *dependence* or *control* relationship between constituents of a linguistic form is depicted (Langacker, 1997). But such trees may be not powerful enough to differentiate those Chinese phrases that comprise the same content words but hold different meanings due to their word order or involved function words. As an example, consider 1) and 2)[1].

1) 走私 /zousi/ smuggle　汽车 /qiche/ car

2) 汽车 /qiche/ car　走私 /zousi/ smuggle

Notice 1) and 2) contain the same content words, but hold different word order. Regarding their meanings, 1) is an ambiguous phrase, corresponding with two English translation phrases as 3) and 4).

3) to smuggle cars

4) smuggled cars

The translation phrase for 2) is 5).

5) the smuggling of cars

So, there are altogether three meanings held by the two phrases. But the two content words can only form two dependent trees, listed in 6) and 7).

6) 汽车 (/qiche/, car)
↑
走私(/zousi/, smuggle)

7) 走私(/zousi/, smuggle)
↑
汽车 (/qiche/, car)

Obviously, these two dependent trees cannot code the three meanings listed in 3), 4) and 5). Only if we could see the same word 走私(/zousi/, smuggle) semantically different in 1) and 2), we could add another dependent tree 8) to code 5), with 6) and 7) corresponding with 3) and 4) respectively.

8) 走私'(/zousi/, smuggle)[2]
↑
汽车 (/qiche/, car)

But this view is quite unintuitive, and will lead to contradictory. Consider other two phrases 9) and 10).

9) 走私 /zousi/ smuggle　集团 /jituan/ bloc
smuggling bloc

10) 汽车 /qiche/ car　走私 /zousi/ smuggle　集团 /jituan/ bloc
car smuggling bloc

Intuitively, the word 走私(/zousi/, smuggle) in 2) holds the same meaning as the word in 10), which subsequently is equivalent with the same word in 9). On the other hand, there is no reason to treat the same word 走私(/zousi/, smuggle) semantically differently in 1) and 9), two typical noun

[1] In this paper, whenever listing a Chinese word, we always list its Pinyin included within two symbols '/', and its English translation. For a Chinese phrase, we furthermore list its English translation when necessary.

[2] To differentiate the two words, we add one quotation mark.

phrases. Particularly, they are both followed by a typical noun in the two phrases.

The second problem for dependent tree to semantically annotate linguistic forms is that due to its tree nature, it cannot represent *multi-dependence* relationship, in which one node is *controlled* by several nodes. For example, consider 11).

11) 喜欢 自己 的 人
/xihuan/ /ziji/ /de/ /ren/
like self of people
the people who like oneself

Conventionally, its dependent tree should be 12).

12) 人 (/ren/, people)
↑
喜欢 (/xihuan/, like)
↑
自己 (/ziji/, self)

But intuitively, there should be some *dependence* relationship between 人(/ren/, people) and 自己 (/ziji/, self). If we add this relationship, it will become a graph.

## 2.2 Conceptual Graph

Conceptual graph is another diagram for semantic annotation of linguistic forms, which comprises *concepts* and *conceptual relationship* denoted by linguistic forms (Eklund, 1996). Although it is claimed to be a directed graph in its original form, it is equivalent to an undirected graph in nature, with its relationship nodes and their directed edges replaced with an undirected edge to directly denote the relationship.

One problem with this diagram for semantic annotation is that it cannot code the information about *head*, if any, in a linguistic form, which intuitively specifies the main information carried by a linguistic form. This will lead to severe problems when using the graph to represent linguistic forms. For example, both phrases 1) and 2) with all three meanings 3), 4) and 5) would be represented by the same diagram as in 13)[3].

13) 走私 ———— 汽车
(/zousi/, smuggle) (/qiche/, car)

To differentiate the three meanings held by the two phrases, we suggest using the following two weighted graphs and one unweighted graph, i.e., 14), 15) and 16) to represent 3), 4) and 5) respectively.

14) 走私 ———— 汽车
(/zousi/, smuggle) (/qiche/, car)

15) 走私 ———— [汽车]
(/zousi/, smuggle) (/qiche/, car)

16) [走私] ———— 汽车
(/zousi/, smuggle) (/qiche/, car)

Here we basically use undirected graphs to annotate phrases, and introduce a rectangle to denote the *head* of a linguistic phrase, if any. Notice that we don't mark a head in 14), which means that we don't take the verb 走私(/zousi/, smuggle) as the head of the verb phrase as usual. In general, for most verb phrases like 14) in Chinese, they correspond with two modifier-center phrases like 15) and 16) that comprise the same content words but with different meanings. For such phrases, we generally use a headword to differentiate between the verb phrase and the two modifier-center phrases, and then use different headword to distinguish the two modifier-center phrases.

Another problem with conceptual structure is concerned with its ability to deal with hierarchical structures. Although *nested conceptual structure* is introduced to

[3] Unless necessary, we don't list relationship in the conceptual graph.

describe *nested belief*, one particular kind of hierarchical structures (Geneviève, 1998), some simple hierarchical structures cannot be distinguished or annotated appropriately. As an example, consider 17) and 18).

17) 漂亮 的 走私 汽车
/piaoliang/ /de/ /zousi/ /qiche/
beautiful of smuggle car
beautiful smuggled cars

18) 走私 漂亮 的 汽车
/zousi/ /piaoliang/ /de/ /qiche/
smuggle beautiful of car
to smuggle beautiful cars

Using conceptual graph, we can annotate both of them as 19), in which case the two phrases cannot be distinguished.

19) 走私——汽车——漂亮

If based on undirected graph plus head, 17) can be annotated as 20).

20) 

But there will be no appropriate annotation for 18), because on the one hand, 汽车(/qiche/,car) should be coded as a *head* due to its relationship with 漂亮(/piaoliang/, beautiful), on the other hand, it's role as the object of the verb 走私(/zousi/, smuggle) makes it illegal to be a *head*.

To differentiate 17) and 18), we further suggest specifying the embedded structures in linguistic forms in some way, and use *circles* to denote them. In such opinion, 17) can be annotated as 21) and 22) respectively.

21) 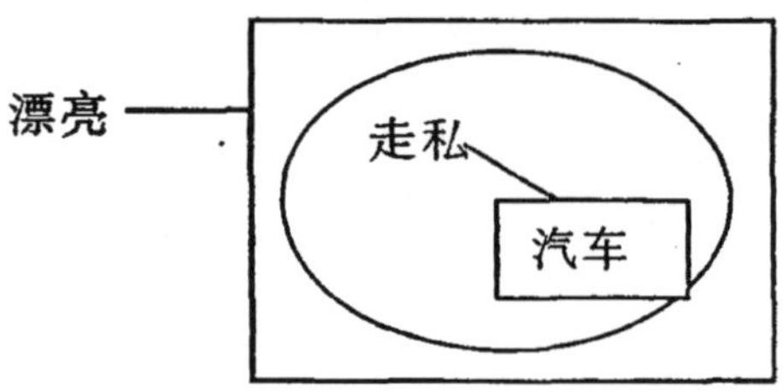


In this diagram, the smaller rectangle denotes the head of the modifier-center phrase 走私汽车 (/zousiqiche/, smuggled cars), the circle codes the phrase as an embedded structure of the whole phrase, while bigger rectangle denotes the head of the whole phrase.

22) 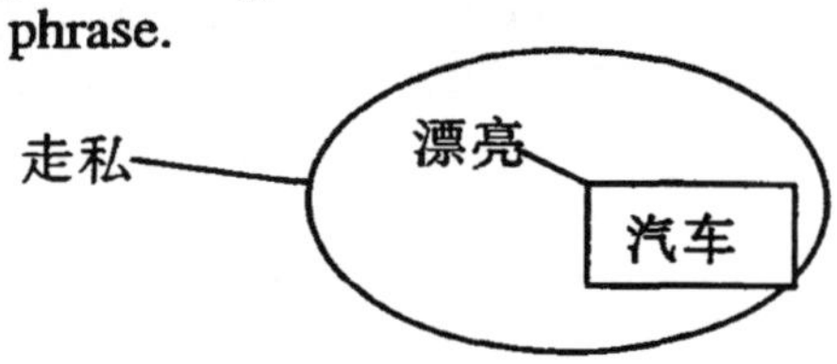


In this diagram, the circle denotes the embedded structure 漂亮的汽车(/piaoliang de qiche/, beautiful cars), while the rectangle denotes the head of the embedded structure. Notice the phrase on the whole is a verb phrase, so there is no head coded here.

## 3. Recursive Graph

One major concern for semantic annotation of linguistic forms is what semantic information will be coded, or more generally, what is their semantic information, which has long been a quite controversial question. From the point of view of *concepts*, linguistic forms including phrases semantically refer to *concepts*, which we think generally fall within four categories:

*a) preliminary concept*. For example, we may see the word 物(/wu/, thing) denotes a preliminary concept.

*b) compositional concept or situation*, which consists of some *concepts* and their *relation*[4]. For example, phrase 1) with the meaning 3) denotes a *situation* including the concepts the two content words, 走私(/zousi/, smuggle) and 汽车(/qiche/, car), denote respectively, and their relationship, 受事(/shoushi/, patient).

[4] *relation* is also a specific kind of concepts, e.g., 受事(/shoushi/, patient) is a *relation* between 走私(/zousi/, smuggle) and 汽车(/qiche/, car).

c) *subordinate concept or specific concept within a situation*, for example, phrase 1) with the meaning 4) refers to the concept denoted by 汽车(/qiche/, car) in the *situation* mentioned in *b*).

d) *subordinate feature, or specific feature of a situation or a concept*, which generally stands for the *relationship* between a *situation* or a *concept* and another unknown *concept*. Consider 23).

| | | |
|---|---|---|
| 23) 姑娘 | 的 | 外貌 |
| /guniang/ | /de/ | /waimao/ |
| girl | of | appearance |
| the appearance of girls | | |

In this phrase, the word 外貌 (/waimao/, appearance) denotes a *feature* of the concept the word 姑娘 (/guniang/, girl) denotes, and the *value* of this *feature* doesn't occur in this phrase.

Notice that the concepts within one situation themselves may be compositional concepts, subordinate concepts or subordinate features, so the concepts that linguistic forms including phrases denote generally presents a kind of hierarchical structure. In fact, this hierarchical structure in return represents the main semantic information of linguistic forms.

We introduce *recursive graph* as formal diagram to represent the hierarchical structure of linguistic forms. Let $P_0$ be the set of *preliminary points*, we call $p \in P_0$ a *0-level graph*. Suppose $P_1 \subseteq P_0$, $E_1(\subseteq P_0)$ is the set of the *edges* between *points* in $P_1$, $R_1(\subseteq(P_1 \times E_1))$ is the set of *relations* between *points* in $P_1$ and *edges* in $E_1$[5], then:

i) $\langle P_1, E_1, R_1\rangle$ *is a 1-level compositional graph;*

ii) $\langle\langle P_1, E_1, R_1\rangle, p\rangle$ $(p \in P_1)$ *is a 1-level point-headed graph;*

iii) $\langle\langle P_1, E_1, R_1\rangle, e\rangle$ $(e \in E_1)$ *is a 1-level edge-headed graph;*

iv) *1-level concepts comprise 1-level compositional graphs, 1-level point-headed graphs, and 1-level edge-headed graphs.*

Let $\Sigma_0 = P_0$, $\Sigma_{n-1}$ be the set of *(n-1)-level graphs*, suppose $P_n \subseteq (\Sigma_0 \cup \Sigma_1 \cup, \ldots, \Sigma_{n-1})$, $(P_n \cap \Sigma_{n-1}) \neq NIL$, $E_n(\subseteq P_n)$ is the set of the *edges* between *points* in $P_n$, $R_n(\subseteq(P_n \times E_n))$ is the set of *relations* between *points* in $P_n$ and *edges* in $E_n$, then:

v) $\langle P_n, E_n, R_n\rangle$ *is a n-level compositional graph;*

vi) $\langle\langle P_n, E_n, R_n\rangle, p\rangle$ $(p \in P_n)$ *is a n-level point-headed graph;*

vii) $\langle\langle P_n, E_n, R_n\rangle, e\rangle$ $(e \in E_n)$ *is a n-level edge-headed graph;*

viii) *n-level concepts comprise n-level compositional graphs, n-level point-headed graphs, and n-level edge-headed graphs.*

Intuitively, *0-level graph* corresponds with *preliminary points*, *compositional graph* corresponds with *situation*, *point-headed graph* corresponds with *subordinate concept*, and *edge-headed graph* corresponds with *subordinate feature*.

## 4. Annotation Guidelines

In general, Chinese phrases can roughly be classified into five categories, i.e., sub-predicate, verb-object, modifier-center, verb-complement, and coordinate. We give some examples in the following for each category.

4.1 Sub-predicate

[5] Here, Edges are also points. An edge point connecting two other points here equals an edge in a traditional definition of graph.

In general, the phrase in this category denotes a *compositional concept*. For example, 24) can be annotated as 25).

24) 姑娘 漂亮
/guniang/ /piaoliang/
girl beautiful
Girls are beautiful

25) 姑娘 ———————— 漂亮
外貌

Intuitively, the concept the word 姑娘(/guniang/, girl) denotes has a feature, 外貌(/waimao/, appearance), and its value is 漂亮(/piaoliang/, beautiful). In other words, there exists a relationship, i.e., 外貌(/waimao/, appearance), between the two concepts denoted by 姑娘(/guniang/, girl) and 漂亮(/piaoliang/, beautiful) respectively[6].

4.2 Verb-object

Similar with sub-predicate phrases, the phrase in this category also denotes a *compositional concept*. Phrase 1) with the meaning 3) is an example, and can be annotated as 26).

26) 走私 ———————— 汽车
受事

Intuitively, there exists a relationship, i.e., 受事(/shoushi/, patient), between the two concepts denoted by 走私(/zousi/, smuggle) and 汽车(/qiche/, car) respectively.

4.3 Modifier-center

The phrase in this category generally denotes a *subordinate concept*. The center here in the phrase can be a verb, a noun or an adjective. As examples, 27) and 28) are annotated as 29) and 30).

27) 漂亮 的 姑娘
/piaoliang/ /de/ /guniang/
beautiful of girl
beautiful girls

28) 姑娘 的 漂亮
/guniang/ /de/ /piaoliang/
girl of beautiful
the beauty of girls

29) [姑娘] ———————— 漂亮
外貌

30) 姑娘 ———————— [漂亮]
外貌

Intuitively, the two concepts denoted by the two content words 姑娘(/guniang/, girl) and 漂亮(/piaoliang/, beautiful) in 27) and 28) hold the same relationship, i.e., 外貌(/waimao/, appearance) as in 24). The difference lies in that the phrases 27) and 28) both have a *head*, i.e., 姑娘(/guniang/, girl) and 漂亮(/piaoliang/, beautiful) respectively.

Another example is 23), it denotes an *subordinate feature*, annotated as 31)[7].

31) 姑娘 ———— [外貌]

Intuitively, the concept denoted by 姑娘(/guniang/, girl) has a feature 外貌(/waimao/, appearance), which is the head of this phrase.

4.4 Verb-complement

For the phrase in this category, the semantic relationship between its two parts, i.e., verb and complement, is very complicated (Ma, 1987); even there is no direct semantic links

[6] Unless necessary, we don't list the link between concepts and relation names.

[7] The link between 姑娘(/guniang/, girl) and 外貌(/waimao/, appearance) denotes a relation between concepts and relationships.

between them sometimes. Consider 32) and 33).

32) 吃 饱
/chi/ /bao/
eat full
to eat and be full

33) 跑 快
/pao/ /kuai/
run fast
to run fast

In 32), 饱(/bao/, full) has a direct link with the agent of 吃(/chi/, eat), in which sense the two concepts denoted by 饱(/bao/, full) and 吃(/chi/, eat) has no direct semantic link. We don't consider such phrases in our annotation temporarily. In contrast, in 33), 快(/kuai/, fast) acts as the value of one feature 速度(/sudu/, speed) of 跑(/pao/, run), in which sense it has a direct semantic link with 跑(/pao/, run). They form a subordinate concept, annotated as 34).

34) 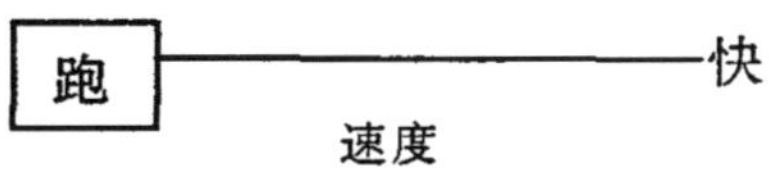


4.5 Coordinate

In general, the phrase in this category denotes a compositional concept. As an example, consider 35).

35) 师 生
/shi/ /sheng/
teacher student
teacher and student

Intuitively, there is a relationship, i.e., 并(/bing/, and), between the two concepts denoted by the two words. So, it can be annotated as 36).

36) 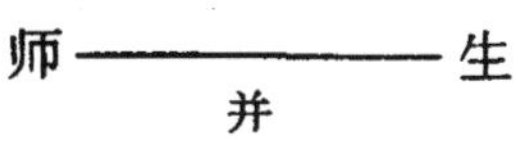


# 5 Conclusion and Future Work

In this paper, we propose a recursive graph based scheme for semantic annotation of Chinese phrases. This scheme can fully differentiate those Chinese phrases that comprise the same content words but with different meaning due to their different word order or some involved function words. It can also capture the hierarchical conceptual structures of Chinese phrases, which determine their main semantic information.

Now, we have annotated about 5,000 Chinese phrases using this scheme. One methodological issue is that we also choose multi-character Chinese words as candidate annotation phrases. The reason is that unlike western languages, there is no clear-cut between words and phrases in Chinese, for most multi-character Chinese words, their components may also be words, and the meaning of the multi-character words tends to be strongly related with that of their component words. In this sense, the words can be treated as *basic* phrases. More importantly, such basic annotation examples can be more complete in the sense of coverage.

Future work will extend to 50,000 Chinese phrases. Another future work is to learn the rules that determine the mapping between linguistic forms and meanings based on this annotation, and apply the rules to new phrases and sentences. If this can be successful, we can develop a semantic analyzer for Chinese without any syntactic analysis. In particular, we can avoid part-of-speeches or syntactic structures that have long been difficult notions for Chinese languages.

# Acknowledgments

I would like to thank Prof. Dong Zhendong and Prof. Huang Changning for their insightful discussions, and the anonymous reviewers for their comments.

## References

J.Allen, Natural Language Understanding, Second Edition, the Benjamin/Cumming Publishing Company, INC, 1995.

Chomsky, 1968, Language and Mind, Enlarged edition, Harcourt Brace Jovanovich, Publishers.

Eklund, Peter W., Gerard Ellis, & Graham Mann, eds. (1996) Conceptual Structures: Knowledge Representation as Interlingua, Lecture Notes in Artificial Intelligence 1115, Springer-Verlag, Berlin.

Geneviève Simonet, 1998, Two FOL Semantics for Simple and Nested Conceptual Graphs, in proceedings of international conference on Conceptual Graph.

R. W. Langacker, 1997, Constituency, dependency, and concept grouping, Cognitive Linguistics, 8(1): 1-32.

Ma Xiwen, 1987, Some sentential patterns related with verb-result verbs, Zhong Guo Yu Wen (Chinese in China), 201 (6): 424-441. (in Chinese)

Zhu Dexi, Yu Fa Da Wen (in Chinese), Beijing University Press, 1982.

# Text Meaning Representation for Chinese

**Wanying Jin**
Computing Research Laboratory
New Mexico State University
Las Cruces, NM 88003-8001
U.S.A.
wanying@crl.nmsu.edu

## Abstract

This paper describes text meaning representation for Chinese. Text meaning representation is composed of a set of ontological concept instances along with ontological links among them. It integrates lexical, textual and world knowledge into a single hierarchical framework. In NLP application it serves as an interlingual representation for various processing. The methodology and implementation of text meaning representation is discussed in detail. [1]

## 1 Introduction

In natural language text processing, it becomes inevitable to require a system having capability to automatically extract and represent the information conveyed in a given text. The theory and methodology of text meaning representation (TMR) has been studied in the past decade (Nirenburg, 1991; Mahesh and Nirenburg, 1996; Beale *et al.*, 1995; Onyshkevych 1997) and its application has been presented in machine translation systems that employ interlingual approach. An ideal text meaning representation will be a language-neutral description of the linguistic information conveyed in a natural language text. TMR captures the meanings of words in the text and represents them in a set of ontological concepts interconnected through ontological relations. In addition, TMR provides information about the lexicon-semantic dependencies as well as stylistic factors. Based on this study, two supportive resources to compose TMR are ontology and semantic lexicon. An ontology is a set of knowledge concepts about the world. It is composed of thousands of concepts organized into a particular hierarchy so that each concept is related to other concepts through semantic links (Carlson *et al.*, 1990; Bateman, 1993; Dowell *et al.* 1995; Nirenburg *et al.*, 1995; Bouaud, *et al.* 1995; Mahesh *et al.* 1995;). Semantic lexicon represents the senses of the words. Each lexicon entry is a framework that maps a word sense to an ontological concept. It also includes information about syntax, semantics, morphology and pragmatics, as well as annotation that keep the record of data management. Over the years, various methodologies have been investigated carrying out the structure of a computational lexicon entry within a knowledge-based framework(Onyshkevych *et al*, 1995; Viegas and Raskin, 1998; Viegas, 1999; Viegas, *et al*, 1998a, 1998b). A semantic parser uses information in the semantic lexicon and makes a decision on word sense disambiguation based on the strategy proposed by Beale *et al.* (1995) and Beale(1997).

This paper presents the development and application of text meaning representation for Chinese. Detailed discussion about the principle for building a computational semantic Chinese lexicon is illustrated in Jin (1999). The methodology and implementation of word sense disambiguation is fully discussed in Viegas, Jin and Beale(1999a, 1999b, 1999c).

## 2 Overview of Ontology

An ontology is a body of knowledge about the world. It is a repository of concepts used in meaning representations. All concepts are organized in a tangled subsumption hierarchy and further interconnected using a system of semantic relations defined among the concepts. The ontology is put into well-defined

[1] This work has been supported by the Department of Defense of the United States under contract number MDA-904-92-C-5189.

relationships with knowledge sources in the system. In an NLP application the ontology supplies world knowledge to lexical, syntactic, semantic and pragmatic processes.

In the MikroKosmos project,[2] the ontological concepts consist of: OBJECT, the static things existing in the world; EVENT, any activities happening in the world, and PROPERTY, the properties of OBJECTs and EVENTs. The ontology organizes terminological nouns into a taxonomy of objects, verbs into a taxonomy of events, and adjectives into a taxonomy of attributes. It further includes many ontological relations between objects and events to support a variety of disambiguation tasks. Currently, the ontology in the MikroKosmos project contains about 5,000 concepts covering a wide range of categories in the world. Each concept, on average, has 14 relation links. An example below presents the top three level of the ontology, which differentiates between OBJECT; EVENT and PROPERTY.

```
+ ALL
  + EVENT
    + MENTAL-EVENT
    + PHYSICAL-EVENT
    + SOCIAL-EVENT
  + OBJECT
    + MENTAL-OBJECT
    + INTANGIBLE-OBJECT
    + PHYSICAL-OBJECT
    + SOCIAL-OBJECT
  + PROPERTY
    + ATTRIBUTE
    + RELATION
    + ONTOLOGY-SLOT
```

Each concept is a frame in which a collection of ontological slots such as DEFINITION, IS-A, SUBCLASSES, INVERSE; case roles such as AGENT, THEME and properties such as HEADED-BY, HAS-MEMBER, etc. link one concept to other concepts in the ontology. Below is an example of a concept frame of GOVERNMENT-ACTIVITY:

[2]The MikroKosmos project is a knowledge-based machine translation system using an interlingual approach. The source languages are Spanish, Chinese and Japanese. The target language is English.

```
Concept        GOVERNMENT-ACTIVITY
DEFINITION:    an activity commonly
               carried out by a
               government.
IS-A:          POLITICAL-EVENT
AGENT:         HUMAN
THEME:         EVENT OBJECT
ACCOMPANIER:   HUMAN
LOCATION:      PLACE
```

This example indicates that the concept GOVERNMENT-ACTIVITY is a subclass of the concept POLITICAL-EVENT; its case role AGENT requires its semantic value as HUMAN and its THEME requires its value as either OBJECT or EVENT; the GOVERNMENT-ACTIVITY can also have case role ACCOMPANIER with value as HUMAN and LOCATION with value as PLACE. Any lexicon entry mapping to the concept GOVERNMENT-ACTIVITY gets extended information through this frame.

## 3 Semantic Lexicon

Semantic lexicon is another knowledge source for text meaning representation. In the MikroKosmos project each lexicon entry is designed as a frame with 11 zones corresponding to information relevant to orthography, morphology, syntax, semantics, syntax-semantic linking, stylistics, and database type management record, etc. The core of the lexicon frame is syntactic zone SYN-STRUC, semantic zone SEM-STRUC and their link SYNSEM zone. Syntax particular to a given language is described in the syntactical zone. The semantic zone maps a sense into an ontological concept in the case of single sense, or to several concepts in the case of multiple senses. Through the syntactic-semantic link zone the information of each word in the text can be extracted directly from lexicon database and its relevant world knowledge also can be retrieved. The general template of semantic lexicon entry is shown as follows. For a detailed description see Viegas and Raskin (1998).

```
Entry Elements =
[FORM:        Word Form
 CAT:         Part of speech
 MORPH:       Morphology
 ANNO:        Annotation
 TRANS:       Translation
```

```
SYNSEM:      Syntax-Semantic link
SYN-STRUC:   Syntactic structure
SEM-STRUC:   Semantic structure
LEX-RULES:   Lexical rules
PRAGM:       Pragmatic information
STYL:        Stylistic information]
```

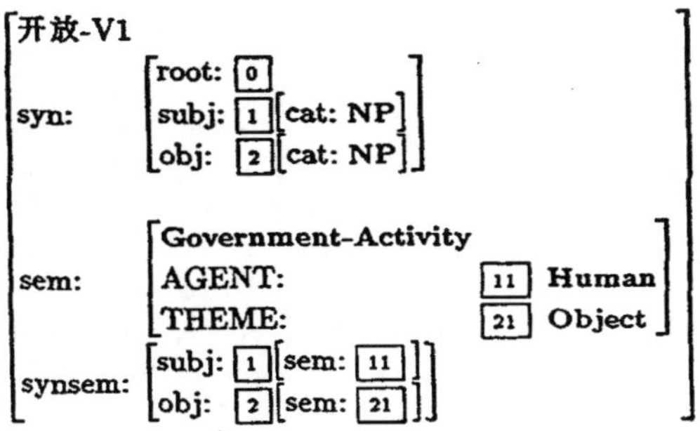


Figure 1: Sense for the Chinese lexicon 开放.

Figure 1. is a simplified structure of a Chinse lexicon entry 开放 in the sense of {GOVERNMENT-ACTIVITY. The SYN zone indicates that when parsing a sentence containing this entry, subcategories SUBJ and OBJ are required. The SEM zone presents the semantic value of each case role, i.e. AGENT with value HUMAN, and THEME with value EVENT or OBJECT. The SYNSEM zone provides information about the syntax-semantic linking. That is, SUBJ [1] is linked to AGENT [11] with value HUMAN and OBJ [2] is linked to THEME [21] with value EVENT or OBJECT.

Due to the lack of morphological information in Chinese, it is often the case that the same Chinese word form can be mapped to a different part of speech and has multiple senses, such as the word 开放:

- in the context 鲜花 开放 *flowers bloom*, can be an intransitive verb mapping to a concept BLOOM with the definition *to produce flower*.
- in the context 政府 开放 对外 贸易 政策 *the government opens the foreign trade policy*, can be a transitive verb mapping to a concept GOVERNMENT-ACTIVITY with the definition *an activity that is commonly carried out by a government at any level*.
- in the context 政府 实行 开放 政策 *the government carries open policy*, can be an adjective mapping to OPEN-TO-PUBLIC with the definition *to be available to the public*.
- in the context 图书馆 开放 *the library is open*, can be an intransitive verb with the same concept OPEN-TO-PUBLIC.

Using the ontological concepts as the value of semantic variables and linking them to syntactic variables makes the lexicon very informative. Figure 2. and Figure 3. present each sense and POS of the lexicon entries for the Chinese word 开放.

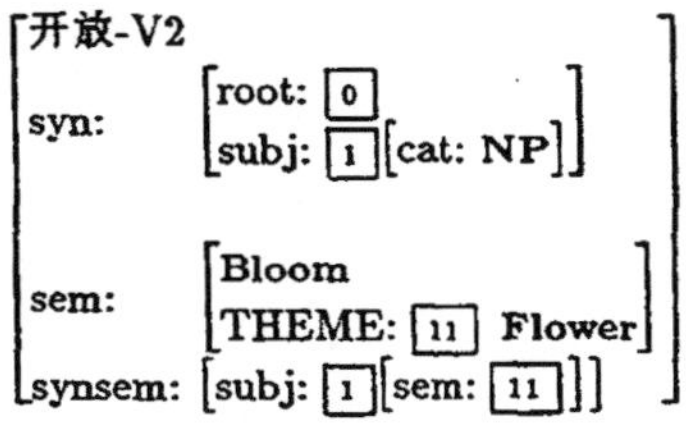


Figure 2: Sense for the Chinese lexicon 开放.

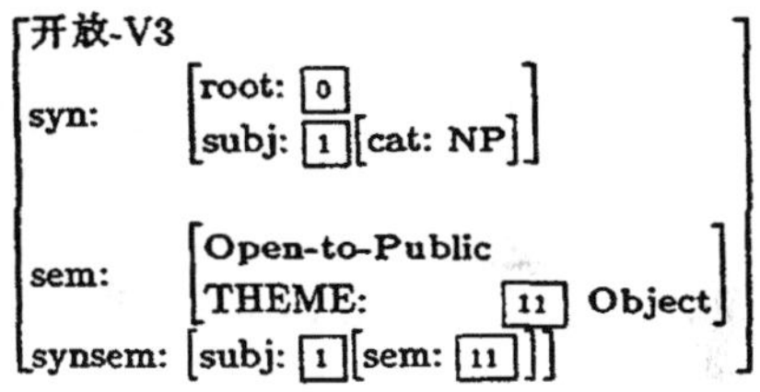


Figure 3: Sense for the Chinese lexicon 开放.

## 4 Semantic Analysis for Word Sense Disambiguation

The task of a semantic analyzer is to combine the knowledge contained in the ontology and lexicon and apply it to the input text to produce text meaning representation output. The central tasks involved are to retrieve the appropriate semantic constraints for each possible word sense, test each sense in context, and construct the output TMRs by instantiating the concepts in semantic zones of the word senses that best satisfy the combination of constraints. Figure 4. illustrates the process of text meaning representation. Below illustrates the process through a sentence 中国

政府 开放 了 对外 贸易 政策. *The Chinese government has opened foreign trade policy.* The syntactic analysis gives the following output:

```
((ROOT 开放)(CAT V)(TRANS open)
  (SUBJ
   (MODS 中国)(CAT N)(TRANS China)
   (ROOT 政府)(CAT N)(TRANS government))
  (OBJ
   (MODS
    (MODS 对外)(CAT ADJ)(TRANS foreign)
    (ROOT 贸易)(CAT N)(TRNAS trade))
   (ROOT 政策)(CAT N)(TRANS policy)  ))
```

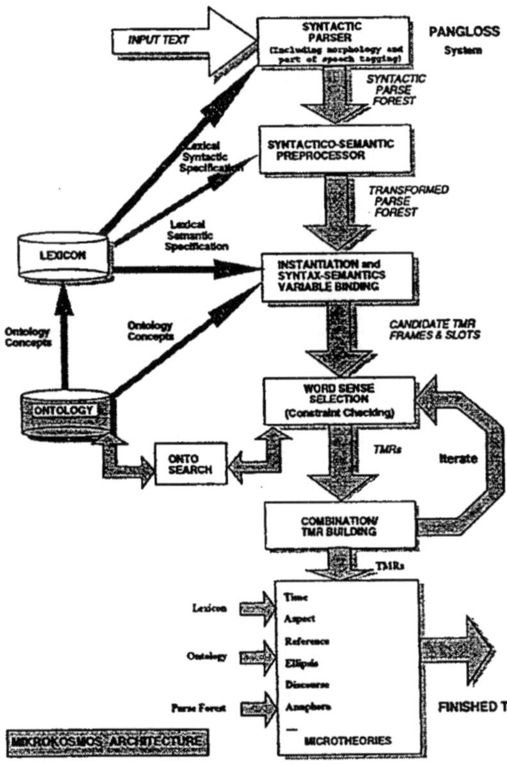


Figure 4: The Architecture of TMR.

The semantic analysis process takes the following steps:

- to gather all of the possible lexicon for each of the words with instantiated each concepts.

```
中国  N     CHINA-6
政府  N     FEDERATION-1
开放  V1    BLOOM-2-1
      V2    GOVERNMENT-ACTIVITY-2-2
      V3    OPEN-TO-PUBLIC-2-3
      ADJ   OPEN-TO-PUBLIC-2-4
对外  ADJ1  INTERNATIONAL-ATTRIBUTE-5-1
      ADV1  OUTWARD-5-2
贸易  N     COMMERCE-EVENT-4-1
      V     COMMERCE-EVENT-4-2
政策  N     LAW-3
```

Syntactic variables are bound to one another using the syntactic patterns in the lexical entries to establish syntactic dependencies. In addition, ontological concepts referred to the semantic zones of the lexical entries are instantiated and linked through ontological relations to establish semantic dependencies. For example, the syntactic structure of the text requires 开放 to be a verb. Thus, the ADJ category with sense OPEN-TO-PUBLIC-2-4 is rejected. From Figure 2. and Figure 3. both SYN zones indicate an intransitive verb that violates the required syntax. Therefore, the concepts BLOOM and OPEN-TO-PUBLIC are also rejected. In the same way, the adverb 对外 with sense OUTWARD-5-2 and the verb 贸易 with sense COMMERCE-EVENT-4-2 are also rejected because of the violation of required POS. Finally the ADJ 对外 with the sense INTERNATIONAL-ATTRIBUTE-5-1 and the NOUN 贸易 with COMMERCE-EVENT-4-1 are selected. After all senses are determined, SYN-SEM zone binds all syntactic variables with semantic variables, i.e. SUBJ FEDERATION-1 is bound to the AGENT of GOVERNMENT-ACTIVITY-2-2, OBJ LAW-3 is bound to the THEME of GOVERNMENT-ACTIVITY-2-2.

- In the next step, selectional constraints are retrieved from the ontology. Individual selectional constraints are checked. In the example, the concept GOVERNMENT-ACTIVITY requires AGENT to be HUMAN and THEME to be EVENT or OBJECT. The lexical information indicates that the SUBJ 政府 with sense FEDERATION must satisfy the AGENT of GOVERNMENT-ACTIVITY with value HUMAN. An inference rule described below checks the satisfaction. The OBJ 政策 with the sense LAW satisfies THEME of GOVERNMENT-

ACTIVITY with value OBJECT. Through IS-A links it is found that LAW is a descendant of OBJECT. Therefore, the semantic constraints are satisfied.

- Seeking satisfaction through inference rules, the semantic analyzer does more than match selectional constraints or find the distance along IS-A links. The search inside the ontology also involves looking for metonymic type links, such as FEDERATION in a metonymic relation with HUMAN through the property HAS-REPRESENTATIVE:

```
Concept:  HAS-REPRESENTATIVE
IS-A:     ORGANIZATION-RELATION
DOMAIN:   ORGANIZATION
RANGE:    HUMAN BUSINESS-ROLE
          GOVERNMENTAL-ROLE
INVERSE:  REPRESENTATIVE-OF
```

  in which DOMAIN is ORGANIZATION that has subclass FEDERATION and RANGE is HUMAN. Thus, the constraint of AGENT of GOVERNMENT-ACTIVITY to be HUMAN is satisfied.

- In case multiple senses all satisfy the constraints, the concept with the shortest path is selected as the best choice. An ontological search program, Onto-Search, is presented in Onyshkevych (1997). The resulting preference values for each constraint are combined in an efficient control and search algorithm called Hunter-Gatherer that combines constraint satisfaction, branch and bound, and solution synthesis techniques to pick the best combination of word senses of the entire sentence in near linear time, as described in Beale (1997).

- Chosen word senses are assembled into TMR frames.

## 5 Text Meaning Representation

A text meaning representation(TMR) is a language-neutral description of the meaning conveyed in a text. It is derived by syntactic and semantic analysis. TMR captures not only the meaning of individual words in the text, but also the relation between those words. It provides information about the lexicon-semantic dependencies. In addition, it also represents stylistic and other factors presented in the text. From the result of word sense disambiguation, TMR integrates lexical, ontological and textual information into a single hierarchical framework. Below is a TMR for the example sentence 中国 政府 开放 了 对外 贸易 政策. *Chinese government has opened foreign trade policy.*

```
(FEDERATION-1
 (AGENT-OF
   (VALUE GOVERNMENT-ACTIVITY-2))
 (RELATION (VALUE CHINA-6))
 (INSTANCE-OF (VALUE FEDERATION)))
(GOVERNMENT-ACTIVITY-2
 (AGENT (VALUE FEDERATION-1))
 (THEME (VALUE LAW-3))
 (INSTANCE-OF
   (VALUE GOVERNMENT-ACTIVITY)))
(LAW-3
 (THEME-OF
   (VALUE GOVERNMENT-ACTIVITY-2))
 (INSTANCE-OF (VALUE LAW)))
(COMMERCE-EVENT-4
 (EVENT-OBJECT-RELATION (VALUE LAW-3))
 (INSTANCE-OF (VALUE COMMERCE-EVENT)))
(INTERNATIONAL-ATTRIBUTE-5
 (DOMAIN (VALUE COMMERCE-EVENT-4))
 (RANGE (VALUE INTERNATIONAL))
 (INSTANCE-OF
   (VALUE INTERNATIONAL-ATTRIBUTE)))
(CHINA-6
 (INSTANCE-OF (VALUE CHINA)))
(ASPECT-7
 (SCOPE (VALUE GOVERNMENT-ACTIVITY-2))
 (TELIC (VALUE YES)))
(TIME-8
 (DOMAIN (VALUE GOVERNMENT-ACTIVITY-2))
 (RANGE (VALUE *speaker-time*)))
(INFERENCE (TYPE METONYMY)
  (HUMAN
    (REPRESENTATIVE-OF
      (VALUE FEDERATION-1))))
```

After semantic analysis, a variety of microtheories are applied to further analyze elements of text meaning such as time, aspect, propositions, sets, co-reference, and so on, to produce a complete TMR. In the example, ASPECT-7 is applied within the scope of GOVERNMENT-ACTIVITY in which TELIC with value YES indicates the GOVERNMENT-ACTIVITY is complete that means the action of opening foreign trade policy is done. TIME-8 indicates the GOVERNMENT-ACTIVITY happens at the time the speaker make the utterance. Thus, the meaning of the Chinese sentence 中国 政府 开放 了 对外 贸易 政策 is completely represented in the TMR.

## 6 Discussion

A knowledge-based machine translation can be viewed as extracting and representing the meaning of a text and generating a text in target language based on the meaning presented. Thus, text meaning representation plays the key role in an interlingual approach to machine translation. The approach described in this article enables integrating linguistic knowledge of source languages with general world knowledge to reach high quality translation. It is because TMR represents meaning deeper and broader than what the context presents. For example, in the context 提供 服务 *provide service*, the linguistic information indicates syntactic-semantic dependency as SUBJ*(human)* -V*(service-event)*-OBJ*(event)*. In an ontology, the SERVICE-EVENT concept frame contains information about AGENT and THEME as well as BENEFICIARY, ACCOMPANIER, INSTRUMENT, LOCATION, etc. which extends the meaning of the given text 提供 服务 to 某人 在 某处 为 某人 提供 服务 *Someone provides service to someone else at some place.* If the extended information is not explicitly presented in the text, the default value provides the assumption based on the world knowledge. In machine translation, it enables the generation of high quality text, especially in the case where the syntax in source language is different from that in target language or in the case where ellipsis is allowed in one language such as *He plays Bach* in English, but is not allowed in other language such as in Chinese, where one must say 他 演奏 巴哈 的 作品 *He plays Bach's work.*

With the rapid development of internet, information retrieval plays the key role in search engin. The extended information about the world knowledge allows to retrieve relevant data through the ontology that is implicitly specified in the query. As result, more broad and deep information can be extracted. It is extremely valuable to the development of next generation of internet search engin. All in all, using ontology strengthens all NLP systems.

## References


Bateman, J. A. 1993. Ontology Construction and Natural Language. *Proc. International Workshop on Formal Ontology*, Padua, Italy.

Beale, S. 1997. *Hunter-Gatherer: Applying Constraint Satisfaction, Branch-and-Bound and Solution Synthesis to Computational Semantics.* Ph.D. Diss., Carnegie Mellon University.

Beale, S., Nirenburg, S. and K. Mahesh. 1995. Semantic Analysis in the MikroKosmos Machine Translation Project. *Proc. of the 2nd SNLP-95*, Bangkok, Thailand.

Bouaud, J., Bachimont, B., Charlet, J., and Zweigenbaum, P. 1995. Methodological Principles for Structuring an ONTOLOGY. *Proc. the Workshop on Basic Ontological Issues in Knowledge Sharing*, International Joint Conference on Artificial Intelligence (IJCAI-95), Montreal, Canada.

Carlson, L. and Nirenburg, S. 1990. *World Modeling for NLP.* Technical Report CMU-CMT-90-121, Center for Machine Translation, Carnegie Mellon University, Pittsburgh, PA.

Dowell, M., Stephen, L., and Bonnell, R. 1995. Using a Domain Knowledge Ontology as a Semantic Gateway among Database. *Proc. the Workshop on Basic Ontological Issues in Knowledge Sharing*, International Joint Conference on Artificial Intelligence (IJCAI-95), Montreal, Canada.

Jin, W., Viegas, E. and Beale, S. 1999. Building a Chinese Computational Semantic Lexicon *Proc. of International Symposium on Machine Translation and Computer Language Information Processing-1999 (ISMT & CLIP)*, Beijing, China.

Mahesh, K. and Nirenburg, S. 1995c. Semantic Classification for Practical Natural Language Processing. *Proc. Sixth ASIS SIGICR Classification Research Workshop: An Interdisciplinary Meeting.* Chicago, IL.

Mahesh, K and Nirenburg, S. 1996. Meaning Representation for Knowledge Sharing in Practical Machine Translation. *Proc. the FLAIRS-96 Track on Information Interchange.* Florida AI Research Symposium.

Mahesh, K. 1996. *Ontology Development for Machine Translation: Ideology and Method-*

*ology*. MCCS-96-292, Computing Research Laboratory, New Mexico State University.

Nirenburg, S., Raskin, V. and Onyshkevych, B. 1995. Apologiae Ontologiae. *Proc. of The Conference on TMI*, Leuven, Belgium.

Nirenburg, S. 1991. Application-Oriented Computational Semantics. *Computational Linguistics and Formal Semantics*, R. Johnson and M. Rosner (eds.)

Onyshkevych, B. 1997. *An Ontological-Semantic Framework for Text Analysis.* Ph.D. Diss., School of Computer Science, Carnegie Mellon University.

Onyshkevych, B. and Nirenburg, S. 1995. A Lexicon for Knowledge-Based MT. *Machine Translation Issue on Building Lexicon for MT*, B. Dorr and J. Klavens (eds.) 10:1-2, 5-57.

Viegas, E. and Raskin. V. 1998. *Computational Semantic Lexicon Acquisition: Methodology and Guidelines.* MCCS-98-315. Computing Research Laboratory, New Mexico State University.

Viegas, E. 1999. An Overt Semantics with a Machine-guided Approach for Robust LKBs. In Proc. of *SIGLEX99 Standardizing Lexical Resources*, University of Maryland.

Viegas, E., Beale, S. and S. Nirenburg. 1998. The Computational Lexical Semantics of Syntagmatic Relations. *Proc. of the 36th ACL and the 17th COLING*, Montréal, Québec, Canada.

Viegas, E., Jin, W. and Beale, S. 1999. A Knowledge-based Approach for Chinese-English Translations *Proc. of 5th Natural Language Processing Pacific Rim Symposium (NLPRS-99)*, Beijing, China.

Viegas, E., Jin, W. and Beale, S. 1999. Long Time No See: Overt Semantics for Machine Translation *Proc. of Conference on Theoretical and Methodological Issues in Machine Translation (TMI-99)*, England.

Viegas, E., Jin, W. and Beale, S. 1999. Using Computational Semantics for Chinese Translation *Proc. of Machine Translation Summit-99*, Singapore.

# How Should a Large Corpus Be Built?–A Comparative Study of Closure in Annotated Newspaper Corpora from Two Chinese Sources, Towards Building A Larger Representative Corpus Merged from Representative Sublanguage Collections

**John Kovarik (kovariks@worldnet.att.net)**
U.S. Department of Defense

## Abstract

This study measures comparative lexical and syntactic closure rates in annotated Chinese newspaper corpora from the Academica Sinica Balanced Corpus and the University of Pennsylvania's Chinese Treebank. It then draws inferences as to how large such corpora need be to be representative models of subject-matter-constrained language domains within the same genre. Future large corpora should be built incrementally only by combining smaller representative sublanguage collections.

## 1 Prior Work

Practically speaking, earlier attempts at building corpora, such as the IBM/Lancaster approach, have taken an all-inclusive perspective toward text selection proposing that (Garside and McEnery, 1993) raw texts for parsed corpora should come from a variety of sources. The IBM/Lancaster group used the Canadian Hansards collection of parallel parsed English and French sentences as a base of English parsed sentences and then focused on the Computer Manuals domain, in which they attempted to randomly select texts with some additional non-Computer Manual material selected as "a measure of 'light relief' " supposedly for the benefit of the annotators. A broad approach was also used in the Hong Kong element of the International Corpus of English (ICE) project (Greenbaum, 1992) which sought to assemble a range of both spoken and written texts along with a range of both formal and informal situations to provide a reasonably large, well-documented and detailed snapshot of the use of educated English. (Bolt, 1994) Both the IBM/Lancaster approach and the ICE project build millions of tokens worth of corpora.

But from a more principled perspective, Douglas Biber, in speaking on representativeness in corpus design, pointed out that the linguistic characterization of a corpus should include both its central tendency and its range of variation. (Biber, 1993) Similarly Geoffrey Leech has stated that a corpus, in order to be representative, must somehow capture the magnitude of languages not only in their lexis but also in their syntax. (Leech, 1991) *This suggests we should build corpora focusing on how well they can approach lexical and syntactic closure, rather than by merely fixating on ever larger amounts of text. To build representative corpora why not first select representative texts constrained by genre of writing?*

In general one possible technique for methodical corpus selection would be to build large corpora out of representative sub-collections constrained by genre and subject matter. Zelig Harris said, "Certain proper subsets of the sentences of a language may be closed under some or all of the operations defined in the language, and thus constitute a sublanguage of it." (Harris, 1968) Calling this an inductive definition of sublanguage Satoshi Sekine has embarked on studies involving new trends in the analysis of sublanguages (Sekine, 1994). Both Harris and Sekine recognized that sublanguages are an efficient way to observe and measure the properties of natural language in smaller, representative blocks.

Getting down to specifics, McEnery and Wilson (McEnery and Wilson, 1996) have hypothesized that genres of writing, such as the style used in newspapers and similar printed publications to report news stories, represent a constrained subset of a natural language. Thus newspaper texts constitute a sublanguage – a version of a natural language which does not display all of the creativity of that natural language. The newspaper sublanguage can be further constrained by subject matter to divide it into smaller, more manageable subsets.

A key mathematical feature of a sublanguage is that it will show a high degree of closure at various levels of description, setting it apart from unconstrained natural language. This closure property of a sublanguage is analogous to the mathematical property of transitive closure. McEnery and Wilson used the closure property to measure and compare rates of lexical and syntactic closure in three corpora: the IBM computer manual corpus, the Canadian Hansards, and the American Printing House for the Blind corpus. To date, however, there has been little work in a similar vein in other languages.

## 2 Overview

This work applies the methodology of McEnery and Wilson to examine closure rates in a comparative study of all available tagged Chinese newspaper corpora. First I define lexical and syntactic closure for this study in section 3. Then, section 4 begins this study with an examination of all the newspaper texts of the Academica Sinica Balanced Corpus (ASBC). Section 5 extends this study to an examination of the newspaper texts of the UPenn Chinese Treebank (CTB). Section 6 presents my findings and section 7 discusses some implications for future corpus building.

## 3 Lexical and Syntactic Closure

### 3.1 Tokenization in Chinese

It should be pointed out that Chinese is an agglutinative, not an inflected language. Moreover, while Chinese tokens can concatenate, Chinese has no extensive morphology like many Indo-European languages. Chinese, of course, has no white space separating lexemes, as a result, all Chinese text must first be segmented into word lengths. However, once a text has been segmented, no stemming is needed so each segmented Chinese word can be counted as it occurs without the need of finding its lemma.

### 3.2 Lexical Closure

Lexical closure is that property of a collection of text whereby given a representative sample, the number of new lexical forms seen among every additional 1,000 new tokens begins to level off at a rate below 10 per cent.

### 3.3 Syntactic Closure

Syntactic closure is that property of a collection of text whereby given a representative sample of a type of text, then the number of new syntactic forms seen among every additional 1,000 new tokens begins to level off. A syntactic form is the combination of token plus type. Thus syntactic closure approaches as the number of new grammatical uses for a previously observed token plus the number of new tokens, regardless of syntactic use, level off to a growth rate below 10 per cent.

## 4 Academica Sinica Balanced Corpus (ASBC)

While it is common practice to attempt to build huge annotated corpora, it is of course very tedious, very expensive, and especially challenging for annotators to maintain consistency over such a huge task. Consequently one must hope that once an annotated corpus of newspaper texts is created, it can be statistically measured and confirmed to be a representative sample. I first measured lexical and syntactic closure rates in all ASBC newspaper texts but found that when viewed as a whole this newspaper sub-collection of the ASBC does not approach closure (see graphs below).

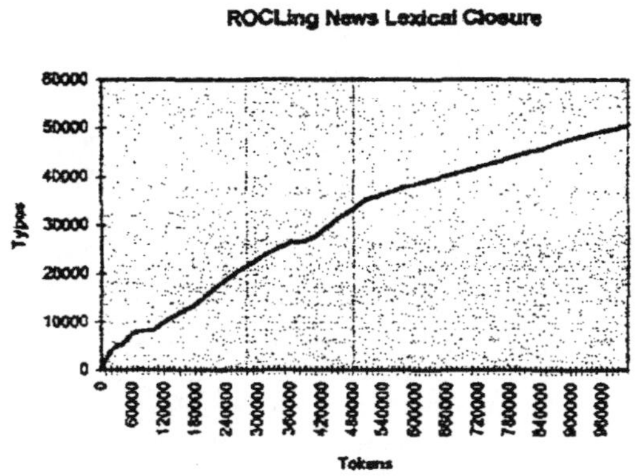

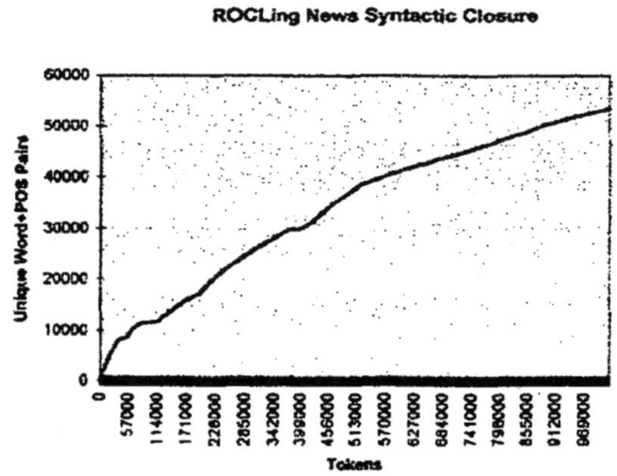


This raises the question *how can we hope for NLP applications to learn on large corpora if they themselves never approach statistical closure, never approach being statistically confirmed as a representative model of the language?*

I then focused downward on subsections of the newspaper corpus–grouping them by similar filename. I searched the ASBC corpus looking for files of annotated newspaper text and found a total of 57 files (18.7 Mb); my findings are summarized in the following table.

Academica Sinica Balanced Corpus News

| Files | Size | Filenames | Subject Matter |
|---|---|---|---|
| 05 | 01.9Mb | A.... | '94 Academics |
| 16 | 01.5Mb | C.... | '93 Various News |
| 01 | 00.2Mb | SSSLA | '91 Politics etc. |
| 36 | 15.1Mb | T.... | '91-'95 Sports etc. |

The large single file, named "SSLA", dealt with a wide assortment of subject matter and thus was significantly different from the other 3 newspaper collections. Not only was its individual file size rather large; it was not even close to the size and homogeneity of the other three newspaper multi-file collections. I rejected it from further study.

The other sub-collections were more similar. Topically speaking, the ASBC "A" newspaper collection was focused primarily on news (77 per cent) while at the same time focusing narrowly on academic events in 1994. The ASBC "C" newspaper collection was less narrowly focused on news (73.5 per cent) but expanded its focus to other than academia while limiting itself to events of 1993. The ASBC "T" newspaper collection, however, spanned the period 1991 through 1995 and dealt with many different subjects, the most frequent of which were sports, news, and domestic politics, but even each of these most frequent subjects only represented 9 per cent of the whole.

Let us consider the three ASBC newspaper sub-collections ("A", "C", and "T" filenames) to be potentially representative sublanguages. If we can observe relatively high degrees of closure at various levels of description, we can propose that such sub-collections are representative sublanguages within the newspaper genre of Chinese natural language. Conversely, those which do not have a high degrees of closure are definitely not sublanguage corpora and not of further interest for this study. The following graphs depict the observed lexical and syntactic closure rates of the three ASBC newspaper sub-collections under study.

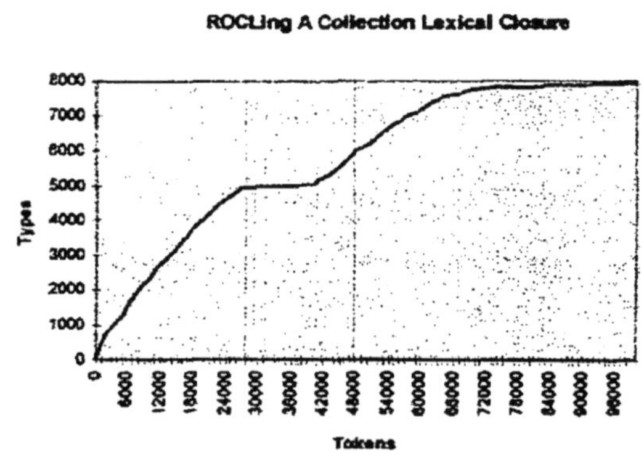


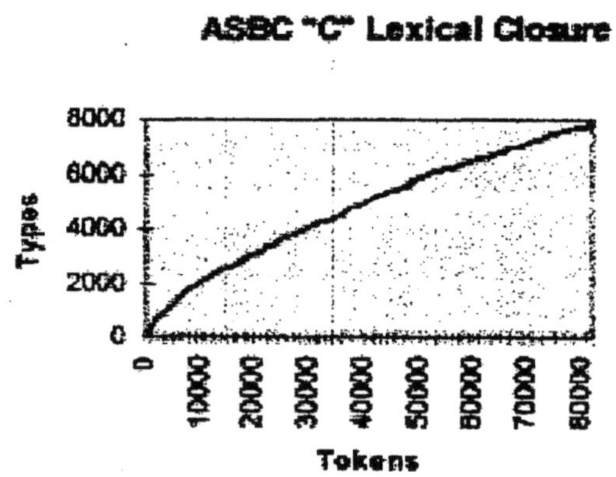

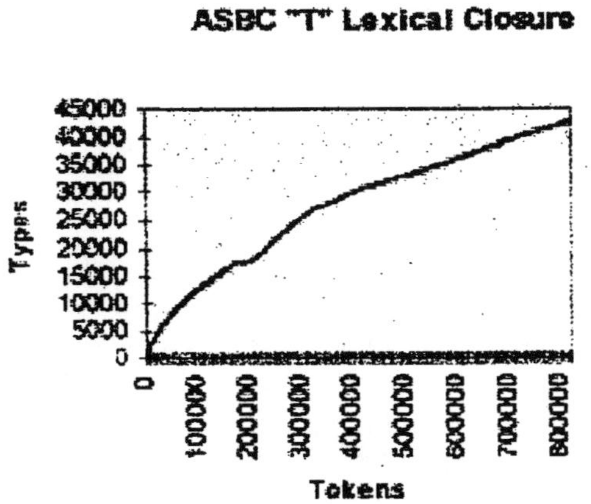


It appears that the ASBC "A" newspaper sub-collections does approach lexical closure; while the "C" and "T" newspaper sub-collections definitely do not.

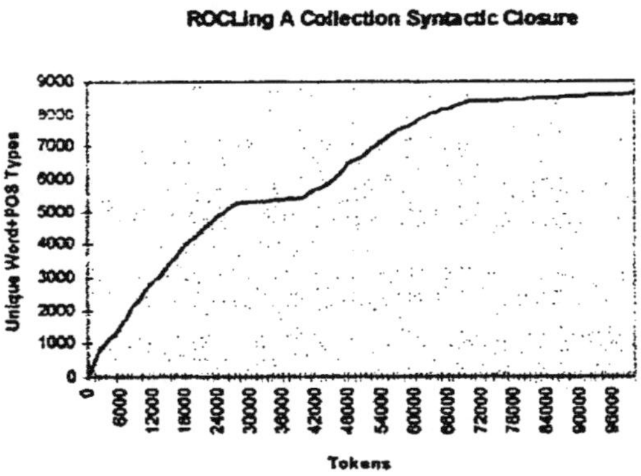


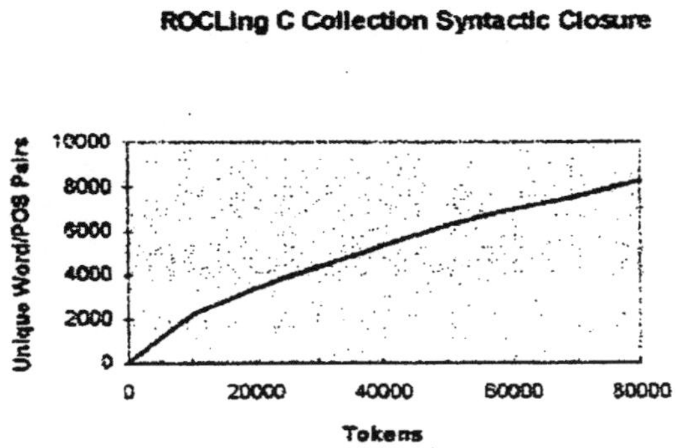


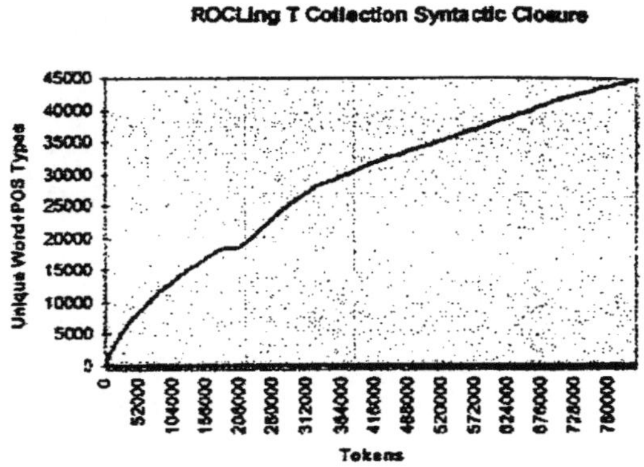


It appears that the ASBC "A" newspaper sub-collection also approaches syntactic closure; while the "C" and "T" newspaper sub-collections do not.

## 5 UPenn Chinese Treebank

I next applied the same measures on the UPenn Chinese Treebank corpus. I wanted to compare the rate at which the UPenn collection approaches lexical and syntactic closure with that of the ASBC "A" and "T" sub-collections. The 329 Xinhua newswire documents in the UPenn Chinese Treebank annotated corpus came from two sub-collections and total 3,289 sentences averaging 27 words or 47 characters per sentence excluding newspaper headlines which are characteristically highly abbreviated clauses. The Perl script written to do this analysis is freely available at *http://home.att.net/~ kovariks/closure.htm.*

UPenn Chinese Treebank Newspaper Texts

| Files | Size | Sub-Collection | Subject |
|---|---|---|---|
| 121 | .322Mb | One | '94 Economics |
| 040 | .114Mb | Two | '96 Economics |
| 076 | .406Mb | Two | '97 Economics |
| 054 | .181Mb | Two | '98 Economics |
| 038 | .060Mb | One | General |

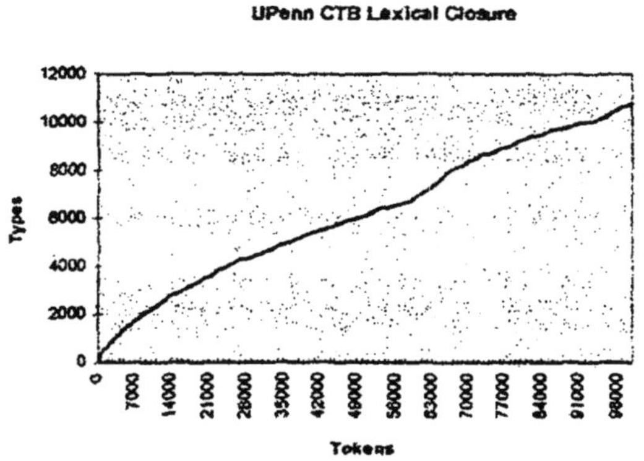


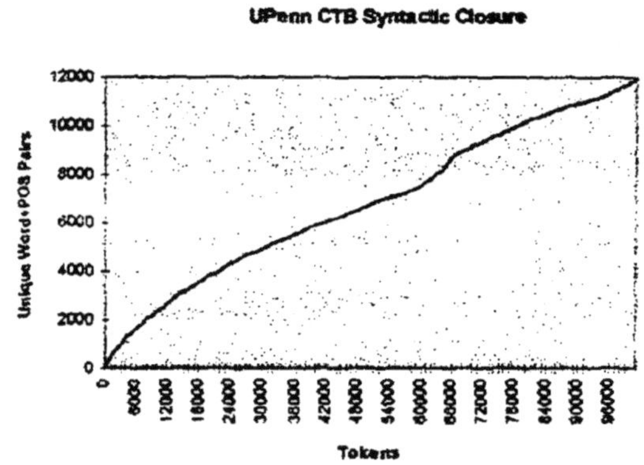


## 6 Findings

The UPenn data initially approaches lexical and syntactic closure at a rate which can be favorably compared with the ASBC "A" Chinese newspaper sub-corpus. By the time 59,000 tokens of the UPenn corpus were tagged, only 56 new token+tag combinations were observed in the preceding 1,000 tokens and 27 of those were new proper nouns. In comparison, at this point the closure rate in the ASBC "A" corpus was not quite as good (see table below). But continuing to the 69,000 token mark, the ASBC "A" closure rate had overtaken that of the UPenn CTB.

| Tokens | Corpus | New token+tags |
|---|---|---|
| 59,000 | UPenn CTB | 56 (27 NR) |
| | ASBC A | 77 (34 N...) |
| 69,000 | UPenn CTB | 61 (36 NR) |
| | ASBC A | 67 (49 N...) |

Interestingly the graphs for both the ASBC "A" and the UPenn CTB data reveal two-humped curves. At approximately the 60,000 token mark on both UPenn CTB graphs the curve was starting to flatten only to suddenly shift into a sharper climb.

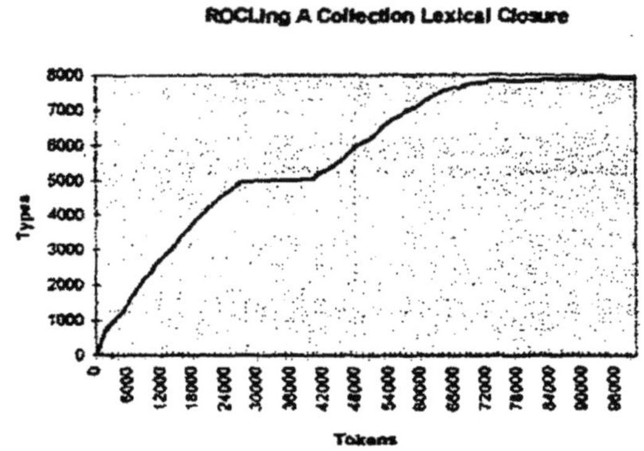


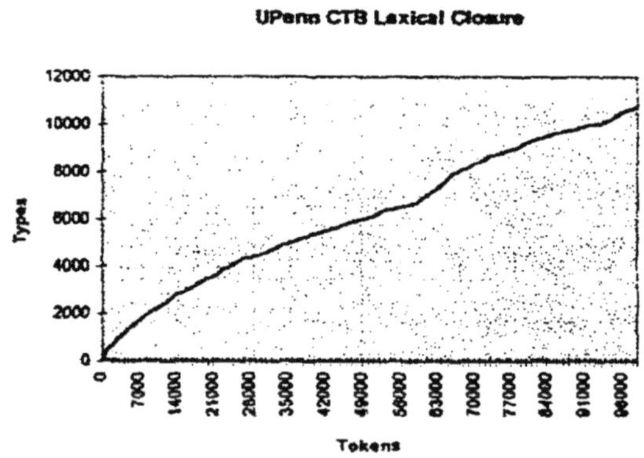


An investigation of the UPenn CTB data revealed that the vast majority of the documents at this point dealt with international aspects of the Chinese economy [1], whereas previously the vast majority of documents had focused on Chinese domestic economic growth [2]. And similarly on the ASBC "A" collection closure graphs around the 30,000 token mark, both

[1] Headlines of articles in UPenn CTB from 66,800-68,300 tokens– 66809: 英宣布参加入侵海地的多国部队 ; 66976: 西班牙外交大臣反对美国封锁古巴 ; 67114: 法批评美国对古巴的禁运政策 ; 67282: 德、俄将加强反核走私行动 ; 67439: 日本科学试验卫星入轨无望 ; 67920: 俄货运飞船与"和平"号轨道站 ; 68298: 法将不参与对海地的军事干预.

[2] Topics of articles in UPenn CTB from 28,000-32,000 tokens– 28071: 中保财险公司 ; 28345: 中国税务部门规定： ; 28745: 广东科技产出指标 ; 29197:

curves start to flatten only to suddenly around the 40,000 token mark shift back into a climb until about 70,000 tokens. An investigation of the ASBC data also showed a subtle shift in subject matter, most of the documents from 29,000 to 39,000 tokens were short notes and simple bulletins on shifts in academic positions, whereas the later data had more long stories on subjects of greater complexity [3], whereas the later data had more long stories on subjects of greater complexity [4].

Thus the ASBC "A" collection, more so than the UPenn CTB corpus, did eventually seem to approach closure. By the time we reach 80,000 tokens, the ASBC "A" collection only saw 14 new token+tag combinations in the last thousand tokens of new text(see table below). Six of those 14 new combinations were nouns, seven were verbs, and one was a preposition [5], having nearly reached lexical closure on newspaper articles regarding academics. In contrast the CTB collection instead logged 146 new token+tag combinations at the 80,000 token mark and its new vocabulary ranged widely across 12 different parts of speech [6]. While the majority of this new vocabulary were nouns, this continuing influx of new words was due primarily to the late inclusion of international news in the CTB's collection of newspaper articles regarding Chinese economics.

---

天津开发区近百家外资企业 ; 29444: 中国三家企业获 ; 29948: 江苏开放型经济 ; 31003: 陕西将向海内外 ; 31499: 台湾一经济学家指出 ; 31890: 陕西引进外资 ; 32246: 甘肃经济 .

[3] Topics of articles in ASBC "A" from 29,300-32,000 tokens– 29306: 29337: 29382: 讯息: 康乐会消息 ; 29537: 29581: 讯息: 小启 ; 29636: 环保: 读者来文 ; 30087: 讯息: 动态报导 ; 30153: 讯息: 「兰屿观点」在法国获佳作奖 ; 30342: 30402: 30449: 30478: 30539: 讯息: 人事动态 ; 30590: 30677: 30772: 30822: 30944: 讯息: 小启 ; 30976: 31093: 讯息: 学术研讨会 .

[4] Topics of articles in ASBC "A" from 56,000-57,000 tokens– 56183: 人事: 历史语言研究所徵组助理 ; 56232: 讯息: 康乐会活动 ; 56274: 讯息: 房屋出租 ; 56323: 讯息: 「台湾近代经济史」座谈会 ; 56475: 讯息: 「亲子互动与伤害」研讨会 ; 56635: 人物: 动态报导 ; 56798: 人事: 李院长获聘为高普考典试委员长 ; 56852: 讯息: 欧美所邀贾化乐博士来访 ; 56930: 讯息: 生医所协办「台湾问题」研讨会 ; 57019: 讯息: 「第七届傅斯年汉学讲座」 .

[5] ASBC Subcollection A* at 80,000 tokens, 14 New token+types observed: Na 检, Na 民间团体, Na 天文学家, Na 语汇词, Na 正教授, Nc 五组, P 据, VA 过路, VC 奖, VC 签, VC 现存, VF 奉, VF 助, VJ 费; Total tags: 7, Total new items: 14.

[6] UPenn CTB at 80,000 tokens, 146 New token+types observed: AD遂, AD为何, AD武装, AD行将, AD原则, AD正好, AD转瞬, CD１・２万, CD１７１６亿, CD２００, CD２００余, CD２１００多, CD２８００万, CD４００万, CD５５, JJ反法西斯, JJ军工, JJ老牌, JJ统一, JJ专属, LC东半部, LC东边, LC南端, LC西边, M等, M海里, NN阿方, NN阿军, NN捕鱼, NN参与者, NN得益者, NN电信, NN东西方, NN短评, NN对比, NN防务, NN风潮, NN副外长, NN附图, NN管辖权, NN管制, NN海域, NN合并, NN后人, NN后裔, NN环形, NN较量, NN尽头, NN巨人, NN句号, NN剧变, NN军政府, NN控制线, NN盟国, NN旗帜, NN前线, NN桥头堡, NN侵略者, NN热战, NN日, NN世人, NN势力, NN水域, NN牺牲, NN小岛, NN血泪, NN印方, NN英方, NN英国人, NN英军, NN渔牧业, NN渔业, NN渔业区, NN占领军, NN战, NN殖民地, NN中叶, NN终结, NN主岛, NN转折, NN组长, NR阿, NR柏林, NR大马尔维纳, NR大西洋, NR东北亚司, NR东德, NR东欧, NR东西欧, NR福克兰, NR华约, NR联秘希夫香卡尔・梅农, NR洛克希德, NR马丁, NR马丁・玛丽埃塔, NR斯坦利港, NR索莱达, NR唐家璇, NR王楠, NR西德, NR希特勒, NR夏治沔, NR新德里, NR雅尔塔, NR印, NT１１月, NT１８３３年, NT１８世纪, NT１９３９年, NT１９８２年, NT１９８６年, NT１９８９年, NT近来, PU布同i, P据据, P凭借, VA安宁, VV波及, VV独立, VV对峙, VV遏制, VV分区, VV扶植, VV攻占, VV共睹, VV共管, VV合并, VV画上, VV划分, VV击败, VV解体, VV借重, VV进攻, VV剧变, VV看不到, VV冷战, VV沦为, VV难以为继, VV派, VV逝去, VV瓦解, VV危机重重, VV显而易见, VV一分为二, VV愈演愈烈, VV遭到; Total tags: 12, Total new items: 146.

| Tokens | Corpus | New token+tags |
|---|---|---|
| 80,000 | UPenn CTB | 146 (24 NR) |
| | ASBC A | 14 (6 N...) |

## 7 Corpus Building Implications

The fact that the UPenn Chinese Treebank data approaches lexical and syntactic closure at rates comparable to the ASBC "A" file newspaper collection suggests that if the UPenn data had been selected more narrowly, it might have reached closure for the economics domain in the newspaper genre even sooner. Some day corpus linguistics may only need much smaller collections of annotated corpora than is the practice today, relying on new directions in sublanguage research. In the case of the ASBC "A" collection, for example, a robust learning structure should be able to build a useable model on 100,000 words worth of data like this which exhibits strong tendencies to lexical and syntactic closure in the Chinese newspaper genre constrained to a given domain.

If the UPenn CTB were enlarged by the infusion of more news stories on international aspects of Chinese economic development, the CTB might better reach lexical and syntactic closure. The following graph shows that the blind addition of 20K additional Chinese economic news stories does not aid closure much. This additional data spanned many topics not seen in the original 100K collection. If it had been selected precisely to aid closure by measuring its potential contribution before extensive hand annotation, the result could have been better.

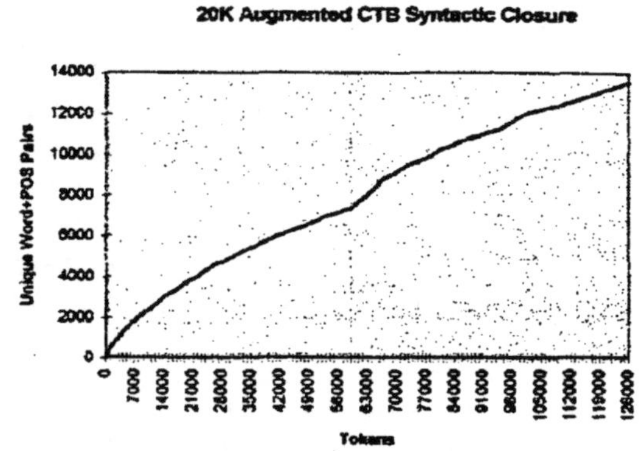


Nevertheless, this expanded CTB collection is sufficiently improved that the rate of closure toward of the expanded collection is better (see table below).

| Tokens | New Tokens | New Token+Tags |
|---|---|---|
| 121,000 | 55 | 64 (12 NR) |
| 122,000 | 61 | 68 (17 NR) |
| 123,000 | 61 | 76 (23 NR) |
| 124,000 | 78 | 82 (18 NR) |
| 125,000 | 48 | 63 (11 NR) |
| 126,000 | 52 | 61 (16 NR) |

Consequently, this expanded CTB collection is sufficiently improved that merging it with the ASBC "A" collection results in a far more measurably representative larger corpus as shown in the final two graphs below. The creation of such measurably representative large corpora out of such smaller, better focused sublanguage building blocks would be cheaper and faster without the resulting tools developed against such corpora suffering much degradation in speed or accuracy.

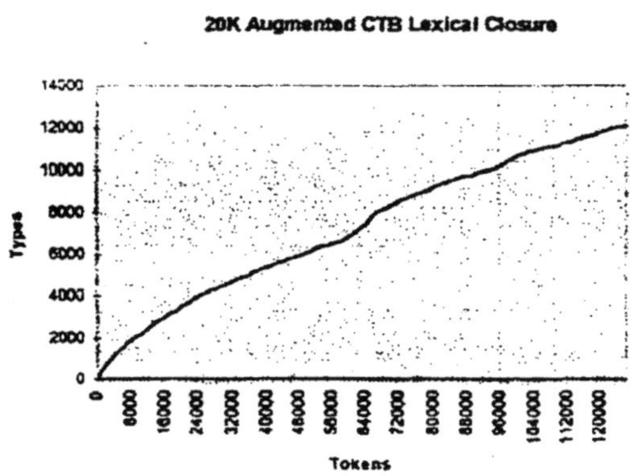


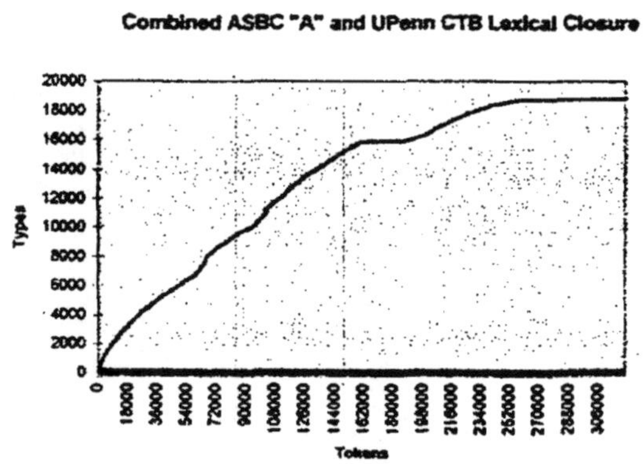

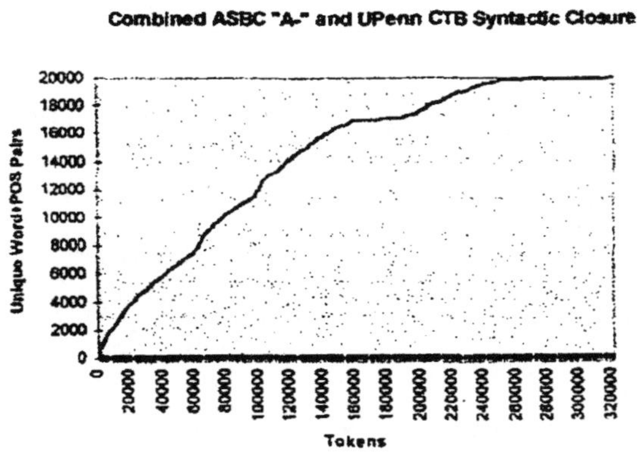


## 8 Discussion

Since only two Chinese tagged corpora are available at the present time, only about 200,000 words of Chinese corpora have been so studied. But to see more work in this vein, one need only consult McEnery and Wilson's study of three English corpora: the IBM computer manual corpus, the Canadian Hansards, and the American Printing House for the Blind corpus (McEnery and Wilson, 1996). Their study (exhaustively detailed in Chapter 6 of their book) spans more than 2.2 million words of tagged English text in three different domains. Consequently the total of 2.3 million words from McEnery and Wilson's results in tagged English texts when combined with these results in tagged Chinese newspaper texts should satisfy any who might argue that there is insufficient data upon which to draw some general conclusions.

This paper does not argue that the two closure measures used are the only measures possible. The argument here is simply that these two closure measures are used to spot when a sublanguage corpus approaches closure–that is, when the curve of new types and new combinations of type with token begins to flatten at a rate below ten percent. One can readily point out that no natural language corpus can ever guarantee closure. The best anyone can aspire to do today, given the current state of our art, is to only approach closure.

## 9 References

### References


D. Biber. 1993. Representativeness in corpus design. volume 8(4), pages 243–257.

P. Bolt. 1994. The international corpus of english project–the hong kong experience. pages 15–24.

R. Garside and A. McEnery. 1993. Treebanking: the compilation of a corpus of skeleton parsed sentences. pages 17–35.

S. Greenbaum. 1992. A new corpus of english: Ice. pages 171–179.

Z. Harris. 1968. *Mathematical Structures of Language*. New York: John Wiley and Sons.

G. Leech. 1991. The state of the art in corpus linguistics. pages 8–29.

T. McEnery and A. Wilson. 1996. *Corpus Linguistics*. Edinburgh: Edinburgh University Press.

S. Sekine. 1994. A new direction for sublanguage nlp. In *Proceedings of the International Conference on New Methods in Language Processing, CCL, UMIST*, pages 123–129.

# A Clustering Algorithm for Chinese Adjectives and Nouns[1]

Yang Wen[1], Chunfa Yuan[1], Changning Huang[2]

[1]State Key Laboratory of Intelligent Technology and System

Deptartment of Computer Science & Technology, Tsinghua University,

Beijing 100084, P.R.C.

[2]Microsoft Research, China

Email: ycf@s1000e.cs.tsinghua.edu.cn

**Key Words:**

bidirectional hierarchical clustering, collocations, minimum description length, collocational degree, revisional distance

## Abstract

This paper proposes a bidirctional hierarchical clustering algorithm for simultaneously clustering words of different parts of speech based on collocations. The algorithm is composed of cycles of two kinds of alternate clustering processes. We construct an objective function based on Minimum Description Length. To partly solve the problem caused by sparse data two concepts of collocational degree and revisional distance are presented.

## 1 Introduction

Recently research on the compositional frames (classification and collocational relationship of words) for Chinese words has been described in Ji et al. (1996)[1], Ji (1997)[2]. The objective of their work is to obtain the clusters of words of different parts of speech and to derive the collocational relationship between different clusters from the collocational relationship between words of different categories.

There are two ways to construct the clusters: One is to get clusters from thesaurus classified manually by linguists. But the fact is that words with the same meanings do not always have the same ability of collocating with other words. The method isn't fit for the NLP problems under our consideration. Another way is to get clusters automatically by computing on the distribution environments of words based on statistical method. The distribution environment of a word is the set of words of other parts of speech that can be collocated with it. We employ the second method in our work.

Previous research usually gets the clusters of words of a certain part of speech based on their distribution environments. But

[1] Supported by National Natural Science Foundation of China (69773031) and "973" Project (G1998030507).

we accept the assumption that the clustering processes of words of different parts of speech are inherently related. For example, having collocations between Chinese adjectives and nouns and if we take on nouns as entities and adjectives as features of nouns' distribution environments, we can obtain clusters of nouns and vice versa. The key of the relationship of the two clustering processes is that they use the same collocations. Therefore we consider the question of clustering the nouns and adjectives simultaneously. Li's work shows that they optimize the clustering results based on this viewpoint (Li et al., 1997)[3]. But they don't explain how to get initial clusters and their scale of problem is too small.

In this paper, we propose an algorithm named bidirectional hierarchical clustering to attempt answering the question.

# 2 Concepts

## 2.1 Problem Description

Our problem can be described as follows: given the set of adjectives $A$, the set of nouns $N$ and the collocation instances, our system will construct a partition $P_N$ over $N$ and a partition $P_A$ over $A$ that respectively contain sets of nouns and sets of adjectives. And both partitions meet the condition that words in the same set (called cluster) have similar semantic distribution environment.

## 2.2 Partitions and Clusters

Let $S$ be a set, $S_i \subset S (i = 1,2,\cdots,n)$. If $P_S = \{S_i\}$ satisfies that

(1) $\bigcup_{i=1}^{n} S_i = S$

(2) $S_i \cap S_j = \varnothing, \forall i,j = 1,2,\cdots n, i \neq j$

Then $P_S$ is a partition over $S$.

In this paper, we call $A_i \in P_A$ an "adjective cluster" and $N_i \in P_N$ a "noun cluster". And we want to obtain the composition of partitions $< P_A, P_N >$ as the clustering result.

## 2.3 Distance between Clusters

In order to measure the distance between clusters of the same part of speech, we use the following equations:

$$dis_A(A_i, A_j) = 1 - \frac{|\Phi_i \cap \Phi_j|}{|\Phi_i \cup \Phi_j|} \quad (1)$$

and

$$dis_N(N_i, N_j) = 1 - \frac{|\Psi_i \cap \Psi_j|}{|\Psi_i \cup \Psi_j|} \quad (2)$$

where $\Phi_i$ is the distribution environment of $A_i$ and is make up of nouns which can be collocated with $A_i$. $\Psi_i$ is the distribution environment of $N_i$ and is composed of adjectives which can be collocated with $N_i$. $\Phi_j$ and $\Psi_j$ follow similar definitions. This distance is a kind of Euclidean distance.

### 2.4 Collocational Degree

Since redundant collocations might be created during clustering, the concept "collocational degree" is used to measure the collocational relationship between a cluster and its distribution environment. The collocational degree is defined as the ratio of the existing collocation instances between the cluster and its distribution environment to all possible collocations generated by them. Thus,

$$\deg A_i = \frac{|\{a\phi \mid a \in A_i, \phi \in \Phi_i, a\phi \in C\}|}{|A_i||\Phi_i|} \quad (3)$$

and

$$\deg N_i = \frac{|\{n\psi \mid n \in N_i, \psi \in \Psi_i, n\psi \in C\}|}{|N_i||\Psi_i|} \quad (4)$$

where $C$ is the set of all existing instances.

### 2.5 Redundant Ratio

After we get the collocational degree of a cluster, redundant ratio (marked as $r$) is calculated to measure the whole performance of the clustering result. We define the redundant ratio as 1 minus the ratio of all existing instances to all possible collocations generated by all clusters (including nouns and adjectives) and their distribution environments. So $r$ is calculated as

$$r = 1 - \frac{2|C|}{\sum_i |A_i||\Phi_i| + \sum_i |N_i||\Psi_i|} \quad (5)$$

## 3 A Bidirectional Hierarchical Clustering Algorithm

Usually a hierarchical clustering algorithm [7] constructs a clustering "tree" by combining small clusters into large ones or dividing large clusters into small ones. The bidirectional hierarchical clustering algorithm proposed by us is composed of two kinds of alternate clustering processes.

The algorithm flow is described as follows:

1) Initially, regard every noun and adjective each as a cluster. Calculate the distances between clusters of the same part of speech.
2) Suppose without loss of generality that we choose to cluster nouns first. Select two noun clusters $N_i$ & $N_j$ of the minimum distance and integrate them into a new one $N_i'$.
3) Calculate the collocational degree of the new cluster. Adjust the sequence numbers of the original clusters and the relational information of adjective clusters.
4) Calculate the distances between the new cluster and other clusters.
5) Repeat from step 2) to 4) until the satisfaction of certain condition. For example, the number of the clusters has decreased to certain amount.[2]
6) Similarly, we can follow the same steps from 2) to 5) for constructing adjective clusters, completing one cycle of clustering processes of nouns and adjectives.
7) Repeat from step 2) to 6) until the

[2] In this paper, we set the proportion is 20%.

objective function[3] reaches the minimum value.

One advantage of this algorithm is that: when two clusters of nouns have similar distribution environments, they might be classified into one cluster. This information can be delivered to the clusters of adjectives that respectively collocate with them by the clustering process of nouns. Thus these clusters of adjectives have great possibility to be combined into one cluster, while the ordinary hierarchical clustering algorithm can not do it.

## 4 An Objective Function Based on MDL

The objective function is designed to control the processes of clustering words based on the Minimum Description Length (MDL) principle. According to MDL, the best probability model for a given set of data is a model that uses the shortest code length for encoding the model itself and the given data relative to it [4] [5]. We regard the clusters as the model for the collocations of adjectives and nouns. The objective function is defined as the sum of the code length for the model ("model description length") and that for the data ("data description length"). When the clustering result minimises the objective function, the bidirectional processes should be stopped and the result is the best probable one. The objective function based on MDL trade-offs between the simplicity of a model and its accuracy in fitting to the data, which are respectively quantified by the model description length and the data description length.

[3] Described later in section 4.

The following are the formulas to calculate the objective function $L$:

$$L = L_{mod} + L_{dat} \tag{6}$$

$L_{mod}$ is the model description length calculated as

$$\begin{aligned} L_{mod} &= -\sum_{i=1}^{k_A} \frac{1}{k_A} \log_2 \frac{1}{k_A} - \sum_{i=1}^{k_N} \frac{1}{k_N} \log_2 \frac{1}{k_N} + 1 \\ &= \log_2(k_A k_N) + 1 \end{aligned} \tag{7}$$

Where $k_A$ and $k_N$ respectively denote the number of clusters of adjectives and nouns. "+1" means that the algorithm needs one bit to indicate whether the collocational relationship between the two clusters exists.

$L_{dat}$ is composed of the data description length of adjectives and that of nouns, namely

$$L_{dat} = L_{dat}(A) + L_{dat}(N) \tag{8}$$

And the two types of data description length are calculated as follows

$$L_{dat}(A) = -\sum_{i=1}^{k_A} \frac{1}{k_A k_N} \sum_{j=1}^{|\Phi_i|} \log_2 \frac{1}{|A_i||N_k|} \tag{9}$$

$$\forall j, \phi_j \in \Phi_i \text{ and } \phi_j \in N_k$$

$$L_{dat}(N) = -\sum_{i=1}^{k_N} \frac{1}{k_A k_N} \sum_{j=1}^{|\Psi_i|} \log_2 \frac{1}{|N_i||A_k|} \tag{10}$$

$$\forall j, \psi_j \in \Psi_i \text{ and } \psi_j \in A_k$$

## 5 Our Experiment

We take the words and collocations

gathered in Ni's Thesaurus [6] to test our algorithm. From Ni's thesaurus, we obtain 2,569 adjectives, 4,536 nouns and 37,346 collocations between adjectives and nouns.

Table 1 shows results of using 5 different revisional distance formulas discussed in the next section. Because the length of this paper is limited, we only give some examples (10 clusters for each part of speech) of clusters in section 8. We can see that the redundant ratio obviously decreases by using the revisional distance, and the result that has the lowest redundant ratio corresponds of the minimum value of the objective function. By human evaluation, most clusters contain the words that have similar meanings and distribution environments. So our algorithm proves to be effective for word clustering based on collocations.

## 6 Discussions

### 6.1 Rivisional Distance

When we combine clusters into a new cluster, their distribution environments will be combined as well. The combination of clusters and their distribution environments might very likely generate redundant collocations that are not listed in the thesaurus. With the word clustering processes going on, there might be more and more redundant collocations. They will obviously affect the accuracy of the distances between clusters. When calculating the distances, the redundant collocations must be considered. So the question is how to revise the distance equation. Notice that the collocational degree defined in the above measures the collocational relationship between a cluster and its distribution environment. Obviously under the same distance, clusters having higher collocational degree have more higher similarity between each other (because they have more actual collocations) than those having lower collocational degree. So the collocational degree can be used to revise the distance equations.

Table 1: Results of different revisional distances

| Revisional distance | $k_A$ | $k_N$ | $L$ | r |
|---|---|---|---|---|
| Not used | 409 | 550 | 20. 067 | 99. 01% |
| $dis' = -\overline{\deg}\ln dis$ | 397 | 610 | 20. 082 | 86. 96% |
| $dis' = dis/\overline{\deg}$ | 383 | 595 | 20. 002 | 78. 78% |
| $dis' = dis/\sqrt{\overline{\deg}}$ | 373 | 586 | 20. 017 | 80. 39% |
| $dis' = -dis\ln\overline{\deg}$ | 395 | 557 | 20. 007 | 80. 08% |

However, the redundant ratio is still very large. The main cause is that existing instances are too sparse, covering only 0.32% of all possible collocations. So another advantage of our algorithm is that we can acquire many new reasonable collocations not gathered in the thesaurus. If we add the new collocations into initial thesaurus and execute the algorithm on new data set, the performance will have great potential to improve. It is further work that can be carried out in the future.

There are two problems that should be considered when we design the revisional distance equations. The first one is to convert the collocational degrees of two clusters into one collocational degree as the revisional factor for distance equations. It is the average collocational degree, marked as $\overline{\deg}$, calculated by

$$\overline{\deg}_A = \frac{\deg A_i |\Phi_i||A_i| + \deg A_j |\Phi_j||A_j|}{(|A_i| + |A_j|)|\Phi_i \cup \Phi_j|} \quad (11)$$

and

$$\overline{\deg}_N = \frac{\deg N_i |\Psi_i||N_i| + \deg N_j |\Psi_j||N_j|}{(|N_i| + |N_j|)|\Psi_i \cup \Psi_j|} \quad (12)$$

In fact it is the collocational degree of the new cluster into which if we assume combining the two original clusters.

The second problem is that the revisonal distance equations should keep coherent of monotonicity with the original distance. It means that under the same average collocational degree, the revional distance should keep the same (or opposite) monotonicity with the original distance, and under the same original distance, the revional distance should keep the same (or opposite) monotonicity with the average collocational degree.

In this paper, four simple revisional distance equations are presented based on consideration of the upper two problems. They are:

a) $dis' = -\overline{\deg} \ln dis$

b) $dis' = \dfrac{dis}{\overline{\deg}}$

c) $dis' = \dfrac{dis}{\sqrt{\overline{\deg}}}$

d) $dis' = -dis \ln \overline{\deg}$

Where $dis'$ denotes the revional distance and $dis$ denotes the original distance.

From the comparison of the upper different results (shown in Table 1), we can draw the conclusion that using revisonal distance equations can increase the clustering accuracy remarkably.

## 6.2 Determinant of Objective Function's Minimum Value

The clustering algorithm terminates when the objective function is minimized. As a result it is very important to find out the function's minimum value. After analyzing the objective function, we find that it normally monotonically declines with clustering processes going on until it gets minimized. At the beginning, there are a large number of clusters with only one element in each of them. So the model description length is quite large while the data description length is quite small. Because the clustering process is hierarchical, every time when the combination occurs the number of clusters will decrease by one with the model description length's decreasing as well. At the same time the number of a certain cluster's elements will increase by one with the data description length's increment as well. However, the decrement is larger than the increment and it is getting smaller while the increment is getting larger. In this way, the objective function declines until the objective function reach its minimum value. If we continue to execute the algorithm, we will see that the value of the objective function rises very fast like as is shown in Figure 1.

addition, the clustering algorithm may help to find new collocations that are not in the thesaurus. This algorithm can also be extended to other collocation models, such as verb-noun collocations.

Figure 1: Values of the Objective Functions

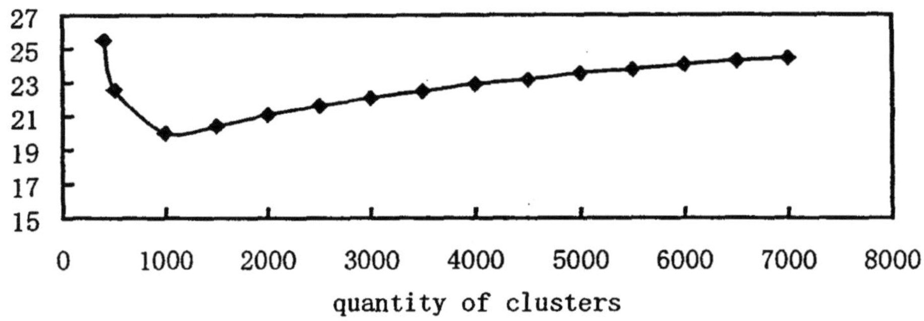


Therefore we choose a fairly simple way to avoid the appearance of the local optimum: When there are two consecutive increases in the objective function during one clustering process, stop the process and start another one. When two consecutive clustering processes are stopped due to the same reason, we assume that we have got the minimum value and stop the whole clustering process. In our future work we will try to find a better way to determine the minimum value of the objective function.

## 7 Conclusion & Future Work

In this paper we have presented a bidirctional hierarchical clustering algorithm of simultaneously clustering Chinese adjectives and nouns based on their collocations. Our preliminary experiments show that it can distinguish different words by their distribution environments. In addition, the clustering algorithm may help to find new collocations that are not in the thesaurus. This algorithm can also be extended to other collocation models, such as verb-noun collocations.

Our future work includes:

1) Because the sparsity of collocations is a main factor of affecting the word clustering accuracy, we can use the clustering results to discover new data and enrich the thesaurus.
2) As there are yet no adjustments to the hierarchical clustering results, we are considering using some iterative algorithm, such as K-means algorithm, to optimise the clustering results.

## 8 Attachment (Examples)

We give 10 clusters of each part of speech clustered by our algorithm (using revisional distance formula b) as follows:

### 8.1 Chinese Adjective clusters (10 of 383)

A1 风趣 天生 雄辩

A2 慷慨 荒唐 虚伪 乐观 糊涂 天真 冷静 单纯 缓和 荒谬 苦闷 悲观 烦恼 灰心 慎重 果断 苦恼 清醒 稚嫩 稚气 清高 迫切

A3 空虚 纯洁 脆弱 忧郁 消遥 充实 狂热

A4 糟糕 出色 优秀 杰出 卓越 合格 逊色 低劣 香

A5 卑劣 庸俗 卑鄙 下流 无耻 文明 狠毒 恶毒 残酷 野蛮 凶恶 凶残 黑暗 阴险 丑恶 残忍 残暴 刻薄 刻毒 凶暴 严酷 可耻 狂妄 凶狠 狡猾 蛮横

A6 无赖 坚定 稳 婉转 坚决 强硬 虔诚

A7 和气 红润 狠心 宏观 富有 阔

A8 耐心 积极 消极 主观 主动 顽固 保守 谨慎

A9 温厚 凌厉 凛然 磅礴

A10 贤惠 花哨 起劲 荣幸 傻 伤感 体面 内疚

8.2 Chinese noun clusters (10 of 595)

N1 老板娘 漫画 徒工 喜剧 小丑 小贩 小品 寓言

N2 阿飞 盗匪 地痞 地震 赌棍 官府 坏蛋 火灾 奸商 流氓 盲流 骗子 品性 小青年 小偷 阴谋 罪犯

N3 阿姨 见证人 奶奶 年头 售票员 信徒 助手 走狗

N4 哀乐 后母 计谋 教训 良策 内行 亲人 生路 知情人

N5 哀思 春意 光明 情操 柔情 深情 诗意

N6 爱 表格 地址 古书 经书 去向 图表 图象 渊源 帐目 哲学

N7 爱好 标语 风俗 角度 年龄 深度 体型 兴趣

N8 爱情 抱负 感情 理想 青春 情感 情谊 友谊

N9 爱人 旅客 妻子 同学

N10 案犯 部下 敌军 革命家 心态 信仰

## References


[1] Donghong Ji & Changning Huang, A Semantic Composition Model for Chinese Noun and Adjective, Communications of COCIPS 6(1): P25-P33, 1996

[2] Donghong Ji, Computational Research on Issues of Lexical Semantics, Post-doctoral Research Report, Tsinghua University , P14~P26, 1997

[3] Juanzi Li et al., Two-dimensional Clustering Based on Compositional Examples, Language Engineering, P164-P169, Tsinghua University Press, 1997

[4] Hang Li & Naoki Abe，Clustering Words with the MDL Principle，cmp-lg/9605014 v2，1996

[5] Wei Xu, The Study of Syntax-Semantics Integrated Chinese Parsing, Thesis for the Degree of Master in Computer Science, Tsinghua University, 1997

[6] Wenjie Ni et al., Modern Chinese Thesaurus, China People Press, 1984

[7] Zhaoqi Bian et al., Pattern Recognition, Tsinghua University Press, 1997

# Extraction of Chinese Compound Words – An Experimental Study on a Very Large Corpus

**Jian Zhang**
Department of Computer Science and Technology of Tsinghua University, China
ajian@s1000e.cs.tsinghua.edu.cn

**Jianfeng Gao, Ming Zhou**
Microsoft Research China
{jfgao, mingzhou}@microsoft.com

**Abstract**

This paper is to introduce a statistical method to extract Chinese compound words from a very large corpus[1]. This method is based on *mutual information* and *context dependency*. Experimental results show that this method is efficient and robust compared with other approaches. We also examined the impact of different parameter settings, corpus size and heterogeneousness on the extraction results. We finally present results on information retrieval to show the usefulness of extracted compounds.

## 1 Introduction

Almost all techniques to statistical language processing, including speech recognition, machine translation and information retrieval, are based on words. Although word-based approaches work very well for western languages, where words are well defined, it is difficult to apply to Chinese. Chinese sentences are written as characters strings with no spaces between words. Therefore, words in Chinese are actually not well marked in sentences, and there does not exist a commonly accepted Chinese lexicon.

Furthermore, since new compounds (words formed with at least two characters) are constantly created, it is impossible to list them exhaustively in a lexicon. Therefore, automatic extraction of compounds is an important issue. Traditional extraction approaches used rules. However, compounds extracted in this way are not always desirable. So, human effort is still required to find the preferred compounds from a large compound candidate list. Some statistical approaches to extract Chinese compounds from corpus have been proposed (Lee-Feng Chien 1997, WU Dekai and Xuanyin XIA 1995, Ming-Wen Wu and Keh-Yih Su 1993) as well, but almost all experiments are based on relatively small corpus, it is not clear whether these methods still work well with large corpus.

In this paper, we investigate statistical approaches to Chinese compound extraction from very large corpus by using statistical features, namely *mutual information* and *context dependency*. There are three main contributions in this paper. First, we apply our procedure on a very large corpus while other experiments were based on small or medium size corpora. We show that better results can be obtained with a large corpus. Second, we examine how the results can be influenced by parameter settings including *mutual information* and *context dependency* restrictions. It turns out that *mutual information mainly affects precision while context dependency affects the count of extracted items.* Third, we test the usefulness of the extracted compounds for information retrieval. Our experimental results on IR show that the new compounds have a positive effect on IR.

The rest of this paper is structured as follows. In section 2, we describe the techniques we used. In section 3, we present several sets of experimental results. In section 4, we outline the related works as well as their results. Finally, we give our conclusions in section 5.

## 2 Technique description

Statistical extraction of Chinese compounds has been used in (Lee-Feng Chien 1997)(WU Dekai and Xuanyin XIA 1995) and (Ming-Wen Wu and Keh-Yih Su 1993). The basic idea is that a

[1] This work was done while the author worked for Microsoft Research China as a visiting student.

Chinese compound should appear as a stable sequence in corpus. That is, the components in the compound are strongly correlated, while the components lie at both ends should have low correlations with outer words.

The method consists of two steps. At first, a list of candidate compounds is extracted from a very large corpus by using *mutual information*. Then, *context dependency* is used to remove undesirable compounds. In what follows, we will describe them in more detail.

## 2.1 Mutual Information

According to our study on Chinese corpora, most compounds are of length less than 5 characters. The average length of words in the segmented-corpus is of approximately 1.6 characters. Therefore, only word *bi-gram*, *tri-gram*, and *quad-gram* in the corpus are of interest to us in compound extraction.

We use a criterion, called *mutual information*, to evaluate the correlation of different components in the compound. *Mutual information* $MI(x,y)$ of a *bi-gram* $(x, y)$ is estimated by:

$$MI(x,y) = \frac{f(x,y)}{f(x)+f(y)-f(x,y)}$$

Where $f(x)$ is the occurrence frequency of word $x$ in the corpus, and $f(x,y)$ is the occurrence frequency of the word pair $(x,y)$ in the corpus. The higher the value of $MI$ is, the more likely $x$ and $y$ are to form a compound.

The mutual information MI(x,y,z) of tri-gram (x,y,z) is estimated by:

$$MI(x,y,z) = \frac{f(x,y,z)}{f(x)+f(y)+f(z)-f(x,y,z)}$$

The estimation of *mutual information* of *quad-grams* is similar to that of tri-grams. The extracted compounds should be of higher value of $MI$ than a pre-set threshold.

## 2.2 Context Dependency

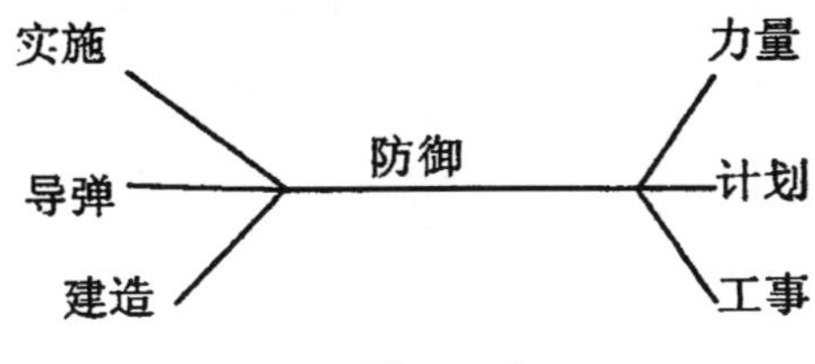


Figure 1

The extracted Chinese compounds should be complete. That is, we should generate a whole word, not a part of it. For example, 导弹防御计划(missile defense plan) is a complete word, and 导弹防御 (missile defense) is not, although both have relatively high value of mutual information.

Therefore, we use another feature, called *context dependency*. The contexts of the word 防御(defense) are illustrated by figure 1.

A compound $X$ has NO left context dependency if

$$LSize = |L| > t1 \text{ or}$$

$$MaxL = MAX_{\alpha} \frac{f(\alpha X)}{f(X)} < t2$$

Where $t1$, $t2$ are threshold value, $f(.)$ is frequency, $L$ is the set of left adjacent strings of $X$, $\alpha \in L$ and $|L|$ means the number of unique left adjacent strings. Similarly, a compound $X$ has NO right context dependency if

$$RSize = |R| > t3 \text{ or}$$

$$MaxR = MAX_{\beta} \frac{f(\beta X)}{f(X)} < t4$$

Where $t1$, $t2$, $t3$, $t4$ are threshold value, $f(.)$ is frequency, $R$ is the set of right adjacent strings of $X$, $\beta \in R$ and $|R|$ means the number of unique left adjacent strings.

The extracted complete compounds should have neither left nor right *context dependency*.

# 3 Experimental results

In our experiments, three corpora were used to test the performance of the presented approach. These corpora are described in table 1. Corpus A consists of local news with more than 325 million characters. Corpus B consists of documents from different domains of novel, news, technique report, etc., with approximately 650 million characters. Corpus C consists of People's Daily news and Xinhua news from TREC5 and TREC6 (Harman and Voorhees, 1996) with 75 million characters.

Table 1: Characteristics of Corpora

| Corpus | Source | Size(char#) |
|---|---|---|
| Corpus A | political, economic news | 325 M |
| Corpus B | Corpus A + novels + technique reports, etc. | 650 M |

| | | |
|---|---|---|
| Corpus C | TREC 5/6 Chinese corpus | 75 M |

In the first experiment, we test the performance of our method on corpus A, which is homogeneity in style. We then use corpus B in the second experiment to test if the method works as well on the corpus that is heterogeneity in style. We also use different parameter settings in order to figure out the best combination of the two statistical features, i.e. *mutual information* and *context dependency*. In the third experiment, we apply the results of the method to information retrieval system. We extract new compounds on corpus C, and add them to the indexing lexicon, and we achieve a higher average precision-recall. In all experiments, corpora are segmented automatically into words using a lexicon consisting of 65,502 entries.

### 3.1 Compounds Extraction from Homogeneous Corpus

Corpus A contains political and economic news. In this series of tests, we gradually loosen the conditions to form a compound, i.e. *MI* threshold becomes smaller and *MaxL/MaxR* becomes larger. Results for *quad-grams, tri-grams* and *bi-grams* are shown in tables 2,3,4. Some compounds extracted are listed in table 5.

Table2: Performance of *quad-gram* compounds extraction

| | Parameter setting (*MI, LSize, MaxL, RSize, MaxR*) | Number of New compounds found | Precision (correct compounds/compounds checked) |
|---|---|---|---|
| 1 | 0.01 1 0.75 1 0.75 | 27 | 100% (27/27) |
| 2 | 0.005 1 0.85 1 0.85 | 92 | 98.9% (91/92) |
| 3 | 0.002 1 0.90 1 0.90 | 513 | 95.8% (113/118) |
| 4 | 0.001 1 0.95 1 0.95 | 1648 | 96.2% (179/186) |
| 5 | 0.0005 1 0.95 1 0.95 | 4707 | 96.7% (206/213) |

Table3: Performance of *tri-gram* compounds extraction

| | Parameter setting (*MI, LSize, MaxL, RSize, MaxR*) | Number of New compounds found | Precision (correct compounds/compounds checked) |
|---|---|---|---|
| 1 | 0.02 2 0.70 2 0.70 | 167 | 100% (167/167) |
| 2 | 0.01 2 0.75 2 0.75 | 538 | 100% (205/205) |
| 3 | 0.005 2 0.80 2 0.80 | 1607 | 100% (262/262) |
| 4 | 0.003 2 0.80 2 0.80 | 3532 | 98.3% (341/347) |
| 5 | 0.001 2 0.80 2 0.80 | 16849 | 96.6% (488/501) |

Table4: Performance of *bi-gram* compounds extraction

| | Parameter setting (*MI, LSize, MaxL, RSize, MaxR*) | Number of New compounds found | Precision (correct compounds/compounds checked) |
|---|---|---|---|
| 1 | 0.05 3 0.5 3 0.5 | 1622 | 98.9% (184/186) |
| 2 | 0.05 3 0.6 3 0.6 | 1904 | 98.6% (309/212) |
| 3 | 0.03 3 0.6 3 0.6 | 3938 | 97.8% (218/223) |
| 4 | 0.01 3 0.5 3 0.5 | 14666 | 97.5% (354/363) |
| 5 | 0.005 3 0.5 3 0.5 | 32899 | 97.3% (404/415) |

Table 5: Some *N-gram* compounds found by our method

<table>
<tr><th>N-gram</th><th>Extracted Compounds</th></tr>
<tr><td>N=2</td><td>粮|库(grain depot)、光盘|驱动器(CD-ROM Driver)、盖|茨(Bill Gates)</td></tr>
<tr><td>N=3</td><td>宣|武|门(XuanWu Gate)、异步|传输|模式(asynchronous transfer model)、亚|马|逊(Amazon)</td></tr>
<tr><td>N=4</td><td>爱|丽|舍|宫(Elysee)、俄|亥|俄|州(Ohio)、董|建|华|先生(Mr. Dong Jianhua)</td></tr>
</table>

It turns out that our algorithm successfully extracted a large number of new compounds (>50000) from raw texts. Compared with previous methods described in the next section, the precision is very high. We can also find that there is little precision loss when we loose restriction. The result may be due to three reasons. First, the two statistical features really characterize the nature of compounds, and provide a simple and efficient way to estimate the possibility of a word sequence being a compound. Second, the corpus we use is very large. It is always true that more data leads to better results. Third, the corpus we used in this experiment is homogeneity in style. The raw corpus is composed of news on politics, economy, science and technology. These are formal articles, and the sentences and compounds are well normalized and strict. This is very helpful for compound extraction.

### 3.2 Compounds Extraction from Heterogeneous Corpus

In this experiment, we use a heterogeneous corpus. It is a combination of corpus A, and some other novels, technique reports, etc. For simplicity, we discuss the extraction of *bi-gram* compounds only. In comparison with the first experiment, we find that the precision is strongly affected by the corpus we used. As shown in table 6, for each corpus, we use the same parameter setting, say *MI* >0.005, *LSize* >3, *MaxL* <0.5, *RSize*>3 and *MaxR*<0.5.

Table 6: Impact of heterogeneousness of corpora

| Corpus | Compounds extracted | Extract precision |
|---|---|---|
| Corpus A | 32899 | 97.3% (404/415) |
| Corpus B | 36383 | 88.3% (362/410) |

As we mentioned early, the larger the corpus we use, the better results we obtain. Therefore, we intuitively expect better result on corpus B, which is larger than corpus A. But, the result shown in table 6 is just the opposite.

There are mainly two reasons for this. The first one is that our method works better on homogeneous corpus than on heterogeneous corpus. The second one is that it might not be suitable to use the same parameter settings on two different corpora. We then try different parameter settings on corpus B.

There are two groups of parameters. *MI* measures the correlation between adjacent words, and other four parameters, namely *LSize, RSize, MaxL,* and *MaxR,* measure the context dependency. Therefore, each time, we fix one parameter, and relax another from tight to loose to see what happens. The Number of extracted compounds and precision of each parameter setting are shown in table 7.

Table 7: Extraction results with different parameter settings
(*MI=Mutual Information, CD = Context Dependency=(LSize, MaxL, RSize, MaxR)*)

| MI\CD | (2, 0.8, 2, 0.8) | (6, 0.7, 6, 0.7) | (10, 0.6, 10, 0.6) | (14, 0.5, 4, 0.5) | (18, 0.4, 18, 0.4) | (22, 0.3, 22, 0.3) | (26, 0.2, 6, 0.2) |
|---|---|---|---|---|---|---|---|
| 0.0002 | 1457781 (39.06%) | 809502 (42.24%) | 570601 (43.98%) | 426223 (44.67%) | 314810 (43.96%) | 209910 (43.38%) | 96383 (40.93%) |
| 0.0004 | 784082 (48.98%) | 485143 (46.84%) | 359499 (52.53%) | 277673 (49.25%) | 209634 (53.92%) | 141215 (49.55%) | 63907 (52.53%) |
| 0.0006 | 530723 (51.28%) | 349882 (53.96%) | 266068 (60.39%) | 208921 (52.48%) | 159363 (49.49%) | 108120 (63.35%) | 48683 (61.65%) |
| 0.0008 | 396602 (54.63%) | 273231 (58.00%) | 211044 (55.19%) | 167660 (65.24%) | 128819 (60.54%) | 87869 (64.40%) | 39502 (54.86%) |
| 0.0010 | 313868 (59.11%) | 223827 (66.51%) | 175050 (61.14%) | 140197 (57.66%) | 108322 (67.38%) | 74104 (63.08%) | 33354 (67.50%) |
| 0.0012 | 257990 (58.94%) | 189014 (59.50%) | 149315 (60.98%) | 120312 (65.28%) | 93323 (70.47%) | 64079 (65.32%) | 28879 (64.65%) |
| 0.0014 | 217766 (58.93%) | 163189 (67.91%) | 129978 (60.19%) | 105334 (65.84%) | 82083 (66.83%) | 56582 (67.50%) | 25486 (65.46%) |

Table 7 shows the extraction results with different parameters. These results fit our intuition. While parameters become more and more strict, less and less compounds are found and precisions become higher. This phenomena is also illustrated in figure 2 and 3, in which the "correct compounds extracted" is an estimation from table7, i.e. ***number of compounds found* × *precision*.** (These two figures are very useful for one who wants to automatically extract a new lexicon with pre-defined size from a large corpus.)

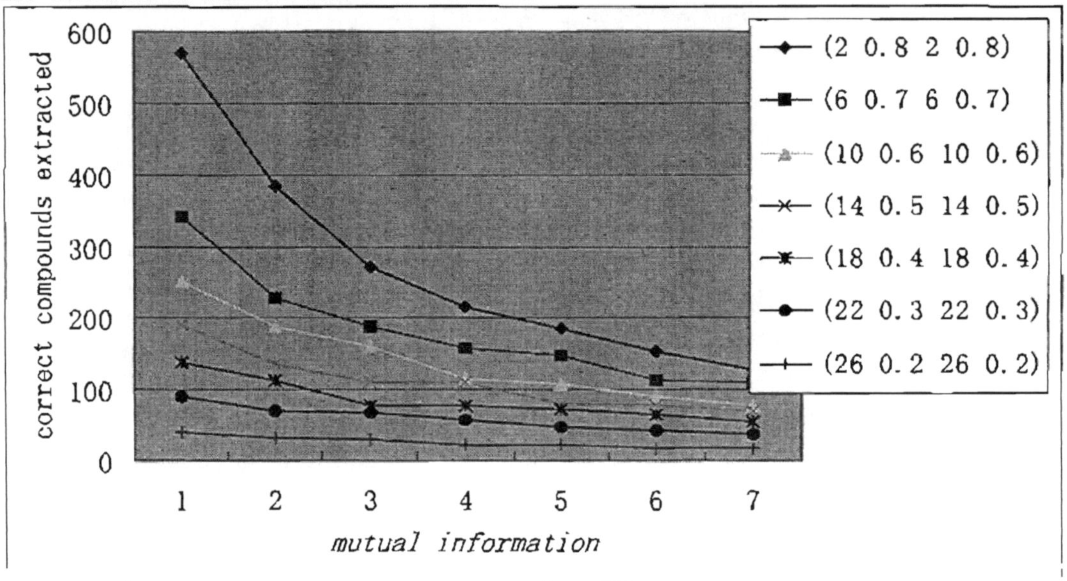


Figure 2 Impact of Parameter *Mutual Information*

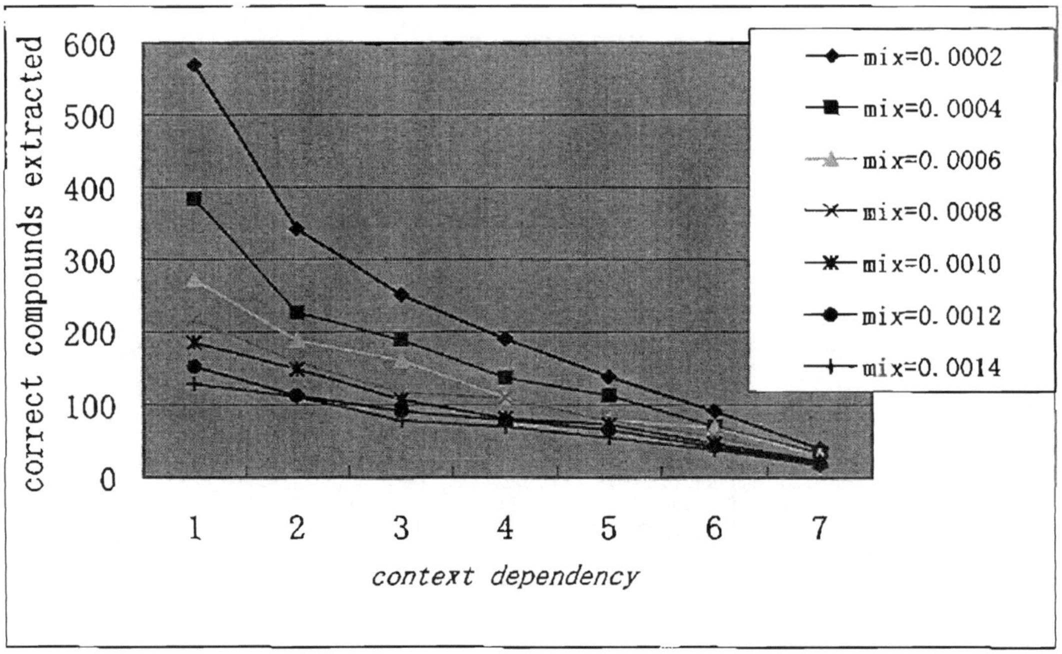


Figure 3 Impact of Parameter *Context Dependency*

The precision of extraction is estimated in the following way. We extract a set of compounds based on a series of pre-defined parameter set. For each set of compounds, we randomly select 200 compounds. Then we merge those selected compounds to a new file for manually check. This file consists of about 9,800 new compounds because there are 49 compounds lists. One person will group these 'compounds' into two sets, say set A and set B. Set A contains the items that are considered to be correct, and set B contains incorrect ones. Then for each original group of about 200 compounds we select in the first step, we check how many items that also appear in set A and how many items in set B. Suppose these two values are *a1* and *b1*, then we estimate the precision as *a1/(a1+b1)*.

So, there are two important points in our evaluation process. First, it is difficult to give a definition of the term "compound" to be accepted popularly. Different people may have different judgement. Only one person takes part in the evaluation in our experiment. This can eliminate the effect of divergence among different persons. Second, we merge those items together. This can eliminate the effect of different time period. One may feel tired after checked too many items. If he checks those 49 files one by one, the latter results are incomparable with the previous one.

The precisions estimated by the above method are not exactly correct. However, as described above, the precisions of different parameter settings are comparable. In this experiment, what we want to show is how the parameter settings affect the results.

Both *MI* and *CD* can affect number of extracted compounds, as shown in table 7. Compared with *MI*, *CD* has stronger effect in this aspect. For each row in table 7, numbers of extracted compounds finally decrease to 10% of that showed in the first column. For each column, while *MI* changes from 0.0002 to 0.0014, the number is decreased of about 20%. This may be explained by the fact that it is difficult for candidate to fulfill all four restrictions in *CD* simultaneously. Many disqualified candidates are cut off. Table 7 lists the precisions of extracted results. It shows that there is no clear increasing/decreasing pattern in each row. That is to say, *CD* doesn't strongly affect the precision. When we check each column, we can see that precision is in a growing progress. As we defined above, *MI* and *CD* are two different measurements. What role they play in our extraction procedure? Our conclusion is that *mutual information mainly affects the precision while context dependency mainly affects the count of extracted items*. This conclusion is also confirmed by Fig2 and Fig3. That is, the curves in Fig2 are more flat than corresponding curves in Fig3.

### 3.3 Testing the Extracted Compounds in Information Retrieval

In this experiment, we apply our method to improve information retrieval results. We use SMART system (Buckley 1985) for our experiments. SMART is a robust, efficient and flexible information retrieval system. The corpus used in this experiment is TREC Chinese corpus (Harman and Voorhees, 1996). The corpus contains about 160,000 articles, including articles published in the People's Daily from 1991 to 1993, and a part of the news released by the Xinhua News Agency in 1994 and 1995. A set of 54 queries has been set up and evaluated by people in NIST(National Institute of Standards and Technology).

We first use an initial lexicon consisting of 65,502 entries to segment the corpus. When running SMART on the segmented corpus, we obtain an average precision of 42.90%.

Then we extract new compounds from the segmented corpus, and add them into the initial lexicon. With the new lexicon, the TREC Chinese corpus is re-segmented. When running SMART on this re-segmented corpus, we obtain an average precision of 43.42%, which shows a slight improvement of 1.2%.

Further analysis shows that the new lexicon brings positive effect to 10 queries and negative effect to 4 queries. For other 40 queries, there is no obvious effect. Some improved queries are listed in table 8 as well as new compounds being contained.

As an example, we give the segmentation results with the two lexicons for query 23 in table 9.

Table 8: Improved Query Samples

| Query ID | Base line precision | New precision | Improvement | Extracted compounds |
|---|---|---|---|---|
| 9 | 0.3648 | 0.4173 | 14.4% | 毒品买卖(drugs sale),中国毒品问题(Drug Problems in China) |
| 23 | 0.3940 | 0.5154 | 30.8% | 联合国安理会(the UN Security Council),和平建议(peace proposal) |
| 30 | 0.3457 | 0.3639 | 5.3% | |
| 46 | 0.3483 | 0.4192 | 20.4% | 中越(China and Vietnam) |
| 47 | 0.5369 | 0.5847 | 8.9% | 皮纳图博火山(Mount Minatubo),臭氧层(ozone layer), 苏比克(Subic) |

Table 9: Segmented Corpus with the Two Lexicons for Query 23

| |
|---|
| Query 23 segment with small lexicon<br>相关 文件 应 提及 苏联 在 海湾战争 中 如何 担任 调停 的 角色，包括 与 伊拉克 之间 的 沟通，苏联 在 [联合国] [安理会] 中 提出 的 停火协议，以及 要求 多国部队 从 伊拉克 撤出 的 [和平] [建议] |
| Query 23 segment with new lexicon<br>相关 文件 应 提及 苏联 在 海湾战争 中 如何 担任 调停 的 角色，包括 与 伊拉克 之间 的 沟通，苏联 在 [联合国安理会] 中 提出 的 停火协议，以及 要求 多国部队 从 伊拉克 撤出 的 [和平建议] |

Another interesting example is query 30. There is no new compound extracted from that query. Its result is also improved significantly because its relevant documents are segmented better than before.

Because the compounds extracted from the corpus are not exactly correct, the new lexicon will bring negative effect to some queries, such as query 10. The retrieval precision changes from 0.3086 to 0.1359. The main reason is that "中国新疆"(Chinese XinJiang) is taken as a new compound in the query.

## 4 Related works

Several methods have been proposed for extracting compounds from corpus by statistical approaches. In this section, we will briefly describe some of them.

(Lee-Feng Chien 1997) proposed an approach based on PAT-Tree to automatically extracting domain specific terms from online text collections. Our method is primary derived from (Lee-Feng Chien 1997), and use the similar statistical features, i.e. *mutual information* and *context dependency*. The difference is that we use n-gram instead of PAT-Tree, due to the efficiency issue. Another difference lies in the experiments. In Chien's work, only domain specific terms are extracted from domain specific corpus, and the size of the corpus is relatively small, namely 1,872 political news abstracts.

(Cheng-Huang Tung and His-Jian Lee 1994) also presented an efficient method for identifying unknown words from a large corpus. The statistical features used consist of string (character sequence) frequency and entropy of left/right neighboring characters (similar to left/right context dependency). The corpus consists of 178,027 sentences, representing a total of more than 2 million Chinese characters. 8327 unknown words were identified and 5366 items of them were confirmed manually.

(Ming-Wen Wu and Keh-Yih Su 1993) presented a method using mutual information and relative frequency. 9,124 compounds are extracted from the corpus consists of 74,404 words, with the precision of 47.43%. In this method, the compound extraction problem is formulated as classification problem. Each bi-gram (tri-gram) is assigned to one of those two clusters. It also needs a training corpus to estimate parameters for classification model. In our method, we didn't make use of any training corpus. Another difference is that they use the method for English compounds extraction while we extract Chinese compounds in our experiments .

(Pascale Fung 1998) presented two simple systems for Chinese compound extraction—CXtract. CXtract uses predominantly statistical lexical information to find term boundaries in large text. Evaluations on the corpus consisting of 2 million characters show that the average precision is 54.09%.

We should note that since the experiment setup and evaluation systems of the methods mentioned above are not identical, the results are not comparable. However, by showing our experimental results on much larger and heterogenous corpus, we can say that our method is an efficient and robust one.

## 5 Conclusion

In this paper, we investigate a statistical approach to Chinese compounds extraction from very large corpora using *mutual information* and *context dependency*.

We explained how the performance can be influenced by different parameter settings, corpus size, and corpus heterogeneousness. We also refine the lexicon with information retrieval system by adding compounds obtained by our methods, and achieve 1.2% improvements on precision of IR.

Through our experiments, we conclude that statistical method based on *mutual information* and *context dependency* is efficient and robust for Chinese compounds extraction. And, *mutual information* mainly affects the precision while *context dependency* mainly affects the count of extracted items.

## Reference

Lee-Feng Chien, (1997) "PAT-tree-based keyword extraction for Chinese Information retrieval", *ACM SIGIR'97*, Phliadelphia, USA, 50-58

WU, Dekai and Xuanyin XIA. (1995). "Large-scale automatic extraction of an English-Chinese lexicon". *Machine Translation* 9(3-4), pp.285-313.

Ming-Wen Wu and Keh-Yih Su. (1993). "Corpus-based Automatic Compound Extraction with Mutual Information and Relative Frequency Count," *Proceedings of R. O. C. Computational Linguistics Conference* VI . Nantou, Taiwan, R. O. C., pp.207-216.

Pascale Fung. (1998). "Extracting Key Terms from Chinese and Japanese texts ". *The International Journal on Computer Processing of Oriental Language, Special Issue on Information Retrieval on Oriental Languages*, pp.99-121.

Cheng-Huang Tung and His-Jian Lee. (1994). "Identification of Unknown Words From a Corpus". *Compouter Processing of Chinese and Oriental Languages* Vol.8, pp.131-145.

Buckley, C. (1985). *Implementation of the SMART information retrieval system*, Technical report, #85-686, Cornell University.

Harman, D. K. and Voorhees, E. M., Eds. (1996). *Information Technology: The Fifth Text Retrieval Conference(TREC5)*, NIST SP 500-238. Gaithersburg, National Institute fo standards and Technology.

# An Algorithm for Situation Classification of Chinese Verbs

**Xiaodan Zhu, Chunfa Yuan**
State Key Laboratory for Intelligent Technology and System, Dept. of Computer Science & Technology, Tsinghua University, Beijing 100084, P.R.C.

**K.F.Wong , Wenjie.Li**
Dept. of System Engineering and Engineering Management, Chinese University of HongKong

## Abstract

Temporal information analysis is very important for Chinese Information Process. Comparing with English, Chinese is quite different in temporal information expression. Based on the feature of Chinese a phase-based method is proposed to deal with Chinese temporal information. To this end, an algorithm is put forward to classify verbs into different situation types automatically. About 2981 verbs were tested. The result has shown that the algorithm is effective.

## 1.*Introduction

We are now launching a research project on Events Extraction from Chinese Financial News, which requires us to extract the related temporal information from news. Temporal expressions in Chinese form a complex system. We cannot fully understand the temporal information only by extracting the verbs, adverbs, auxiliary words and temporal phrases. Instead, more profound analysis is needed. In this paper, we first introduce the temporal system of Chinese, then we put forward a method in dealing with Chinese temporal information, in which situation types is very important. Therefore, an algorithm is rendered to classify verbs into several situation types.

* Supported by National Natural Science Foundation of China (69975008) and 973 project (G1998030507)

### 1.1 Temporal System of Chinese

Commonly, Chinese linguists [3][4] think that the temporal system of Chinese includes three parts: phase, tense and aspect. Each of these represents some profile of temporal expression (these definitions are a little different from linguistic theory of English).

(1) Phase. A sentence may describe a static state or an action; an action may be durative or instantaneous; a durative action may indicate a terminal or not. All of these are the research fields of phase. So, static vs. dynamic, durative vs. instantaneous, telic vs. non-telic are three pairs of phase features. Phase depends fully on meaning. According to phase features, we can classify the verbs into different situation types.

(2) Tense. Tense describes the relations between an event (E), reference time (R) and speaking time (S). First, taking S as the origin, we can get three relations between R and S: if R is before S, the sentence describes past; if R is the same time as S, it describes present; if R is after S, it describes future. This is called primary tense. Secondly, we can get three relations between E and S: If E is before R, we call it anterior; if E is the same time as R, we call it simple; otherwise we call it posterior. This is called secondary tense. Therefore, there are nine tenses including anterior past, anterior future, simple future, posterior present, etc.

(3) Aspect . Aspect reflects the way we observe an event. For the same event, there are many perspectives. We can take the event as atomic and not consider its inner structure, and call it perfective. We can consider it being in process, and call it imperfective. For imperfective, we can observe it at a position before it, at the beginning of it, in the middle of it, etc. Different perspectives lead to different expressions in the language.

Phase, tense and aspect are not independent even though they are different conceptions; each of them can influence and restrict the others, ultimately building up the complex temporal system of Chinese.

## 1.2 Phase-based Chinese temporal information analysis

Most languages express temporal information through phase, tense and aspect, however, for different languages, the relative importance of the three parts is different. A very important feature of English is that tense and aspect are expressed by variation of predicates. But for Chinese, predicates keep the same form no matter how the tense and aspect are different.

Therefore, in English, temporal information analysis mainly considers tense and aspect, as well as temporal adjective and time words and phrases. But in Chinese, tense and aspect of a sentence are not very clear, verbs do not vary in form with the change of tense and aspect. So we suggest basing temporal information analysis on phase. We mainly perceive the situation type of a sentence, then roughly acquire tense from adverbs and auxiliary words. After considering the temporal phrases, we can understand the temporal information of single event fully. Finally, according to the absolute temporal information of single event, we can get the temporal relation between two events. Phase-based temporal information analysis has been used in our research on Event Extraction from Financial News, in which the most important and fundamental problem is to acquire the situation types of a sentence.

## 1.3 Situation Classification of Chinese Verbs

In the West, research on situation has a long history. The earliest can be traced to the times of Aristotle. In resent years, Western researchers have published a large volume of papers, which present many points of view. The most important are Vendler(1967), Bache(1982), and Smith (1985) . They approximately classify the situation as four types: state, activity, accomplishment, and achievement.

Chinese researchers have also done considerable work, among which the most typical research were done by Chen[3] and Ma[5].

Ma[5] stated that the situation of a sentence is fully determined by the situation of the main verb of the sentence. He use three phases: static, durative, telic to classify verbs into four situational types V1,V2,V3,V4.

| | Static | Durative | Telic |
|---|---|---|---|
| V1 | + | + | + |
| V2 | - | + | + |
| V3 | - | + | - |
| V4 | - | - | + |

Table 1.1

Chen[3] stated that the situation of a sentence not only depends on the main verb of the sentence but also on other parts of the sentence. That is, although the main verb is the most important in determining a sentence situation, other parts such as adverbs also have effect. Chen's classification is more detailed.

| NO. | Verb types | Instances |
|---|---|---|
| (1) | Attribute | 是(be)，等于(equal) |
| (2) | Mental state | 相信(believe)，抱歉(regret) |
| (3) | Position | 站(stand)，坐(sit)，躺 (lie) |
| (4) | Action and Mental Activity | 跳(jump)，想(think)，猜(guess) |
| (5) | Verb-object Structure | 读书(read (books))，唱歌(sing (songs)) |
| (6) | Change | 变化(change)，成为 (become) |
| (7) | Directional Action | 跑来(run up)，爬上(climb on) |
| (8) | Instantaneous Change | 死(die)，躺(lie)，断(snap) |
| (9) | Instantaneous Action | 坐(sit)，站(stand) |
| (10) | Verb-verb or Verb-adjective | 推到(push down)，切碎(smash (into pieces)) |

Table 1.2

| Phase feture / Situation types | Static | Durative | Telic | verb types (table above) |
|---|---|---|---|---|
| State | + | | | (1) (2) (3) |
| Activity | - | + | - | (3) (4) (5) |
| Accomplishment | - | + | + | (3) (4) |
| Simple change | - | - | + | (6) (7) |
| Complex change | - | - | - | (8) (9) (10) |

Table 1.3

From the tables above, we can find that some words(such as (3) and (4) in table 1.3) can belong to more than one category, so Chen use modifiers, auxiliary words and prepositions to eliminate the ambiguity.

| | State | | | Activity | Accomplishment | Complex change | Simple change |
|---|---|---|---|---|---|---|---|
| | (1) | (2) | (3) | | | | |
| 很+V | - | + | - | - | - | - | - |
| V+着 | - | (-) | + | + | + | - | - |
| 在+V | - | (-) | (-) | + | + | + | - |
| V+(了)+TQP+了(act) | - | - | - | + | + | + | - |
| V+(了)+TQP+了(state) | - | + | + | - | + | + | + |
| TQP: Time Quantity Phrase, (-) : in most case, it is ↩ | | | | | | | |

Table 1.4

## 2. Our Classification Algorithm for Verbs' Situation

### 2.1 Guiding Thoughts

(1) Our algorithm is for information processing

•Ma[5] uses three pairs of phase features in classifying, but from which we can not get an automatic classification algorithm for computers; the classification can only be done manually.

•In linguistics, telicity is a phase feature used in classifying. In table 1.1 the difference between category V2 and V3, in table 1.3, the difference between "activity" and "accomplishment", are attributed to telicity. But in information process, we need not distinguish whether an event is telic or not. For example,

Exp.1
他在吹笛子。 (He is playing the flute)
他在吹"梁祝"。 (He is playing a song "Liangzhu")

Chen[3] thinks that in Exp. 1, the first sentence has the features: dynamicity, and durativity, and non-telicity; it belongs to "activity". The second sentence has the features dynamicity, durativity, and telicity, because in the second sentence, there is a default terminal----when the song "liangzhu" is over, the action "play" is over, so the sentence belongs to "accomplishment" instead of "activity". However we think such discrimination is useless for information extraction, because telicity is an ambiguous concept itself. What we need is to acquire the exact duration of the event. So if we knew the event is durative or not, and got the temporal phrases, we can know terminal time of the event. Besides, whether an event is telic or not can not be attributed to collocation and only can be done manually(as the exp 1 shows). For these reasons, we consider the two verbs in Exp. 1 belonging to the same situational type, that is, we do not use talicity as a phase feature to classifying verbs.

(2) Separate classification of the verb situation from classification of the sentence situation.

Chen[3] points that some verbs belong to more than one category, and gives a method to distinguish these cases. To make the ideal more clear, we use two steps to complete the sentence situation recognition. In this paper, we render an algorithm to classify verbs into different categories, which is the basis of another research---- recognition of sentence situation, which will be discussed in future work.

## 2.2 Classification Method

We classify the verbs into five categories , Att(Attribute), Men(Mentality), Act (Activity) , Ins(Instantaneous) , Amb (Ambiguous).

Att: 是(be), 等于(equal), 包含(include), 合(accord with)
Men: 喜欢(like), 轻视(belittle), 爱(love), 满意 (be satisfied with)
Act: 画(draw), 唠叨(gab), 喝(drink), 跑步(run)
Ins: 爆炸(explore), 熄灭(extinguish), 断(snap), 发现 (discovery)
Amb: 坐(sit), 站(stand), 躺(lie), 跪(kneel), 带(bring), 挂(hang), 戴(wear), 安装(install)

Amb(Ambiguous) include those words which describe different situations in different context. For example:

Exp. 2:
他将照片挂在墙上 (they hung the picture on the wall. )
照片挂在墙上 (Picture is hanging on the wall.)

In Exp. 2, the two sentences have the same predicate "挂 (hang). In the first sentence, "挂 describes an instantaneous action, but the second sentence describes a state. In English, forms of these two predicates are different; while in Chinese, they are the same. For this reason, we consider it ambiguous and indistinguishable without context.

We have pointed out previously that phase depends only on meaning. However different situational types collocate with different words. So the essence of our algorithm is replace semantic judgement with collocational judgement. For example, 'Men(Mentality)' can follow "很 (very) . Verbs in the "Amb" category can followed by "介宾(preposition-object)" structures, etc. The following is the set of collocational features.

| | Static verbs | | Amb | Act | Ins |
|---|---|---|---|---|---|
| | Att | Men | | | |
| Verb+了 | - | + | + | + | + |
| 很+Verb | - | + | - | - | - |
| Verb+着 | - | (-) | + | (+) | - |
| 在+Verb | - | (-) | (-) | + | - |
| Verb+介宾 | - | - | + | - | + |

Table 2.1

## 2.3 Implementation of the algorithm

According to table 2.1, a classification algorithm was designed, and we use two resources to implement our algorithm: The *Contemporary Chinese Cihai* [11] (which we will refer to as the *Cihai* below) dictionary and the *Machine Tractable Dictionary of Contemporary Chinese Predicate Verbs* [12](which we will refer to as the *predicate dictionary* below). The *Cihai* dictionary includes 12,000 entries and 700,000 collocation instances. *predicate dictionary* includes about 3000 verbs with their semantic information, case relations and detailed collocation information. These two dictionaries both include some of the collocation information that the algorithm needs.

Considering the features of these two dictionaries, we adjust part of our algorithm:
(1) In predicate dictionary, there is a slot named 'verb type', which includes 'transitive verb', 'intransitive verb', 'attributive verb', 'linking verb' etc. So, at the beginning of the algorithm, we judge if the verb is a "linking verb" ( 是(be)', 等于(equal)' ,etc) or a 'possessive verb' ('具有' (have)). If it is, we directly classify the verb as "att(attribute)' without further processing.
(2) The *predicate dictionary* provides the case relation of verbs, and their semantic ategories. We restrict the agent of verbs in the 'Men(mentality)' to belong to one of:

"{ 人}"(people), "{ 人类} "(human), "{人群} "(multitude) , {集体}(collectivity)", "{生物}(creatures)", "{信念}(belief)", "{动物}(animal) " (3) Because *Cihai* includes collocation instances instead of collocation relations, we should consider synonyms. To be exact, when we determine whether a verb belongs to "Men(Mentality)" or not, we judge if it can follow 很 (very) and synonyms such as "极其", "十分", "分外", "尤其", "非常". However, some seldom seen instances were included. All these cause some errors.

The final algorithm is as follows:

```
if (a verb is labeled as" linking verb" or "possessive verb"
    in predicate dictionary )
then        the verb belongs to "Att(Attribute)"
else if (the verb can follow "很"(very) and synonyms "极其",
     "十分", "分外", "尤其", "非常") and (its agent's
     semantic belongs to set1*)
  then    the verb belongs to "Men(Mentality)"
  else if  (it can follow "在") or (be followed by"着")
     then if  (it can be followed by "preposition-object"
               structure)
          then    the verb belongs to "Amb(Ambiguous)"
          else    the verb belongs to "Act(Activity)"
     else if  (it can be followed by"了")
          then    the verb belongs to"Ins(Instantaneous)"
          else    the verb belongs to" unknown"
```

*set1={human, multitude, collectivity, creatures, belief, animal }

# 3. Results and Analysis

## 3.1 Results

We use the algorithm above to classify the 2981 words in predicate dictionary, at the same time, we do the classification manually, Table 3.1 is the result:

| | Att | Men | Amb | Ins | Act | Un-known | Totel |
|---|---|---|---|---|---|---|---|
| Human | 20 | 112 | 500 | 662 | 1683 | 4* | 2981 |
| Algo-Rithm | 20 | 111 | 537 | 691 | 1519 | 103 | 2981 |

*this 4 words are not verb.

Table 3.1

Table 2.2 shows the details:

| by algo-rithm | Classifying by human | | | | | | |
|---|---|---|---|---|---|---|---|
| | Att | Men | Amb | Ins | Act | Non-verb | Totel |
| Att | 20 | 0 | 0 | 0 | 0 | 0 | 20 |
| Men | 0 | 99 | 1 | 1 | 10 | 0 | 111 |
| Amb | 0 | 0 | 473 | 9 | 55 | 0 | 537 |
| Ins | 0 | 0 | 3 | 637 | 51 | 0 | 691 |
| Act | 0 | 1 | 12 | 2 | 1504 | 0 | 1519 |
| Un-known | 0 | 12 | 11 | 13 | 63 | 4 | 103 |
| Totel | 20 | 112 | 500 | 662 | 1683 | 4 | 2981 |

Table 3.2

Table 3.3 shows precision and recall:

| | Att | Men | Amb | Ins | Act | Average |
|---|---|---|---|---|---|---|
| Precision | 100.0 | 89.9 | 88.1 | 92.2 | 99.0 | 93.8 |
| Recall | 100.0 | 88.4 | 94.6 | 96.2 | 89.4 | 93.7 |

Table 3.3

## 3.2 Analysis

We mainly analyze the errors:

(1) Failure of algorithm

Chinese is a very complex language. Replacing semantic judgment by using collocations has limitation itself. For example, in most cases, whether a verb is durative or not can be decided by whether it can be used in such structure "verb+ 着" (In most case, " 着" represents an action in progress). But some instantaneous verbs such as "敲(knock)", can also be used in such structure to express a repeated action.

(2) Errors caused by the resources

(2.1) Collocation incompleteness in *Cihai*: for example, "反对(disagree)" can collocate with "很 (very), but this collocation is not included in *Cihai*.

(2.2)Errors caused by *predicate dictionary*: It is obvious that a certain proportion of dictionary errors is inevitable. For example, though "恳求 (beg) can follow "在 to represent the action is in progress, it is not included in the corresponding slot of predicate dictionary.

(2.3) The inconsistency between the two dictionaries: For example, 崇敬 (admire), "在乎 (mind), and "看不起 ( belittle) are included in *predicate dictionary* but not in *Cihai*. Although "抱歉 (regret) is included in *Cihai* , it is taken as an adjective instead of a verb.

## 4. Conclusion

In this paper, we advance a phase-based method to analyze temporal information in Chinese. For this purpose, an algorithm is rendered to classify verbs into different situation types. Because a verb's situation depends on the meaning of the verb, the essence of our algorithm takes advantage of collocations to avoid semantics. The result shows the algorithm is successful. We also believe that if the errors caused by resources were eliminated, the result would be improved significantly.

Although the five categories are defined by us, they can describe basic situations of Chinese. The classification algorithm itself is independent of resources, so it can be applied to other resources (dictionaries) if these resources include sufficient collocation information. Furthermore, Discarding dictionaries and doing classification directly on large-scale real corpus, especially in certain domain, deserve the future research.

Our algorithm is very useful for the future analysis of sentence situation for Information Extraction system and for dictionary construction.

## *References*


[1]Message Understanding Conference Website, http://www.muc.saic.com.

[2]Message Understanding Evaluation and Conference: Proceedings of 3rd-6th APRA Workshops, Morgan Kaufmann Publishers Inc., 1996.

[3]Chen ping. Discussion On Temporal System of Contemporary Chinese: China Chinese Vol.6,1998.

[4]Gong Qianyan. Phase, Tense and Aspect of Chinese, Commercial Press.

[5]Ma Qingzhu. Time Quantity Phrase and Categories of Verbs: China Chinese. Vol.2,1981.

[6]Hu Yushu & Fan Xiao. Research on Verbs, Henan Univ. Press, 1995

[7]Hwang C.H. & Schubert L. K. Interpreting Tense, Aspect and Time Adverbials: A Compositional, Unified Approach : Proceeding of 1st International Conference in Temporal Logic, Bonn, Germany, July 1994.

[8]Allen J.F. Towards a General Theory of Action and Time: Artificial Intelligence, 23,123-154.

[9]Allen J.F. & George, F.. Action and Events in Interval Temporal Logic: Journal of Logic and Computation, Special Issue on Actions and Processes, 1994.

[10]Ion Androutsopoulos , Graeme Ritche & Peter Thanisch . Time ,Tense and Aspect in Natural Language Database Interface, CMP-LG Mar 1998.

[11]Ni Wenjie . Contemporary Chinese Cihai, People China Press, 1994.

[12]Chen Qunxiu . Designing and implement of Machine Tractable Dictionary of Contemporary Chinese Predicate Verbs, Proceedings of ICCC96, Singapore, Jun, 1996.

# Zero Anaphors in Chinese Discourse Processing

Chin-Chuan Cheng
City University of Hong Kong
ctcheng@cityu.edu.hk

**Abstract**

In Chinese, zero anaphors occur frequently. This talk discusses several issues in identification of zero anaphors. Syntactic tagging of words in a running text for detection of anaphora requires specification of argument structure for verbal elements. Verbs requiring a subject or an object can be used to locate the position of zero anaphors. Typical argument structures for verbs, however, often do not take into account the expansion of the structure in discourse such as placing the instrument in object position. Once the place of a zero anaphor is located, the discourse processor will attempt to recover the entity. There may be more than one entity in the previous context that can fit in the argument structure of the verb. It has been discussed in the literature that the recovery of zero anaphors requires extra-linguistic knowledge. However, I will discuss two recovery principles that utilize linguistic information as given in the text. The opening statement of a topic continuity normally provides the element for ellipsis in the statements that follow. So the first principle is to return to the opening statement for recovery. Perceptive verbs, on the other hand, often trigger the search of anaphors in the most recent element. This recency principle can be broken by certain adverbial expressions that mark the turn of the event. These principles apply within a topic continuity. The size of a topic continuity is empirically determined to be about 50 words with some variation.

**Association for Computational Linguistics**
209 N. Eighth Street
Stroudsburg, Pennsylvania 18360

CURRAN ASSOCIATES INC
proceedings
.com